OUR
AMERICAN
HERITAGE

☆ ☆ ☆

OUR
AMERICAN
HERITAGE

☆ ☆ ☆

Edited by
Charles L. Wallis

1817

HARPER & ROW, PUBLISHERS, NEW YORK, EVANSTON, AND LONDON

Acknowledgment is made to the following for permission to reprint copyrighted material:

BRANDT & BRANDT for extract from "The Devil and Daniel Webster" from *13 O'clock*, from *The Selected Works of Stephen Vincent Benét*, copyright 1936 by The Curtis Publishing Company, copyright renewed © 1964 by Thomas C. Benét, Stephanie B. Mahin, and Rachel B. Lewis; extract on Robert E. Lee from *John Brown's Body*, published by Holt, Rinehart & Winston, Inc., copyright 1927, 1928 by Stephen Vincent Benét, copyright renewed 1955, 1956 by Rosemary Carr Benét; extract from "Listen to the People" from *We Stand United*, published by Holt, Rinehart & Winston, Inc., copyright 1941 by Stephen Vincent Benét, copyright renewed © 1969 by Thomas C. Benét, Stephanie B. Mahin, and Rachel B. Lewis; extract from "Nightmare at Noon" from *The Selected Works of Stephen Vincent Benét*, published by Holt, Rinehart & Winston, Inc., copyright 1940 by Stephen Vincent Benét, copyright renewed © 1968 by Thomas C. Benét, Stephanie B. Mahin, and Rachel B. Lewis; "Clipper Ships and Captains" and "Lewis and Clark" from *A Book of Americans*, published by Holt, Rinehart & Winston, Inc., copyright 1933 by Rosemary and Stephen Vincent Benét, copyright renewed © 1961 by Rosemary Carr Benét.

COLLINS-KNOWLTON-WING, INC., for extract from *America Is Americans* by Hal Borland, copyright © 1942, 1969 by Hal Borland; extract from *The Old Country Store* by Gerald Carson, copyright 1954 by Gerald Carson.

CROWN PUBLISHERS, INC., for extract from *The Unvanquished* by Howard Fast, copyright 1942 by Howard Fast.

JOAN DAVES for extract from "I've Been to the Mountain Top," copyright © 1968 by the Martin Luther King, Jr., Estate.

DOUBLEDAY & COMPANY, INC., for "The Peacemaker," copyright 1918 by Current Literature Publishing Co., from *Joyce Kilmer: Poems, Essays & Letters*.

HARCOURT, BRACE & WORLD, INC., for extract from *The People, Yes* by Carl Sandburg, copyright 1936 by Harcourt, Brace & World, Inc.

HARPER & ROW, PUBLISHERS, INC., for extract from *In God We Trust* by Norman Cousins, copyright © 1958 by Norman Cousins; "So Long as There Are Homes" from *Poems of Inspiration and Courage* by Grace Noll Crowell, copyright 1936 by Harper & Row, Publishers, Inc., 1964 by Grace Noll Crowell; adaptation from *The Secret of Victorious Living* by Harry Emerson Fosdick, copyright 1934 by Harper & Row, Publishers, Inc.; extract from *Grandma Moses*, edited by Otto Kallir, copyright 1952 by Grandma Moses Properties, Inc.; extracts from *You Can't Go Home Again* by Thomas Wolfe, copyright 1940 by Maxwell Perkins; extract from *Profiles in Courage* by John F. Kennedy, copyright © 1956 by John F. Kennedy.

HOLT, RINEHART & WINSTON, INC., for "The New England Steeple" from *Road to America* by Frances Frost, copyright © 1937 by Frances Frost, 1965 by Paul Blackburn; "The Gift Outright" from *The Poetry of Robert Frost*, edited by Edward Connery Lathem, copyright 1942 by Robert Frost, copyright © 1970 by Lesley Frost Ballantine.

HOUGHTON MIFFLIN COMPANY for extract from *Paul Revere and the World He Lived In* by Esther Forbes; extract from "America Was Promises," extract from "American Letter," and extract from "Speech to Those Who Say Comrade" from *Collected Poems, 1917–1952* by Archibald MacLeish.

ALFRED A. KNOPF, INC., for "Watch, America" from *The Green Leaf* by Robert Nathan, copyright 1945, 1950 by Robert Nathan.

LITTLE, BROWN AND COMPANY for extract from *John Adams and the American Revolution* by Catherine Drinker Bowen.

THE MACMILLAN COMPANY for "America Was Schoolmasters" from *Collected Poems* by Robert P. Tristram Coffin, copyright 1943 by The Macmillan Company; "Abraham Lincoln Walks at Midnight" from *Collected Poems* by Vachel Lindsay, copyright 1914 by The Macmillan Company, 1942 by Elizabeth C. Lindsay.

MC GRAW-HILL BOOK COMPANY for extract from *The Wild Ocean* by Alan Villiers, copyright © 1957 by Alan Villiers.

HAROLD MATSON COMPANY, INC., for extract from *Midnight on the Desert* by J. B. Priestley, copyright © 1937, 1964 by J. B. Priestley.

HAROLD OBER ASSOCIATES, INC., for extract from "Let America Be America Again" by Langston Hughes, copyright 1938 by Langston Hughes; "A New Wind A-Blowin'" by Langston Hughes, copyright 1943 by Langston Hughes.

RUSSELL & VOLKENING, INC., for extract from *Yankee Storekeeper* by Ralph E. Gould, copyright 1946 by Ralph E. Gould.

CHARLES SCRIBNER'S SONS for extract from *Of Time and the River* by Thomas Wolfe, copyright © 1935 by Charles Scribner's Sons, 1963 by Paul Gitlin, Administrator C.T.A.; extract from *The Poem of Bunker Hill* by Harry Brown, copyright 1941 by Charles Scribner's Sons.

SIMON & SCHUSTER, INC., for extracts from *More about the Art of Living* by Wilferd A. Peterson, copyright © 1966 by Wilferd A. Peterson.

(See additional acknowledgments on page 215.)

CONTENTS

☆ ☆ ☆

Inscribed to
GEORGE AND VERDA ARMACOST
friends of youth

☆ ☆ ☆

PREFACE

The word "America" suggests varied and rich meanings.

America is history. Ours is a history of aspiration and adventure, hope and heartache, sweat and sacrifice. It is a history of a people passionately dedicated to certain ideals profoundly related to the divine and human spirit.

America is people. These people are both settled and restless, rooted and rootless, descendants of *Mayflower* families and children of latter-day immigrants. Some of these people are of imposing stature, but America is no less the chronicle of unnamed and unheralded citizens who did their duty, served responsibly their generation, and left a silent legacy of work and faith.

America is loyalty. Loyalty is expressed in honoring all the flag represents, in obeying the laws, in conviction and patriotism, in love for God and people, and in devotion to the commonweal.

America is revolution. Born in the souls of men who here sought a better, freer life, America is a divine discontent and a dedication to an ever nobler way of life.

America is the promise of a creative tomorrow wherein, guided by the lamps of those who have blazed our trails, we move confidently onward.

One thing more. America is anniversaries. Two hundred years ago fifty-six men signed the Declaration of Independence, pledging their lives, fortunes, and sacred honor to such things as liberty, equality, brotherhood, and the common good. Mirrored in this heritage album are the words men have used to commemorate in each passing generation that day of our nation's birth.

CHARLES L. WALLIS

Keuka College
Keuka Park, New York

I

OUR GOODLY HERITAGE

☆ ☆ ☆

The preservation of the sacred fire of liberty and the destiny of the republican model of government are justly considered, perhaps as deeply, as finally, staked on the experiment intrusted to the hands of the American people.

GEORGE WASHINGTON
FIRST INAUGURAL ADDRESS

HERITAGE AND HARVEST

The heritage of the past is the seed that brings forth the harvest of the future.

NATIONAL ARCHIVES BUILDING
WASHINGTON, D.C.

☆ ☆ ☆

DEVOTION TO AN IDEAL

We have faith that we shall not prove false to the memories of the men of the mighty past. They did their work. They left us the splendid heritage we now enjoy.

We in our turn have an assured confidence that we shall be able to leave this heritage unwasted and enlarged to our children and our children's children.

To do so we must show, not merely in great crises, but in the everyday affairs of life, the qualities of practical intelligence, of courage, of hardihood, and endurance, and above all the power of devotion to a lofty ideal, which made great the men who founded this Republic in the days of Washington, which made great the men who preserved this Republic in the days of Abraham Lincoln.

THEODORE ROOSEVELT

☆ ☆ ☆

LAND AND PEOPLE

What makes a nation is a good piece of geography.

ROBERT FROST

☆ ☆ ☆

FROM AN OLD ALMANAC

O! ye unborn inhabitants of America! Should this page escape its destin'd conflagration at the year's end, and these alphabetical letters remain legible, when your eyes behold the sun after he has rolled the seasons round for two or three centuries more, you will know that in Anno Domini 1758, we dream'd of your times.

NATHANIEL AMES

☆ ☆ ☆

I LOVE AMERICA

I love America for manifold
Inspiring beauty in her vast domain;
Hill, lake, woodland, prairie, desert, shore,
Blue-haloed mountain, valley, stream, and
    plain.

I love America for Pilgrim faith,
The firm foundation of democracy.
I love America for patriots
Who lived and died to keep their homeland
    free.

I love America for many bloods
Now blended into one . . . American.
I love America for guarding well
Her sacred trust, the rights God granted
    man.

I love America for all that she
Has been and is and yet may hope to be.
I love America for standing now . . .
The world's lone citadel of liberty.

GAIL BROOK BURKET

☆ ☆ ☆

LEANING UPON THE PAST

No man has ever been independent; every man has leaned upon the past.

Every liberty we enjoy has been bought at the cost of martyrs' blood; every achievement has been made at the cost of incredible toil.

We drink every day from wells that we have not dug; we warm by fires we have not kindled; we live by liberties we have not won; we are protected by institutions we have not set up.

Our governments rest upon the foundations cemented in place by the blood of soldiers who tracked their way, barefoot, through icy battlefields or over burning sands.

Our courts are reared upon the bodies of those who died for freedom.

ROY L. SMITH

☆　☆　☆

HERITAGE

Once upon a time, the story goes,
This land was new, the soil untried.
On these acres, vast, untamed,
Men and women toiled on side by side.

Farmhouses were slowly built,
And bits of land fenced in;
And women cooked and passed the food
To the weary toiling men.

Livestock was made captive,
The sod was turned, the soil made free,
And winters came with snow and cold,
And toil went on unceasingly.

And from these years of endless toil
There blossomed forth in history's page
The dreams of sturdy pioneers—
The story of our heritage.

IRENE BENNETT

☆　☆　☆

CHAIN OF DESTINY

No man can be President without looking back upon the effort given to the country by the thirty Presidents who in my case have preceded me. No man of imagination can be President without thinking of what shall be the course of his country under the thirty more Presidents who will follow him. He must think of himself as a link in the long chain of his country's destiny, past and future.

HERBERT HOOVER

☆　☆　☆

I have but one lamp by which my feet are guided, and that is the lamp of experience. I know of no way of judging of the future but by the past.

PATRICK HENRY

☆　☆　☆

HIGHEST LOYALTY

Americanism implies loyalty to the Founding Fathers, but the highest loyalty consists in meeting the issues of our generation with the same intelligence and sense of responsibility with which they met the issues of their generation.

GLENN FRANK

☆　☆　☆

From PAUL REVERE'S RIDE

So through the night rode Paul Revere;
And so through the night went his cry of alarm
To every Middlesex village and farm,
A cry of defiance, and not of fear,
A voice in the darkness, a knock at the door,
And a word that shall echo forevermore!
For, borne on the night-wind of the Past,
Through all our history, to the last,
In the hour of darkness and peril and need,
The people will waken and listen to hear
The hurrying hoof-beats of that steed,
And the midnight message of Paul Revere.

HENRY WADSWORTH LONGFELLOW

☆　☆　☆

HE RODE INTO HISTORY

So away, down the moonlit road, goes Paul Revere and the Larkin horse, galloping into history, art, editorials, folklore, poetry; the beat of those hooves never to be forgotten. The man, his bold dark face bent, his hands light on the reins, his body giving to the flowing rhythm beneath him, becoming, as it were, something greater than himself—not merely one man riding one horse on a certain lonely night of long ago, but a symbol to which his countrymen can yet turn. Paul Revere had started on a ride which, in a way, has never ended.

ESTHER FORBES
From PAUL REVERE AND THE WORLD
HE LIVED IN

☆　☆　☆

10

From NIGHTMARE AT NOON

There are certain words,
Our own and others', we're used to—words
    we've used,
Heard, had to recite, forgotten. . . .
Liberty, equality, fraternity.

I am merely saying—what if these words
    pass?
What if they pass and are gone and are no
    more?

They were bought with belief and passion, at
    great cost.
They were bought with the bitter and anony-
    mous blood
Of farmers, teachers, shoemakers, and fools
Who broke the old rule, and the pride of
    Kings. . . .

It took a long time to buy these words.
It took a long time to buy them and much
    pain.

STEPHEN VINCENT BENÉT

☆   ☆   ☆

PRAYER

God of our fathers, give unto us, thy servants, a true appreciation of our heritage, of great men and great deeds in the past, but let us not be intimidated by feelings of our own inadequacy for this troubled hour.

Remind us that the God they worshiped, and by whose help they laid the foundations of our Nation, is still able to help us uphold what they bequeathed and to give it new meanings.

Remind us that we are not called to fill the places of those who have gone, but to fill our own places, to do the work thou hast laid before us, to do the right as thou hast given us to see the right, always to do the very best we can, and to leave the rest to thee.

PETER MARSHALL

☆   ☆   ☆

Every ship that comes to America got its chart from Columbus.

RALPH WALDO EMERSON

☆   ☆   ☆

GRATITUDE IN EVERY TONGUE

All hail, Columbus, discoverer, dreamer, hero, and apostle!

We of every race and country recognize the horizon which bounded his vision and the infinite scope of his genius.

The voice of gratitude and praise for all the blessings which have been showered upon mankind by his adventure is limited to no language but is uttered in every tongue.

Neither marble nor brass can fitly form his statue.

Continents are his monument, and unnumbered millions present and to come, who enjoy in their liberties and their happiness the fruits of his faith, will reverently guard and preserve, from century to century, his name and fame.

CHAUNCEY DEPEW

☆   ☆   ☆

AND SO—AMERICA

Before America became the land it is today,
    There was a dream;
A dream that men could say
The things they wished to say.

Before America became to us a nation,
    There was a hope,
A hope that men could come and go at will,
And without fear.

Before America was born, and here to stay,
    There was a prayer,
A prayer that men could speak of God
And worship each in his own way.

And so that dream, that hope, that prayer
    Became America.

GRACE ELIZABETH BUSH

☆ ☆ ☆

HEROES OF FAITH

By faith the voyaging *Mayflower* embarked from Old England and found harbor off the bleak New England shores. By faith the Pilgrim Fathers set up a government on a new continent dedicated to God and inspired by a desire to do his will on earth as it is done in heaven.

By faith Thomas Jefferson was stirred to strike a blow for political independence and wrote the thrilling document that declared that all men are created equal and endowed with certain inalienable rights. By faith he said, "Love your neighbor as yourself and your country more than yourself."

By faith George Washington left his spacious mansion at Mount Vernon and espoused the cause of the tax-burdened colonists. By faith he forsook ease and comfort, choosing rather to suffer hardship with his men at Valley Forge than to enjoy the favor of a king. By faith he became the President of the newly born republic and endured as seeing Him who is invisible.

By faith Alexander Hamilton established the financial credit of the nation. In the eloquent words of Daniel Webster: "He touched the corpse of public credit and it sprang into life. He smote the rock of national resources and abundant streams of revenue flowed." By faith James Madison gave richly of his scholarly mind to form the Federal Constitution. By faith Andrew Jackson fought the battle of the impoverished and underprivileged many against the privileged few.

By faith Abraham Lincoln bore the awful burden of four purgatorial years seeking to preserve the Federal Union. By faith he carried a dreadful war to its conclusion without hate in his heart, saying, "I have not only suffered for the South, I have suffered with the South."

By faith Woodrow Wilson in the dreadful heartbreak of a world war dreamed a dream of a warless world in which the nations should be leagued together to keep the peace. By faith he glimpsed that promised land which, like Moses, he might not enter.

And what shall I more say? For time would fail me if I should tell of that unnumbered host, the unnamed and obscure citizens who bore unimagined burdens, sacrificed in silence and endured nobly, that a government of the people, for the people, and by the people might not perish from the earth.

EDGAR DE WITT JONES

☆ ☆ ☆

GOD'S FOOTSTOOL

America is the greatest force that God has ever allowed to exist on his footstool.

DWIGHT D. EISENHOWER

☆ ☆ ☆

THE FIRST TRUE PIONEERS

There had been settlers in plenty who sailed westbound across the North Atlantic before, but the Pilgrim Fathers may be regarded as the first of the true pioneers.

They set out from Europe not with an eye over their shoulders at the land which they had left and intending to return at the first opportunity, nor misled by promoters seeking to make a quick profit out of them, careless of what then might be their fate.

They were the first cohesive and united body of men, women, and children who sailed for the new land seeking neither a way around it to a richer East nor a quick wealth from the easy exploitation of precious metals.

They sailed for the new land to make a new life in and of that new land, to bring up their children and their children's children there, with a new freedom, a freedom of body, of spirit, and of mind.

ALAN VILLIERS
From THE WILD OCEAN

☆ ☆ ☆

12

SOURCE OF WISDOM

It is refreshing to turn to the early incidents of our history, and learn wisdom from the acts of the great men who have gone to their account.

JOHN MC LEAN

☆   ☆   ☆

MEN OF IRON

We run our memory back over the pages of history for about eighty-two years, and we discover that we were then a very small people, in point of numbers vastly inferior to what we are now, with a vastly less extent of country, with vastly less of everything we consider desirable among men.

We look upon the change as exceedingly advantageous to us and to our posterity, and we fix upon something that happened away back as in some way or other being connected with this rise of prosperity.

We find a race of men living, in that day, whom we claim as our fathers and grandfathers; they were iron men; they fought for the principle that they were contending for; and we understood by what they then did it has followed the degree of prosperity which we now enjoy has come to us. "We hold these truths to be self-evident, that all men are created equal." That is the electric cord in the Declaration that links the hearts of patriotic men as long as the love of freedom exists in the minds of men throughout the world.

ABRAHAM LINCOLN

☆   ☆   ☆

RICH INHERITANCE

While the people of other countries are struggling to establish free institutions, under which man may govern himself, we are in the actual enjoyment of them—a rich inheritance from our fathers.

JAMES K. POLK

☆   ☆   ☆

From WATCH, AMERICA

Where the northern ocean darkens,
    Where the rolling rivers run,
Past the cold and empty headlands,
    Toward the slow and westering sun,
There our fathers, long before us,
    Armed with freedom, faced the deep;
What they won with love and labor,
    Let their children watch and keep.

By our dark and dreaming forests,
    By our free and shining skies,
By our green and ripening prairies,
    Where the western mountains rise;
God who gave our fathers freedom,
    God who made our fathers brave,
What they built with love and anguish,
    Let their children watch and save.

ROBERT NATHAN

☆   ☆   ☆

I always consider the settlement of America with reverence and wonder as the opening of a grand scene and design in Providence for the illumination of the ignorant and the emancipation of the slavish part of mankind all over the world.

JOHN ADAMS

☆   ☆   ☆

He is an American, who, leaving behind him all his ancient prejudices and manners, receives new ones from the new mode of life he has embraced, the new government he obeys, and the new rank he holds.

He becomes an American by being received in the broad lap of our great alma mater. Here individuals of all nations are melted into a new race of men, whose labors and prosperity will one day cause great changes in the world.

The American is a new man, who acts upon new principles; he must therefore entertain new ideas and form new opinions.

MICHEL GUILLAUME JEAN DE CRÈVECOEUR

☆　☆　☆

A nation's character is the sum of its splendid deeds.

They constitute one common patrimony, the nation's inheritance.

They awe foreign powers, and they arouse and animate our own people.

HENRY CLAY

☆　☆　☆

WHO SPEAKS FOR AMERICA?

The hope of the United States in the present and in the future is the same that it always has been: it is the hope and confidence that out of unknown homes will come men who will constitute themselves the masters of industry and of politics. The average hopefulness, the average welfare, the average enterprise, the average initiative of the United States are the only things that make it rich. We are not rich because a few gentlemen direct our industry; we are rich because of our own intelligence and our own industry.

America does not consist of men who get their names into newspapers; America does not consist politically of the men who set themselves up to be political leaders; she does not consist of the men who do most of her talking—they are important only so far as they speak for the great voiceless multitude of men who constitute the body and the saving force of the nation.

Nobody who cannot speak the common thought, who does not move by the common impulse, is the man to speak for America, or for any of her future purposes. Only he is fit to speak who knows the thoughts of the great body of citizens, the men who go about their business every day, the men who toil from morning to night, the men who go home tired in the evenings, the men who are carrying on the things of which we are so proud.

WOODROW WILSON

☆　☆　☆

TRIBUTE IN FANEUIL HALL, BOSTON

A few days ago I stood on the cupola of your statehouse, and overlooked for the first time this venerable city and the country surrounding it.

Then the streets, and hills, and waters around me began to teem with the life of historical recollections, recollections dear to all mankind, and a feeling of pride arose in my heart, and I said to myself, I, too, am an American citizen.

There was Bunker Hill; there Charlestown, Lexington, and Dorchester Heights not far off; there the harbor into which the British tea was sunk; there the place where the old liberty tree stood; there John Hancock's house; there Benjamin Franklin's birthplace.

And now I stand in this grand old hall, which so often resounded with the noblest appeals that ever thrilled American hearts, and where I am almost afraid to hear the echo of my own feeble voice.

No man that loves liberty, wherever he may have first seen the light of day, can fail on this sacred spot to pay his tribute to Americanism. And here, with all these glorious memories crowding upon my heart, I will offer mine.

I, born in a foreign land, pay my tribute to Americanism? Yes, for to me the word Americanism, true Americanism, comprehends the noblest ideas which ever swelled a human heart with noble pride.

CARL SCHURZ

☆　☆　☆

History interposes with evidence that tyranny and wrong lead inevitably to decay; that freedom and right, however hard may be the struggle, always prove resistless.

GEORGE BANCROFT

☆　☆　☆

ON HIS NINETIETH BIRTHDAY

Freedom is the open window through which pours the sunlight of the human spirit and of human dignity. With the preservation of these moral and spiritual qualities and with God's grace will come further greatness for our country.

HERBERT HOOVER

☆ ☆ ☆

AMERICAN IDEALS AND VALUES

Five basic values and ideals have developed out of the American tradition.

1. *Faith in the moral law.* When the Declaration of Independence and the Constitution were written, faith in the moral law was almost universal. Before it all men were equal, and from it they derived equal rights and privileges. Faith in its immutability and permanence gave men a sense of certainty and security.

2. *The ideal of the free individual.* The free individual, in the conception of the founders of the United States, was not licentious and unprincipled. He did not do anything he pleased. On the contrary, he was one who knew the moral law and lived according to it. He was self-disciplined and self-directive. He stood on his own feet and faced the world with the confidence and courage that came from a faith in the moral law.

3. *The team method of solving group problems and promoting common concerns.* Frontier living promoted cooperation among equals. All free men had the right to participate in government. The rights and freedoms of the individual were imbedded in the Constitution. Sovereignty was vested in the people. Suffrage became universal.

4. *Faith in reason.* Faith in reason is derived from the Greeks. It was reinforced by frontier conditions, the advances of modern science, and the success of our form of government and way of life.

5. *Faith in the mission of America.* This faith has been pronounced in American history. It inspired Lincoln during the dark days of the War between the States and has been a source of strength and fortitude in other times of danger.

I. JAMES QUILLEN

☆ ☆ ☆

THE AMERICAN DREAM

"The American Dream" is a phrase constantly used by orators and writers. What does it mean? It is the dream that inspired the founding families to give up the security of their lives in Europe and come across the forbidding Atlantic to a wilderness world—in the *Mayflower* and other ships—seeking . . . seeking what? Freedom and the opportunities that go with it.

"The American Dream" means the dream, and the challenge of widening opportunity, which inspired the covered-wagon pioneers to head out westward across the rugged mountains, the wild prairies and the waterless desert to settle a vast new territory. It is the bright light of hope and adventure that has motivated tens of thousands of Americans and American families who started with only freedom and opportunity and achieved great success—benefiting themselves and, more importantly, their fellowman.

"The American Dream" is the latent fire that lies buried, awaiting a spark, in the breast of every American boy and girl, young man and woman—the dream of achieving, the dream of contributing, the dream of fulfillment. It is all this, and much, much more—and all of it comes from a bedrock foundation of spiritual understanding, faith in God, a dedication to God's laws.

GEORGE S. BENSON

☆ ☆ ☆

Too much time cannot be spent in a task that is to endure for centuries.

AUGUSTUS SAINT-GAUDENS

AMERICAN FABRIC

The games men have played and the songs they have sung, the delusions they have had and the victories and defeats they have experienced, the homes they have built and the clothing they have worn, the aberrations from which they have suffered and the soaring, inexpressible ideals they have served—all of these, in one way or another, go to make up the heritage which we as Americans have today.

The fabric of American life is a seamless web. Everything fits in somewhere. History is a continuous process; it extends far back into the past, and it will go on—in spite of today's uneasy qualms—far into the future.

Our American heritage is greater than any one of us. It can express itself in very homely truths; in the end, it can lift our eyes beyond the glow in the sunset skies.

BRUCE CATTON

☆ ☆ ☆

INSCRIPTION

U.S.
In loving memory
of
"Uncle Sam"
The name
Originating with
Samuel Wilson
1766–1854
During the War of 1812
And since adopted by
The United States.

OAKWOOD CEMETERY
TROY, NEW YORK

☆ ☆ ☆

ON ANDREW JACKSON

He does what he thinks is right and does it with all his might.

DANIEL WEBSTER

LIFE LINE

In times of change and danger, when there is a quicksand of fear under men's reasoning, a sense of continuity with generations gone before can stretch like a life line across the scary present.

JOHN DOS PASSOS

☆ ☆ ☆

AMERICA

God built him a continent of glory and
  filled it with treasures untold;
He carpeted it with soft-rolling prairies and
  columned it with thundering mountains;
He studded it with sweet-flowing fountains
  and traced it with long-winding streams;
He planted it with deep-shadowed forests,
  and filled them with song.
Then he called unto a thousand peoples and
  summoned the bravest among them.
They came from the ends of the earth, each
  bearing a gift and a hope.
The glow of adventure was in their eyes, and
  in their hearts the glory of hope.
And out of the bounty of earth and the labor
  of men,
Out of the longing of hearts and the prayer
  of souls,
Out of the memory of ages and hopes of the
  world,
God fashioned a nation in love, blessed it with
Purpose sublime—and called it America!

ABBA HILLEL SILVER

☆ ☆ ☆

EPITAPH TO LUCY EATON

Descended from the Pilgrims
She lov'd their doctrines
And practic'd their virtues.

MIDDLE CEMETERY
LANCASTER, MASSACHUSETTS

☆ ☆ ☆

CREDO

I am an American.

The Golden Rule is my rule.

In humility and with gratitude to Almighty
God,

I acknowledge my undying debt to the
Founding Fathers,

Who left me a priceless heritage,

Which now is *my* responsibility.

With steadfast loyalty,

I will uphold the Constitution of the United
States.

I will treasure my birthright of American
ideals.

I will place moral integrity above worldly
possessions.

Problems of interest to my country shall be
of interest to me.

I will count my right of suffrage to be a
sacred trust,

And I will diligently strive to prove worthy
of that trust.

I will give my full support to upright public
servants,

But those with unclean hands I will firmly
oppose.

Each obligation that comes to me as a true
American,

I will discharge with honor.

My heart is in America, and America is in my
heart!

I am an American.

BENJAMIN E. NEAL

☆ ☆ ☆

Think of your forefathers! Think of your
posterity!

JOHN QUINCY ADAMS

☆ ☆ ☆

If only we are faithful to our past, we shall
not have to fear our future. The cause of
peace, justice, and liberty need not fail and
must not fail.

JOHN FOSTER DULLES

☆ ☆ ☆

From THE AGES

Here the free spirit of mankind, at length,
    Throws its last fetters off; and who shall
        place
A limit to the giant's unchained strength,
    Or curb his swiftness in the forward race?

WILLIAM CULLEN BRYANT

☆ ☆ ☆

PANORAMA

The American record is not flawless, as we all
know. The nation whose literature and history lack vigorous self-criticism is more apt to
illustrate the suppression of free speech than
the attainment of alleged perfection. But on
the whole, from the Founding Fathers on, the
American panorama is one we need not blush
to own, one in which we may often take
hearty pride. This is a history good citizens
need to know, to understand their world and
to be able to improve it. With our faith in
majority government we see the importance
of clearer self-knowledge for those expected
to do the thinking and voting.

DIXON WECTER

☆ ☆ ☆

SOUNDING BOARDS

The use of history is to tell us what we are; for
at our birth we are nearly empty vessels and
we become what our traditions pour into us.

We must needs be sounding boards for
past themes, else we should have to repeat,
each in his own experience, the successes and
the failures of our forebears.

What we take to be our own choices are in
fact imposed upon us from without, pressed
into us by the stamps of our inheritance.

LEARNED HAND

☆ ☆ ☆

18

Full of crooked little streets, but I tell you Boston has opened and kept open more turnpikes that lead straight to free thought and free speech and free deeds than any other city of live men or dead men.

OLIVER WENDELL HOLMES

☆　☆　☆

In Massachusetts there has been a consecutive development of thought since colonial times. Her links with the past have never been broken. The influx of new blood and new idea has not overwhelmed the old blood and old idea.

There is in New England a traceable connection between the whole historic volume and stream of human culture—that moving treasury of human thought and experience which flows down out of antiquity and involves us, surrounds and supports us and makes us the thing we are, no matter how we may struggle or how little we may understand.

In Massachusetts you may still stop the first man you meet in the street and find in his first remark the influence of Wyclif or Samuel Adams.

The spiritual life in New England has never been luxuriant. It is one-sided, sad, and inexpressive in many ways. But it has coherence, and this is what makes it valuable for the young American.

JOHN JAY CHAPMAN

☆　☆　☆

LANDING OF THE PILGRIM FATHERS

The breaking waves dashed high
On a stern and rock-bound coast;
And the woods against a stormy sky,
Their giant branches tossed;
And the heavy night hung dark
The hills and waters o'er—
When a band of exiles moored their bark
On a wild New England shore.

Not as the conqueror comes,
They, the true-hearted, came;
Not with the roll of stirring drums,
And the trumpets that sing of fame;
Not as the flying come,
In silence and in fear;
They shook the depths of the desert's gloom
With their hymns of lofty cheer.

Amidst the storm they sang,
And the stars heard, and the sea!
And the sounding aisles of the dim woods
    rang
To the anthem of the free;
The ocean eagle soared
From his nest by the white wave's foam,
And the rocking pines of the forest roared:
This was their welcome home!

There were men with hoary hair
Amidst that pilgrim band;
Why had they come to wither there,
Away from their childhood's land?
There was woman's fearless eye,
Lit by her deep love's truth;
There was manhood's brow serenely high,
And the fiery heart of youth.

What sought they thus afar?
Bright jewels of the mine?
The wealth of seas? the spoils of war?
They sought a faith's pure shrine!
Aye, call it holy ground,
The soil where first they trod!
They left unstained what there they found—
Freedom to worship God!

FELICIA DOROTHEA HEMANS

☆　☆　☆

A nation which does not remember what it was yesterday, does not know what it is today, nor what it is trying to do. We are trying to do a futile thing if we do not know where we came from or what we have been about.

WOODROW WILSON

19

THE AMERICAN PEOPLE

The genius of the United States
is not best or most
in its executives or legislatures,
nor in its ambassadors or authors
or colleges or churches or parlors,
nor even in its newspapers or inventors,
but always most in the common people.

Their manners, speech, dress, friendships,
the freshness and candor of their physiog-
    nomy,
the picturesque looseness of their carriage,
their deathless attachment to freedom,
their aversion to anything indecorous or
    soft or mean,
the practical acknowledgment of the citizens
    of one state by the citizens of all other
    states,
the fierceness of their roused resentment,
their curiosity and welcome of novelty,
their self-esteem and wonderful sympathy,
their susceptibility to a slight,
the air they have of persons who never knew
    how it felt to stand in the presence of
    superiors,
the fluency of their speech,
their delight in music, the sure symptom
    of manly tenderness and native elegance
    of soul,
their good temper and open-handedness,
the terrible significance of their elections,
the President's taking off his hat to them,
    not they to him—
these too are unrhymed poetry.

WALT WHITMAN

☆   ☆   ☆

Ours is become a nation too great to offend
the least, too mighty to be unjust to the weak-
est, too lofty and noble to be ungenerous to
the poorest and lowliest.

STEPHEN S. WISE

☆   ☆   ☆

PLEDGE OF ALLEGIANCE

I pledge allegiance to the flag of the United
States of America and to the Republic for
which it stands, one Nation under God, indivisible, with liberty and justice for all.

☆   ☆   ☆

GIFT OF GOD

In no other country in the world is aspiration
so definite a part of life as it is in America.
The most precious gift God has given to this
land is not its great riches of soil and forest
and mine but the divine discontent planted
deeply in the hearts of the American people.

WILLIAM ALLEN WHITE

☆   ☆   ☆

THE MESSAGE OF THE BELLS

Listen, America!
Whatever you're doing on July 4th,
pause for a moment and listen
to a message from the bells.
Bells and carillons
in churches, schools, and public buildings
will ring in all fifty states.
They will peal out a reminder
of your freedom;
how hard it was won,
how easily it can be lost.
There are appropriate lyrics
that go well with the musical bells.
The first line goes like this:
"When in the course of human events. . ."
We suggest you re-read the
rest of them
to yourself and to your family.
You might find greater
inspiration and certainly
something more meaningful
about Independence Day than
the usual overdose of sunburn,
heartburn, or breaking 90.

NEWSWEEK

II

FAITH OF OUR FATHERS

✩   ✩   ✩

We on this continent should never forget that men first crossed the Atlantic not to find soil for their ploughs but to secure liberty for their souls.

ROBERT J. MC CRACKEN

SPIRITUAL FORCES

We Americans say that the Constitution made the nation.

Well, the Constitution is a great document and we never would have been a nation without it, but it took more than that to make the nation!

Rather it was our forefathers and fore-mothers who made the Constitution and then made it work.

The government they constructed did get great things out of them, but it was not the government primarily that put great things into them.

What put great things into them was their home life, their religion, their sense of personal responsibility to Almighty God, their devotion to education, their love of liberty, their personal character.

When their government pumped, it drew from profound depths in the lives of men and women where creative spiritual forces had been at work.

HARRY EMERSON FOSDICK

☆　☆　☆

PRAYER

God of our fathers and of our fathers' fathers, who in the crises of our national history hast raised up leaders who through faith in thee have found courage to dare and strength to persevere, be with us today in our hour of national opportunity and of national responsibility. Forgive us our self-satisfaction and our self-indulgence, our love of money and our love of pleasure, our readiness to condemn others and to excuse ourselves. Grant us candor to discern thy will for us as a nation, and resolution to follow it; and at this time of the world's need raise up for us, we beseech thee, leaders to go before us into our promised land.

WILLIAM ADAMS BROWN

☆　☆　☆

From MAHMOOD

Old events have modern meanings; only that survives
Of past history which finds kindred in all hearts and lives.

JAMES RUSSELL LOWELL

☆　☆　☆

NATIONAL HYMN

God of our fathers, whose almighty hand
Leads forth in beauty all the starry band
Of shining worlds in splendor through the skies,
Our grateful songs before thy throne arise.

Thy love divine hath led us in the past,
In this free land by thee our lot is cast;
Be thou our ruler, guardian, guide, and stay,
Thy word our law, thy paths our chosen way.

From war's alarms, from deadly pestilence,
Be thy strong arm our ever-sure defense;
Thy true religion in our hearts increase,
Thy bounteous goodness nourish us in peace.

Refresh thy people on their toilsome way,
Lead us from night to never-ending day;
Fill all our lives with love and grace divine,
And glory, laud, and praise be ever thine.

DANIEL C. ROBERTS

☆　☆　☆

Our institutions of freedom will not survive unless they are constantly replenished by the faith that gave them birth.

JOHN FOSTER DULLES

☆　☆　☆

It is impossible to mentally or socially enslave a Bible-reading people. The principles of the Bible are the groundwork of human freedom.

HORACE GREELEY

☆ ☆ ☆

INSCRIPTION

Sacred to the Memory of
John Cooke
Who was buried here in 1695
The last surviving male Pilgrim
Of those who came over in the
Mayflower
The first white settler of this town
And the pioneer in its religious
Moral and business life
A man of character and integrity
And the trusted agent for this
Part of the Commonwealth
Of the Old Colonial
Civil Government of Plymouth.

COOKE MEMORIAL PARK
FAIRHAVEN, MASSACHUSETTS

☆ ☆ ☆

When England grew corrupt, God brought over a number of pious persons and planted them in New England, and this land was planted with a noble vine.

JONATHAN EDWARDS

☆ ☆ ☆

THE MAYFLOWER COMPACT

In ye name of God, Amen. We whose names are underwritten, the loyall subjects of our dread soveraigne Lord, King James, by ye grace of God, of Great Britaine, France, and Ireland king, defender of ye faith, &c., haveing undertaken, for ye glory of God, and advancement of ye Christian faith, and honor of our king and countrie, a voyage to plant ye first colonie in the Northerne parts of Virginia, doe by these presents solemnly & mutualy in ye presence of God, and one of another, covenant & combine our selves togeather into a civill body politick, for our better ordering & preservation & furtherance of ye ends aforesaid; and by vertue hearof do enacte, constitute, and frame such just & equall lawes, ordinances, acts, constitutions,

& offices, from time to time, as shall be thought most meete & convenient for ye generall good of ye Colonie, unto which we promise all due submission and obedience. In witnes wherof we have hereunder subscribed our names at Cap-Codd ye 11. of November, in ye year of ye raigne of our soveraigne lord, King James, of England, France, & Ireland ye eighteenth, and of Scotland ye fiftie-fourth. Ano. Dom. 1620.

☆ ☆ ☆

In the United States religion exercises but little influence upon the laws and upon the details of public opinion; but it directs the customs of the community, and, by regulating domestic life, it regulates the state.

ALEXIS DE TOCQUEVILLE (1839)

☆ ☆ ☆

THE PILGRIM FATHERS

O God, beneath thy guiding hand
　　Our exiled fathers crossed the sea;
And when they trod the wintry strand,
　　With prayer and psalm they worshipped
　　thee.

Thou heard'st, well pleased, the song, the
　　prayer:
　　Thy blessing came; and still its power
Shall onward through all ages bear
　　The memory of that holy hour.

Laws, freedom, truth, and faith in God
　　Came with those exiles o'er the waves;
And where their pilgrim feet have trod,
　　The God they trusted guards their graves.

And here thy name, O, God of love,
　　Their children's children shall adore,
Till these eternal hills remove,
　　And spring adorns the earth no more.

LEONARD BACON

☆ ☆ ☆

We have a right to be proud of our Pilgrim and Puritan fathers. They were ready to do and to suffer anything for their faith, and a faith which breeds heroes is better than an unbelief which leaves nothing worth being a hero for.

OLIVER WENDELL HOLMES

☆   ☆   ☆

No New Englander who is willing to indulge his native feelings, can stand upon the rock where our ancestors set the first foot after their arrival on the American shore, without experiencing emotions very different from those which are excited by any common object of the same nature.

TIMOTHY DWIGHT

☆   ☆   ☆

PLYMOUTH BICENTENNIAL (1820)
I have seldom had more lively feelings from the associations of place than I had when I stood on this blessed rock; and I doubt whether there be a place in the world where a New England man should feel more gratitude, pride, and veneration than when he stands where the first man stood who began the population and glory of his country. The Colosseum, the Alps, and Westminster Abbey have nothing more truly classical, to one who feels as he ought to feel, than this rude and bare rock.

GEORGE TICKNOR

☆   ☆   ☆

SYMBOLIC APPROACH
Each of us has made his symbolic approach to Plymouth Rock; each is here because someone took a step forward and felt a sustaining firmness underfoot, whether the landing took place from the *Mayflower*, from an Irish "coffin ship," on Ellis Island, or from the last jet at Logan or LaGuardia.

FRANCIS RUSSELL

☆   ☆   ☆

THANKSGIVING PROCLAMATION
Soon the bright flurries in the air, tracing on windowpanes the infinite wonders of heavenly space, will mark the flight of a season that came with snowy petals of dogwood drifting, spray beyond delicate spray, in the early luster of spring. Having in mind this fair course of nature from seedtime to flowering, and from flowering to plentiful harvest, safe now against winter storms, and the light of that shining grace which has followed us round the year, permitting us to live in peace and human kindness above the common hope, I appoint Thursday, the twenty-fifth of November [1937], as a Day of Public Thanksgiving in this State [Connecticut]. Let us then, as our fathers used, praise the Giver of Life for the ample fruit of the earth, sweetened by sun and rain, and for the work of the laborer worthy of his hire in every task and station: for food and clothing and shelter that serve the body's need. Let us praise him especially for the blessings which have warmed and fostered the spirit: for every brave, just, and generous deed, every impulse of brotherly love; for every counsel of wisdom and comfort, every witness of truth, every thought of friends who walk with us still, though lost to our sight—for all tokens of goodness in man, which have deepened faith in our power, looking within the heart, to fix our eyes upon virtue as upon the Pole Star, and by it keep our way even to the mortal end. For these mercies, without name or number, let us rejoice and give praise.

WILBUR L. CROSS

☆   ☆   ☆

REDEDICATION
Men grow in stature
only as they
daily rededicate themselves
to a noble faith.

DWIGHT D. EISENHOWER

☆   ☆   ☆

25

HERITAGE

Puritanism was a cutting edge which hewed liberty, democracy, humanitarianism, and universal education out of the black forest of feudal Europe and the American wilderness.

Puritan doctrine taught each person to consider himself a significant if sinful unit to whom God had given a particular place and duty, and that he must help his fellow men.

Puritanism is an American heritage to be grateful for and not to be sneered at because it required everyone to attend divine worship and maintained a strict code of moral ethics.

SAMUEL ELIOT MORISON

☆　☆　☆

RESOLUTION

To proclaim a true and absolute soul freedom to all the people of the land impartially so that no person be forced to pray, nor pray otherwise than as his soul believeth and consenteth.

ROGER WILLIAMS

☆　☆　☆

AMERICA

My country, 'tis of Thee,
Sweet Land of Liberty
　Of thee I sing;
Land where my fathers died,
Land of the pilgrims' pride,
From every mountain side
　Let Freedom ring.

My native country, thee,
Land of the noble free,
　Thy name I love;
I love thy rocks and rills,
Thy woods and templed hills,
My heart with rapture thrills
　Like that above.

Let music swell the breeze,
And ring from all the trees

Sweet Freedom's song;
Let mortal tongues awake;
Let all that breathe partake;
Let rocks their silence break,
　The sound prolong.

Our fathers' God to Thee,
Author of Liberty,
　To thee we sing,
Long may our land be bright
With Freedom's holy light,
Protect us by thy might
　Great God, our King.

Our glorious Land to-day,
'Neath Education's sway,
　Soars upward still.
Its hills of learning fair,
Whose bounties all may share,
Behold them everywhere
　On vale and hill!

Thy safeguard, Liberty,
The school shall ever be,—
　Our Nation's pride!
No tyrant hand shall smite,
While with encircling might
All here are taught the Right
　With Truth allied.

Beneath Heaven's gracious will
The stars of progress still
　Our course do sway;
In unity sublime
To broader heights we climb,
Triumphant over Time,
　God speeds our way!

Grand birthright of our sires,
Our altars and our fires
　Keep we still pure!
Our starry flag unfurled,
The hope of all the world,
In peace and light impearled,
　God hold secure!

SAMUEL F. SMITH

☆ ☆ ☆

America has much for which to thank Roger Williams: for his religious and intellectual individualism, for his principles of religious toleration and the separation of church and state, and for the precious principle of democracy as a way of life.

Above all, perhaps, America—and other democratic peoples everywhere—may be deeply grateful to him for his courage—the courage to think straight and to fight for the ideals he knew were right, even though he were in a minority of one; the courage to face persecution, banishment, and suffering for his convictions; and the courage to build firmly the first society in the world dedicated to the proposition that all men are free and equal.

MAX SAVELLE

☆ ☆ ☆

From HAIL, COLUMBIA!

Hail, Columbia, happy land!
Hail, ye heroes, heav'n born band!
Who fought and bled in freedom's cause,
Who fought and bled in freedom's cause,
And when the storm of war was gone,
Enjoyed the peace your valor won.
Let independence be our boast,
Ever mindful what it cost;
Ever grateful for the prize,
Let its altar reach the skies.

Behold the chief who now commands,
Once more to serve his country, stands,
The rock on which the storm will beat!
The rock on which the storm will beat!
But armed in virtue, firm and true,
His hopes are fixed on heav'n and you.
When hope was sinking in dismay,
When gloom obscured Columbia's day,
His steady mind, from changes free,
Resolv'd on death or liberty.

JOSEPH HOPKINSON

☆ ☆ ☆

MEMORIAL TABLET

General Charles Cotesworth Pinckney
One of the founders of
the American Republic.

In war
he was the companion in arms
and the friend of Washington.

In peace
he enjoyed his unchanging confidence
and maintained with enlightened zeal
the principles of his administration
and of the Constitution.

As a Statesman
he bequeathed to his country the sentiment,
Millions for defence
Not a cent for tribute.

As a lawyer
his learning was various and profound,
his principles pure, his practice liberal.
With all the accomplishments
of the gentleman
he combined the virtues of the patriot
and the piety of the Christian.

His name
is recorded in the history of his country
inscribed on the charter of her liberties
and cherished in the affections of her
citizens.

SAINT MICHAEL'S CHURCH
CHARLESTON, SOUTH CAROLINA

☆ ☆ ☆

Equality to us is basically a religious ideal. It does not refer to talent, ability, culture or background, for we differ in those respects. It does not even refer to equality of opportunity; this is a consequence, rather than the substance, of our belief. Equality means one simple thing—in the words of Al Smith, "We believe in the common brotherhood of man under the common fatherhood of God."

RICHARD M. NIXON

☆ ☆ ☆

☆ ☆ ☆

In its main features the Declaration of Independence is a great spiritual document.

It is a declaration not of material but of spiritual conceptions.

Equality, liberty, popular sovereignty, the rights of man—these are the elements which we can see and touch.

They are ideals.

They have their source and their roots in the religious convictions.

Unless the faith of the American people in these religious convictions is to endure, the principles of our Declaration will perish.

CALVIN COOLIDGE

☆ ☆ ☆

A SIGNER DECLARES

There is a tide in the affairs of men, a nick of time. We perceive it now before us. To hesitate is to consent to our own slavery.

That noble instrument upon your table, that insures immortality to its author, should be subscribed this very morning by every pen in this house. He that will not respond to its accents, and strain every nerve to carry into effect its provisions, is unworthy of the name of free man.

For my own part, of property, I have some; of reputation, more. That reputation is staked, that property is pledged on the issue of this contest; and although these grey hairs must soon descend into the sepulcher, I would infinitely rather that they descend thither by the hand of the executioner than desert at this crisis the sacred cause of my country.

JOHN WITHERSPOON

☆ ☆ ☆

There is nothing in the Universe that I fear but that I shall not know all my duty, or fail to do it.

MARY LYON

☆ ☆ ☆

A CONGRESSMAN'S PRAYER

Almighty Father! look in mercy down:
　Oh! grant me virtue, to perform my part—
　The patriot's fervour, and the statesman's art
In thought, word, deed, preserve me from thy frown.

Direct me to the paths of bright renown—
　Guide my frail bark, by truth's unerring chart,
　Inspire my soul, and purify my heart;
And with success my stedfast purpose crown.

My country's weal—be that my polar star—
　Justice, thou Rock of Ages, is thy law—
And when thy summons calls me to thy bar,
　Be this my plea, thy gracious smile to draw—
That all my ways to justice were inclin'd—
And all my aims—the blessing of mankind.

JOHN QUINCY ADAMS

☆ ☆ ☆

UNQUENCHABLE FAITH

On the Fourth of July, 1826, America celebrated its jubilee—the Fiftieth Anniversary of Independence. John Adams, second President of the United States, died that day, aged ninety, while from Maine to Georgia bells rang and cannon boomed. And on that same day, Thomas Jefferson died before sunset in Virginia.

In their dying, in that swift, so aptly celebrated double departure, is something which shakes an American to the heart. It was not their great fame, their long lives or even the record of their work that made these two seem indestructible. It was their faith, their bounding, unquenchable faith in the future, their sure, immortal belief that mankind, if it so desired, could be free.

CATHERINE DRINKER BOWEN

☆ ☆ ☆

MOTTOES

Alabama: We dare defend our rights.

Alaska: North to the future.

Arizona: *Ditat Deus* (God enriches).

Arkansas: *Regnat populus* (The people rule).

California: *Eureka* (I have found it).

Colorado: *Nil sine numine* (Nothing without the Deity).

Connecticut: *Qui transtulit sustinet* (He who transplanted continues to sustain).

Delaware: Liberty and independence.

Florida: In God we trust.

Georgia: Wisdom, justice, and moderation.

Hawaii: *Ua Mau Ke Ea O Ka Aina I Ka Pono* (The life of the land is perpetuated in righteousness).

Idaho: *Esto Perpetua* (Mayest thou endure forever!).

Illinois: State sovereignty—national union.

Indiana: The crossroads of America.

Iowa: Our liberties we prize and our rights we will maintain.

Kansas: *Ad astra per aspera* (To the stars through difficulties).

Kentucky: United we stand, divided we fall.

Louisiana: Union, justice, and confidence.

Maine: *Dirigo* (I guide).

Maryland: *Scuto bonae voluntatis tuae coronasti nos* (With the shield of thy goodwill thou hast covered us).

Massachusetts: *Ense petit placidam sub libertate quietem* (By the sword we seek peace, but peace only under liberty).

Michigan: *Si quaeris peninsulam amoenam circumspice* (If you seek a pleasant peninsula, look around you).

Minnesota: *L'Etoile du Nord* (The star of the north).

Mississippi: *Virtute et armis* (By valor and arms).

Missouri: *Salus populi suprema lex esto* (Let the welfare of the people be the supreme law).

Montana: *Oro y plata* (Gold and silver).

Nebraska: Equality before the law.

Nevada: All for our country.

New Hampshire: Live free or die.

New Jersey: Liberty and prosperity.

New Mexico: *Crescit eundo* (It grows as it goes).

New York: Excelsior.

North Carolina: *Esse quam videri* (To be rather than to seem).

North Dakota: Liberty and union, now and forever, one and inseparable.

Ohio: With God, all things are possible.

Oklahoma: *Labor omnia vincit* (Labor conquers all things).

Oregon: The Union.

Pennsylvania: Virtue, liberty, and independence.

Rhode Island: Hope.

South Carolina: *Animis opibusque parati* (Prepared in mind and resources).

South Dakota: Under God the people rule.

Tennessee: Agriculture and commerce.

Texas: Friendship.

Utah: Industry.

Vermont: Freedom and unity.

Virginia: *Sic semper tyrannis* (Thus ever to tyrants).

Washington: *Alki* (By and by).

West Virginia: *Montani semper liberi* (Mountaineers are always freemen).

Wisconsin: Forward.

Wyoming: *Cedant arma togae* (Let arms yield to the gown).

☆ ☆ ☆

AN EDITOR'S CREED

I am in earnest,
I will not equivocate,
I will not excuse,
I will not retreat a single inch,
And I will be heard.

WILLIAM LLOYD GARRISON

☆ ☆ ☆

WASHINGTON

Thank God! the people's choice was just,
The one man equal to his trust.
Wise beyond lore, and without weakness
   good,
Calm in the strength of flawless rectitude.

JOHN GREENLEAF WHITTIER

☆   ☆   ☆

PRAYER

We thank thee for our inheritance in the nation of which we are members, for the land we love, for the calling and privileges of the Republic, for the enrichment of mutual interest and service, for exchange of thought, for brotherly emulation, for mutual aid. We thank thee for the gifts of the past and the hope of the future; for the noble traditions and high ideals committed to our charge; for civil and religious liberty; for the open Bible, and the inviolable conscience; for the Gospel of thy grace; for the awakening sense of brotherhood and social obligation; and for the hope of the coming of thy Kingdom.

RICHARD ROBERTS

☆   ☆   ☆

NEW ENGLAND STEEPLE

Tall on the village hill the church stood
   lonely
against the dark,
shining and white against the stars with
   only
our eyes to mark

its midnight solitude, its soaring steeple
pointed and clean.
Far down the dim-lit street the village
   people
dreamt unseen;

and past the green and past the church there
   slumbered
the quiet dead:
on the bend of the hill the low stones gleamed

unnumbered.
"Look up," you said.

"We are uncounted among the silent sleepers
in this windless land—
we alone and the crying brookside peepers.
Give me your hand.

Here is our love," you said, "in this white
   spire leaping
into the sky:
it will endure though we be awake or sleeping
or if we die."

In that instant of truth, in the clear precipi-
   tate hour,
dark was undone,
and the mellow bell in the sheer incredible
   tower
struck the new day with one.

FRANCES FROST

☆   ☆   ☆

DOUBLY AMERICAN

I am doubly an American, because I am foreign-born. It may be that the native-born Americans take America for granted. Foreign-born Americans like myself do not take America for granted. We look upon American citizenship as the most precious and sacred of boons. We understand what it is that we have left behind us—of denial of the freedoms of man—and we know what it is that has come to be our high destiny, to be a sharer in Amerian freedom, to be a bearer of American responsibility, to be a devotee of the American Democracy, to use American freedom not for one's own advantage but for the service of the American Democracy and for the preservation of its loftiest ideals and purposes.

STEPHEN S. WISE

☆   ☆   ☆

BLESSINGS OF THE GREAT SPIRIT

Brother, we know that the Great Spirit is pleased that we follow the traditions and customs of our forefathers—for in so doing we receive his blessing—we have received strength and vigor for the chase.

The Great Spirit has provided abundance—when we are hungry we find the forest filled with game—when thirsty, we slake our thirst at the pure streams and springs that spread around us. When weary, the leaves of the tree are our bed—we retire with contentment to rest—we rise with gratitude to the Great Preserver.

Renovated strength in our limbs, and bounding joy in our hearts, we feel blessed and happy. No luxuries, no vices, no disputed titles, no avaricious desires, shake the foundations of our society, or disturb our peace and happiness.

We know the Great Spirit is better pleased with his red children, than with his white, when he bestows upon us a hundred fold more blessings than upon you.

RED JACKET

☆   ☆   ☆

EXAMPLES OF DEVOTION

George Washington was one of the richest men in America at the time of the Revolution. His fields were well tilled and fenced. His mansion was beautiful and commodious. Prudence would have kept him out of the war and saved his property, but the love of liberty impelled him to stake his life and fortune on the outcome. When he won, we all won.

Moses could have lived in the King's court in safety, and perhaps succeeded to the Egyptian throne. He preferred hardship with his own people to luxury with the loss of honor and self-respect. And in his daring, the whole world profited.

The Pilgrim Fathers could have made a good living in England, or in Holland, but their dream of independence drove them to America and hardships. In their adventure and prowess was laid the foundation of idealism for the world's greatest nation.

The world owes some of its richest blessings and finest privileges to men who sacrificed the bird they held in their hand for better birds in the bush. It is an old fallacy that the certain is preferable to the possible.

SIMON EDELSTEIN

☆   ☆   ☆

From THE CRISIS (1776)

These are the times that try men's souls. The summer soldier and the sunshine patriot will, in this crisis, shrink from the service of their country; but he that stands it now, deserves the love and thanks of man and woman.

THOMAS PAINE

☆   ☆   ☆

SHADOWS

The lamp Erasmus lighted has burned low;
Its tiny flame is bent beneath the storm,
And in the terrifying shadows go
Barbaric monsters hideous of form.
Soon time shall say that Voltaire lived in
    vain,
That Milton's freedom was an idle dream;
And men shall feel the flicking lash again
And run before the chariot's crashing beam.

Another man must walk through Valley
    Forge,
Another Lincoln face the night alone,
Before the world shakes off its present
    scourge
And men can say that freedom is their own.
Yet if our love to these does not reply,
In agony another Christ must die.

JOHN H. STARIE

☆   ☆   ☆

Our greatest need is to regain confidence in our spiritual heritage.

JOHN FOSTER DULLES

32

III

WE HOLD THESE TRUTHS

☆   ☆   ☆

Among the natural rights of the colonists are these: First a right to life, secondly to liberty, thirdly to property; together with the right to defend them in the best manner they can.

SAMUEL ADAMS

WHAT IS AN AMERICAN?

An American is one who believes in the right of men and women—of whatever creed, class, color, or ancestry—to live as human beings with the dignity becoming the children of God.

An American is one who believes in the right to be free; free not only from crushing coercions and dictatorships and regimentation, but free for that way of life where men may think and speak as they choose and worship God as they see fit.

An American is one who believes in the right to vote, the right to work, the right to learn, the right to live, and—what is equally important—the right to be different; for he knows that if we ever lose our right to be different, we lose our right to be free.

An American is one who believes in democracy, not only for himself, but for all his fellow-Americans, and by democracy he means not simply the rule of the majority, but the rights of minorities—and those minorities have rights, not because they are minorities, but because they are human beings.

An American is one who believes in the responsibility of privilege. What he asks for himself, he is willing to grant to others; what he demands from others, he is willing to give himself. His creed is not alone, "Live and let live," but "Live and help live."

An American is one who acts from faith in others, not fear of others; from understanding, not prejudice; from good will, not hatred. To bigotry he gives no sanction; to intolerance, no support.

The only question the True American ever asks is not, "Are you a Protestant or Catholic, Gentile or Jew, white or colored?" but, "Are you an American? If you are an American, then give me your hand, for I am an American too."

HAROLD W. RUOPP

☆　　☆　　☆

EPITAPH

Here lies the body of
Richard Thomas
An inglishman by birth,
A Whig of '76.
By occupation a cooper,
Now food for worms.
Like an old rumpuncheon,
marked, numbered and shooked,
he will be raised again and finished
by his creator.
America, my adopted country,
my best advice to you is this,
Take care of your liberties.

FORT HILL CEMETERY
WINSLOW, MAINE

☆　　☆　　☆

WORDS OF LIGHT

The sacred rights of mankind are not to be rummaged from among old parchments or musty records. They are written, as with a sunbeam, in the whole volume of human nature, by the hand of the divinity itself, and can never be erased or obscured by mortal power.

ALEXANDER HAMILTON

☆　　☆　　☆

THE AMERICAN'S CREED

I believe in the United States of America as a government of the people, by the people, for the people; whose just powers are derived from the consent of the governed; a democracy in a republic; a sovereign nation of many sovereign states; a perfect union, one and inseparable; established upon those principles of freedom, equality, and humanity for which American patriots sacrificed their lives and fortunes. I, therefore, believe it is my duty to my country to love it, to support its constitution, to obey its laws, to respect its flag, and to defend it against all enemies.

WILLIAM TYLER PAGE
ADOPTED BY CONGRESS (1918)

35

THE DAY THE BELLS RANG
JULY 4, 1776

During the day, the streets of Philadelphia were crowded with people anxious to learn the decision.

In the steeple of the old State House was a bell on which, by a happy coincidence, was inscribed, "Proclaim liberty throughout all the land unto all the inhabitants thereof."

In the morning, when Congress assembled, the bell-ringer went to his post, having placed his boy below to announce when the Declaration was adopted, that his bell might be the first to peal forth the glad tidings.

Long he waited, while the deliberations went on. Impatiently the old man shook his head and repeated, "They will never do it! They will never do it!"

Suddenly he heard his boy clapping his hands and shouting, "Ring! Ring!"

Grasping the iron tongue, he swung it to and fro, proclaiming the glad news of liberty to all the land.

The crowded streets caught up the sound. Every steeple re-echoed it.

All that night, by shouts, and illuminations, and booming of cannon, the people declared their joy.

From A BRIEF HISTORY OF THE UNITED STATES (1871)

☆　☆　☆

AVENUES OF HOPE

God has placed upon our head a diadem and has laid at our feet power and wealth beyond definition or calculation. But we must not forget that we take these gifts upon the condition that justice and mercy shall hold the reins of power and that the upward avenues of hope shall be free to all the people.

BENJAMIN HARRISON

☆　☆　☆

"... from every mountainside, let freedom ring."

If America is to be a great nation, this must become true.

So let freedom ring from the prodigious hilltops of New Hampshire.

Let freedom ring from the mighty mountains of New York.

Let freedom ring from the heightening Alleghenies of Pennsylvania.

Let freedom ring from the snowcapped Rockies of Colorado.

Let freedom ring from the curvacious peaks of California.

Let freedom ring from Stone Mountain of Georgia.

Let freedom ring from Lookout Mountain of Tennessee.

Let freedom ring from every hill and mole of Mississippi.

From every mountainside, let freedom ring.

MARTIN LUTHER KING, JR.

☆　☆　☆

WHAT THEY BELIEVED

The American Founding Fathers believed deeply—

in the ability of a human being to learn enough in order to take part in self-government;

in the capacity of people to make sense of their lives if given reasonable conditions within society itself;

in the responsive power of men when exposed to great ideas;

in people to stand upright spiritually without ornate or complicated props;

in man to live under due process of law;

in man to make basic decisions concerning his religion or his politics or anything else—again given the conditions that made this possible.

NORMAN COUSINS

☆　☆　☆

PREAMBLE OF THE CONSTITUTION

We the People of the United States, in Order to form a more perfect Union, establish Justice, insure domestic Tranquility, provide for the common defence, promote the general Welfare, and secure the Blessings of Liberty to ourselves and our Posterity, do ordain and establish this Constitution for the United States of America.

☆　☆　☆

LETTER TO THE CONSTITUTIONAL CONVENTION

We kept steadily in our view that which appears to us the greatest interest of every true American, the consolidation of our Union, in which is involved our prosperity, felicity, safety, perhaps our national existence.

GEORGE WASHINGTON

☆　☆　☆

FIFTY-SIX SIGNERS

The signers of the Declaration of Independence numbered fifty-six men. They were of varied backgrounds, ages, education, property and experience. Some were already famous—Adams, Franklin; some were unheard of, recruited at the last minute as replacements for men who refused to support independence. Two of the signers were only twenty years of age; sixteen were in their thirties; twenty in their forties; eleven in their fifties; six in their sixties; and only one, Franklin, over seventy. All but two were married; each had an average of six children. Twenty-five were lawyers; twelve were merchants; four were doctors; one a preacher; and a famous one, a printer. Half were college graduates; some were self-educated. Few benefited from their bravery but not one recanted his original declaration of independence.

SUNSHINE MAGAZINE

☆　☆　☆

DEFINITION OF GOVERNMENT

Government. As *society* arises from our wants, so arises *government* from our errors, vices, and crimes. Were man a perfect being the true end and design of government, whatever form insures it with the least expense, consistent also with the general security and happiness, is to be preferred.

Government being therefore necessary for the preservation of social order, it is obvious that the exercise of it should be committed to persons in whom those qualities are most likely to be found, the perfection of which is among the attributes of him who is emphatically styled the Supreme Being; namely, *wisdom, goodness* and *power*; wisdom, to discern the real interest of the community; goodness, to endeavor always to pursue that real interest; and strength, or power, to carry this knowledge and intention into action.

These are the natural foundations of sovereignty; and these are the requisites that ought to be found in every well constituted government.

FAMILY ENCYCLOPEDIA (1834)

☆　☆　☆

THE NEW ORDER

The great seal of the United States, printed on all one dollar bills, carries the Latin inscription *Novus Ordo Seclorum.*

The designers of the great seal knew that behind the actual accomplishments and failures of the political and economic life of this country there is a dream.

Somehow the basic principles of American democracy are felt to be related to the eternal scheme of things.

Implied in the motto "The New Order of the Ages" is the belief that this country in its social life demonstrates a fundamental revision of man's traditional way of conducting his affairs, and his change places him in tune with the universe.

CHARLES DUELL KEAN

☆ ☆ ☆

WHY I BELIEVE IN AMERICA

Because we are free to choose our government, to speak our minds, to observe our different ways.

Because we are generous with our freedom and share our rights with those who disagree with us.

Because we hate no people and covet no people's land.

Because we are blessed with a natural and varied abundance.

Because we set no limit to a man's achievement: in mine, factory, field, or service in business or the arts, an able man, regardless of class or creed, can realize his ambition.

Because we have great dreams and the opportunity to make those dreams come true.

WENDELL WILLKIE

☆ ☆ ☆

To the States or any one of them, or any city
of the States, *Resist much, obey little,*
Once unquestioning obedience, once fully
enslaved,
Once fully enslaved, no nation, state, city,
of this earth, ever afterward resumes its
liberty.

WALT WHITMAN

☆ ☆ ☆

POPULAR SOVEREIGNTY

Sovereignty in America is popular, first and last; government always exists for the people; and the only tenable law of progress is to allow as much freedom as possible to as many people as will stoutly possess themselves of it. "Walk from the people," as the wise proverb runs, "and you walk into night." Our historic eye is on the *people*: "The People, Yes."

T. V. SMITH

☆ ☆ ☆

From BOSTON
We grant no dukedoms to the few,
    We hold like rights and shall;
Equal on Sunday in the pew,
    On Monday in the mall.
For what avail the plough or sail,
Or land, or life, if freedom fail?

RALPH WALDO EMERSON

☆ ☆ ☆

KEY TO PROGRESS

Liberty has been the key to our progress in the past and is the key to our progress in the future. If we can preserve liberty in all its essentials, there is no limit to the future of the American people.

ROBERT A. TAFT

☆ ☆ ☆

PEOPLE'S GOVERNMENT

The Government of the Union is emphatically and truly a government of the people. In form and in substance it emanates from them. Its powers are granted by them and are to be exercised directly on them and for their benefit.

JOHN MARSHALL

☆ ☆ ☆

MORAL DOCUMENT

The ethical and moral concepts of Christianity are found all the way through the Declaration of Independence. It was on July 4, 1776, that fifty men gathered in Independence Hall in Philadelphia to declare this nation free from Great Britain and they affixed their signatures and then the Liberty Bell rang out. It was the birthday of a small nation that was to become the mightiest and greatest nation the world has ever known. Down through the years God has mightily blessed America.

BILLY GRAHAM

☆ ☆ ☆

CREED

I am an American:
That's the way we put it,
Simply, without any swagger, without any
   brag,
In those four plain words.
We speak them softly, just to ourselves.
We roll them on the tongue, touching every
   syllable, getting the feel of them, the
   enduring flavor.
We speak them humbly, thankfully, rever-
   ently:
I am an American.

They are more than words, really.
They are the sum of the lives of a vast
   multitude of men and women and wide-
   eyed children.
They are a manifesto to mankind; speak
   those four words anywhere in the
   world—yes, anywhere—and those who
   hear will recognize their meaning.
They are a pledge. A pledge that stems from
   a document which says: "When in the
   course of human events," and goes on from
   there.
A pledge to those who dreamed that dream
   before it was set to paper, to those who
   have lived it since, and died for it.
Those words are a covenant with a great host
   of plain Americans, Americans who put
   their share of meaning into them.
Listen, and you can hear the voices echoing
   through them, words that sprang white-hot
   from bloody lips, scornful lips, lips a-
   tremble with human pity:
"Don't give up the ship! Fight her till she
   dies. . . Damn the torpedoes! Go ahead!
   . . . Do you want to live forever? . . . Don't
   cheer, boys; the poor devils are dying."
Laughing words, June-warm words, words
   cold as January ice:
"Root, hog, or die. . . I've come from Alabama with my banjo. . . Pike's Peak or bust!
   . . . Busted, by God! . . . When you say that,

smile. . . . Wait till you see the whites of
   their eyes. . . . With malice toward none,
   with charity for all, with firmness in the
   right. . . . I am not a Virginian, but an
   American."
You can hear men in assembly summoned,
   there in Philadelphia, hear the scratch of
   their quills as they wrote words for the
   hour and produced a document for the
   ages.
You can hear them demanding guarantees
   for which they suffered through the hell of
   war, hear a Yankee voice intoning the text
   of ten brief amendments.
You can hear the slow cadences of a gaunt
   and weary man at Gettysburg, dedicating
   not a cemetery, but a nation.

You can hear those echoes as you walk along
   the streets, hear them in the rumble of
   traffic; you can hear them as you stand at
   the lathe, in the roaring factory; hear them
   in the clack of train wheels, in the drum-
   ming throb of the air liner; hear them in
   the corn fields and in the big woods and in
   the mine pits and the oil fields.
But they aren't words any longer; they're a
   way of life, a pattern of living.
They're the dawn that brings another day in
   which to get on the job.
They're the noon whistle, with a chance to get
   the kinks out of your back, to get a bowl of
   soup, a plate of beans, a cup of coffee into
   your belly.
They're evening, with another day's work
   done; supper with the wife and kids; a
   movie, or the radio, or the newspaper or a
   magazine—and no Gestapo snooping at the
   door and threatening to kick your teeth in.
They are a pattern of life as lived by a free
   people, freedom that has its roots in rights
   and obligations:
The right to go to a church with a cross or a
   star or a dome or a steeple, or not to go to
   any church at all; and the obligation to respect others in that same right.

40

The right to harangue on a street corner, to hire a hall and shout your opinions till your tonsils are worn to a frazzle; and the obligation to curb your tongue now and then.

The right to go to school, to learn a trade, to enter a profession, to earn an honest living; and the obligation to do an honest day's work.

The right to put your side of the argument in the hands of a jury; and the obligation to abide by the laws that you and your delegates have written in the statute books.

The right to choose who shall run our government for us, the right to a secret vote that counts just as much as the next fellow's in the final tally; and the obligation to use that right, and guard it and keep it clean.

The right to hope, to dream, to pray; the obligation to serve.

These are some of the meanings of those four words, meanings we don't often stop to tally up or even list.

Only in the stillness of a moonless night, or in the quiet of a Sunday afternoon, or in the thin dawn of a new day, when our world is close about us, do they rise up in our memories and stir in our sentient hearts.

Only then? That is not wholly so—not today!

For today we are drilling holes and driving rivets, shaping barrels and loading shells, fitting wings and welding hulls,

And we are remembering Wake Island, and Bataan, and Corregidor, and Hong Kong and Singapore and Batavia;

We are remembering Warsaw and Rotterdam and Rouen and Coventry.

Remembering, and muttering with each rivet driven home: "There's another one for remembrance!"

They're plain words, those four. Simple words.

You could write them on your thumbnail, if you chose,

Or you could sweep them all across the sky, horizon to horizon.

You could grave them on stone, you could carve them on the mountain ranges.

You could sing them, to the tune of "Yankee Doodle."

But you needn't. You needn't do any of those things,

For those words are graven in the hearts of 130,000,000 people,

They are familiar to 130,000,000 tongues, every sound and every syllable.

But when we speak them we speak them softly, proudly, gratefully:

I am an American.

HAL BORLAND

☆   ☆   ☆

FREEDOM'S PRICE TAG

We have enjoyed so much freedom for so long that we are perhaps in danger of forgetting how much blood it cost to establish the Bill of Rights.

FELIX FRANKFURTER

☆   ☆   ☆

The principal business of government is to further and promote human strivings.

WILBUR L. CROSS

☆   ☆   ☆

The things required for prosperous labor, prosperous manufactures, and prosperous commerce are three. First, liberty; second, liberty; third, liberty.

HENRY WARD BEECHER

☆   ☆   ☆

I have no private purposes to accomplish, no party projects to build up, no enemies to punish—nothing to serve but my country.

ZACHARY TAYLOR

☆   ☆   ☆

☆ ☆ ☆

OATH OF NATURALIZED CITIZENS

I hereby declare, on oath, that I absolutely and entirely renounce and abjure all allegiance and fidelity to any foreign prince, potentate, state, or sovereignty of whom or which I have heretofore been a subject or citizen; that I will support and defend the Constitution and laws of the United States of America against all enemies, foreign and domestic; that I will bear true faith and allegiance to the same; and that I take this obligation freely without any mental reservation or purpose of evasion; so help me God. In acknowledgment whereof I have hereunto affixed my signature.

☆ ☆ ☆

We have accepted a second Bill of Rights under which a new basis of security and prosperity can be established for all—regardless of station, race, or creed. Among these are:

The right of a useful and remunerative job in the industries or shops or farms or mines of the nation.

The right to earn enough to provide adequate food and clothing and recreation.

The right of every farmer to raise and sell his products at a return which will give him and his family a decent living.

The right of every businessman, large and small, to trade in an atmosphere of freedom from unfair competition and domination by monopolies at home or abroad.

The right of every family to a decent home.

The right of adequate medical care and the opportunity to achieve and enjoy good health.

The right to adequate protection from the economic fears of old age, sickness, accident, and unemployment.

The right to a good education.

FRANKLIN D. ROOSEVELT

☆ ☆ ☆

Every genuine American holds to the ideals of justice for all men, of independence, including free speech and free action within the limits of law, of obedience to law, of universal education, of material well-being for all the well-behaving and industrious, of peace and goodwill among men.

CHARLES ELIOT NORTON

☆ ☆ ☆

WHAT IS FREEDOM?

You cannot say what freedom is in a single sentence. It is not necessary to define it. It is enough to point to it.

Freedom is a man lifting a gate latch at dusk, and sitting for a while on the porch before he goes to bed.

It is the violence of an argument outside an election poll; it is the righteous anger of the pulpits.

It is the warm laughter of a girl on a park bench.

It is all the howdys in the world, and all the hellos.

It is you, trying to remember the words of "The Star-Spangled Banner."

It is the sea breaking on wide sands somewhere, and the shoulders of a mountain supporting the sky.

It is the air you fill your lungs with, and the dirt that is your garden.

It is the absence of apprehension at the sound of approaching footsteps outside your closed door.

It is your hot resentment of intrigue, the tilt of your chin, and the tightening of your lips sometimes.

It is all the things you do and want to keep on doing.

It is all the things you feel and cannot help feeling.

Freedom? It is you!

HAZEL PARKER HAYNES

☆ ☆ ☆

Let us strive to build an America of new faith in old dreams—an America eternally vigorous and creative. Let us preserve America as a reservoir of hope and faith in the midst of cynicism and despair.

HUBERT H. HUMPHREY

☆   ☆   ☆

WITHIN OURSELVES

The only place where we can save democracy is within ourselves, by making it worth saving, by trying to live up—as democratic citizens —to the obligations which we assume. I would remind you that the hardest thing on earth to be is a citizen of a democratic society; this is probably why history shows so few democratic societies that have endured.

HERBERT AGAR

☆   ☆   ☆

FAITHFUL AT DUTY

Nearly one hundred years ago, there was a day of remarkable gloom and darkness, still known as the Dark Day—a day when the light of the sun was slowly extinguished as if by an eclipse.

The Legislature of Connecticut was in session, and as the members saw the unexpected and unaccountable darkness coming on, they shared in the general awe and terror. It was supposed by many that the last day, the day of judgment, had come. Someone, in the consternation of the hour, moved an adjournment.

Then there arose an old Puritan legislator, Davenport Stanford, who said that if the last day had come he desired to be found at his post of duty, and therefore moved that candles be brought so that the House could proceed with its business.

So, my son, when in the conflict of life the cloud and the darkness come, stand unflinchingly by your post; remain faithful to the discharge of your duty.

ROBERT E. LEE

☆   ☆   ☆

From THE EMANCIPATION PROCLAMATION

That on the 1st day of January, A.D. 1863, all persons held as slaves within any State or designated part of a State the people whereof shall then be in rebellion against the United States shall be then, thenceforward, and forever free; and the executive government of the United States, including the military and naval authority thereof, will recognize and maintain the freedom of such persons and will do no act or acts to repress such persons, or any of them, in any efforts they may make for their actual freedom.

ABRAHAM LINCOLN

☆   ☆   ☆

Human freedom is not a gift of man. It is an achievement by man and, as it was gained by vigilance and struggle, so it may be lost in indifference and supineness.

HARRY F. BYRD

☆   ☆   ☆

An individual may not be able to write legislation for the entire nation, but he can certainly make his concerns intelligent and important to the people around him.

He can learn how to find essential information and how to evaluate it.

He can learn how to appraise organizations and invest himself in the ones he can trust.

He can communicate his concerns to the group of which he is a part.

What, after all, is a democratic civilization except a congeries of viewpoints leading up to a consensus?

Not every individual may be able to have his viewpoint govern that consensus, but that is part of the democratic chance.

Each idea is an entry; it calls for vitality and staying power of a very high order.

NORMAN COUSINS

☆ ☆ ☆

WILLIAM PENN'S LEGACY

William Penn spent less than four years in the colonies. Yet his influence on their development and his legacy to the future United States were as important a contribution as that made by any settler or other English promoter of the 17th Century.

He shared prominently in establishing three colonies—New Jersey, Delaware, and Pennsylvania.

He saw that humble folk got a chance to start their lives anew under favorable conditions.

He practiced and preached religious freedom.

He was a great humanitarian in an inhumane age.

He wrought so well that his ideals have in the long course of time become primary ingredients in the tradition of democracy in America.

CARL BRIDENBAUGH

☆ ☆ ☆

DEMOCRACY

Democracy is based on the conviction that man has the moral and intellectual capacity, as well as the inalienable right, to govern himself with reason and justice.

Democracy maintains that government is established for the benefit of the individual, and is charged with the responsibility of protecting the rights of the individual and his freedom in the exercise of his abilities.

Democracy has proved that social justice can be achieved through peaceful change.

Democracy holds that free nations can settle differences justly and maintain lasting peace.

HARRY S. TRUMAN

☆ ☆ ☆

CHOICEST OF BLESSINGS

The liberty enjoyed by the people of these States, of worshipping Almighty God agreeably to their consciences, is not only among the choicest of their blessings, but also of their rights.

GEORGE WASHINGTON

☆ ☆ ☆

UNMANIFEST DESTINY

To what new fates, my country, far
  And unforeseen of foe or friend,
Beneath what unexpected star,
  Compelled to what unchosen end,

Across the sea that knows no beach
  The Admiral of Nations guides
Thy blind obedient keels to reach
  The harbor where thy future rides!

The guns that spoke at Lexington
  Knew not that God was planning then
The trumpet word of Jefferson
  To bugle forth the rights of men.

To them that wept and cursed Bull Run,
  What was it but despair and shame?
Who saw behind the cloud the sun?
  Who knew that God was in the flame?

Had not defeat upon defeat,
  Disaster on disaster come,
The slave's emancipated feet
  Had never marched behind the drum.

There is a Hand that bends our deeds
  To mightier issues than we planned,
Each son that triumphs, each that bleeds,
  My country, serves Its dark command.

I do not know beneath what sky
  Nor on what seas shall be thy fate;
I only know it shall be high,
  I only know it shall be great.

RICHARD HOVEY

☆ ☆ ☆

ON ELECTION EVE

In this town, as in every community in our nation, friends and neighbors will gather together around the polling place.

They will discuss the state of the nation, the weather, and the prospect of their favorite football team. They will discuss the political campaign. And I suppose there will be a few warm arguments.

But when you and I step into the voting booth, we can proudly say: "I am an American, and this vote I am casting is the exercise of my highest privilege and my most solemn duty to my country."

We vote as free men, impelled only by the urgings of our own wisdom and our own conscience.

It is that right, the right to determine for themselves who should be their own officers of government, that provides for the people the most powerful safeguard of our democracy.

FRANKLIN D. ROOSEVELT

☆ ☆ ☆

THE DEMOCRACY OF THE FAMILY TREE

More than one ancestor is struggling within you! We are all of mixed blood—very mixed, indeed, but more good than bad. You have two parents, four grandparents, eight great-grandparents, sixteen great-great-grandparents, thirty-two great-great-great-grandparents, and so on! Go back only ten generations and you accumulate 2,046 ancestors on the way. You are descended from possibly 1,024 different people of the generation that saw the *Mayflower* cross the ocean. There is nothing so democratic as a family tree, if you climb into all its branches!

ALBERT W. PALMER

☆ ☆ ☆

If we are to have peace, justice, and freedom in the days ahead, men must be placed above things and institutions. They must be free to think, to express their convictions, to assemble, to criticize and oppose as well as to support causes, and to worship God freely.

Man's right to freedom is not a privilege granted by the state or any group in society, but it is a God-given, human or natural right, depending on the approach one takes. And men can demand only that amount of freedom for which they are willing to accept a similar amount of responsibility. In order for a free society to function well, there must be certain qualities of character in the citizens, a sense of moral responsibility, a concern for the freedom and rights of others, an informed and educated electorate and respect for intelligence.

HAROLD A. BOSLEY

☆ ☆ ☆

THE DEMOCRATIC PATTERN

(1) Respect for the dignity and worth of the individual human personality.

(2) Open opportunity for the individual.

(3) Economic and social security.

(4) The search for truth.

(5) Free discussion, freedom of speech, and freedom of the press.

(6) Universal education.

(7) The rule of the majority, the rights of the minority, and the honest ballot.

(8) Justice for the common man, trial by jury, arbitration of disputes, orderly legal processes, freedom from search and seizure, and right to petition.

(9) Freedom of religion.

(10) Respect for the rights of private property.

(11) The practice of the fundamental social virtues.

(12) The responsibility of the individual to participate in the duties of democracy.

W. W. CHARTERS

☆ ☆ ☆

BALLAD OF THE COMMON MAN
(FOR THE JEFFERSON MEMORIAL)

To him who felt a human sea
Begin to rise for liberty,
   Build, O men, keep building!

To him who raised the human pen
That freed the first American,
   Build, O men, keep building!

For he is in the common star
Of all we live in, all we are
In sons and more sons near and far—
   Build, O men, keep building!

And rear your temple all around
Our common feet and common ground,
Giving our love a common sound—
   Build, O men, keep building!

And let us feel there is no night
Can ever hide the growing light—
The light he saw, the light he spread—
And all our sight, though he is dead—
   Build, O men, keep building!

And even though your labor's done
And the race may rest in Jefferson,
Rise up again, there's more to be done!
   Build, O men, keep building!
    Keep on building Men!

ALFRED KREYMBORG

☆ ☆ ☆

PORTRAIT OF JEFFERSON

Mr. Jefferson is now between eighty-one and eighty-two, above six feet high, of an ample long frame, rather thin and spare. His head, which is not peculiar in its shape, is set rather forward on his shoulders; and his neck being long, there is, when he is walking or conversing, an habitual protrusion of it. It is still well covered with hair, which having once been red, and now turning gray, is of an indistinct sandy color.

His eyes are small, very light, and now neither brilliant nor striking. His chin is rather long, but not pointed. His nose small, regular in its outline, and the nostrils a little elevated. His mouth is well formed and still filled with teeth; it is strongly compressed, bearing an expression of contentment and bears the marks of age and cutaneous affection. His limbs are uncommonly long; his hands and feet very large, and his wrists of an extraordinary size. His walk is not precise and military, but easy and swinging. He stoops a little, not so much from age as from a natural formation. When sitting, he appears short, partly from a rather lounging habit of sitting, and partly from the disproportionate length of his limbs.

His dress, when in the house, is a gray surtout coat, kerseymere stuff waistcoat, with an under one faced with some material of a dingy red. His pantaloons are very long and loose, and of the same color as his coat. His stockings are woollen either white or gray; and his shoes of the kind that bear his name. His whole dress is very much neglected, but not slovenly. He wears a common round hat. His dress, when on horseback, is a gray straight-bodied coat and a spencer of the same material, both fastened with large pearl buttons. When we first saw him, he was riding; and, in addition to the above articles of apparel, wore round his throat a knit white woollen tippet, in the place of a cravat, and black velvet gaiters under his pantaloons. His general appearance indicates an extraordinary degree of health, vivacity, and spirit. His sight is still good, for he needs glasses only in the evening. His bearing is generally good, but a number of voices in animated conversation confuses it.

DANIEL WEBSTER

☆ ☆ ☆

The principles of Jefferson are the definitions and axioms of free society.

ABRAHAM LINCOLN

☆ ☆ ☆

A little rebellion now and then is a good thing, and as necessary in the political world as storms in the physical.

THOMAS JEFFERSON

☆ ☆ ☆

HUMAN DIGNITY

Democracy is the only form of government that is founded on the dignity of man, not the dignity of some men, of rich men, of educated men or of white men, but of all men. Its sanction is not the sanction of force, but the sanction of human nature. Equality and justice, the two great distinguishing characteristics of democracy, follow inevitably from the conception of men, as rational and spiritual beings.

In this light freedom takes on meaning. It is not freedom to do as we please but freedom to achieve that autonomy which we approach in proportion as we develop our rational and spiritual nature. It is not mere freedom to live that concerns us most, but freedom to live human lives. Men must be free to exercise those powers which make them men.

ROBERT M. HUTCHINS

☆ ☆ ☆

Liberty is the absence of coercion of a human being by any other human being. It is a condition where the person may do whatever he desires, according to his wisdom and conscience.

FLOYD ARTHUR HARPER

☆ ☆ ☆

Freedom means self-expression, and the secret of freedom is courage. No man ever remains free who acquiesces in what he knows to be wrong.

HAROLD J. LASKI

☆ ☆ ☆

PATRIOTIC OBLIGATION

The man who takes the oath today to preserve, protect, and defend the Constitution of the United States only assumes the solemn obligation which every patriotic citizen—on the farm, in the workshop, in the busy marts of trade and everywhere—should share with him. The Constitution which prescribes his oath, my countrymen, is yours; the government you have chosen him to administer for a time is yours; the laws and the entire scheme of our civil rule, from the town meeting to the State capitals and the national capital, is yours. Every voter, as surely as your chief magistrate, under the same high sanction, though in a different sphere, exercises a public trust. Nor is this all. Every citizen owes to the country a vigilant watch and close scrutiny of fidelity and usefulness. Thus is the people's will impressed upon the whole framework of our civil policy—municipal, state, and federal; and this is the price of our liberty and the inspiration of our faith in the republic.

GROVER CLEVELAND

☆ ☆ ☆

SEARCH

We go forth all to seek America.
And in the seeking we create her.
In the quality of our search shall be the
    nature of the America that we created.

WALDO FRANK

☆ ☆ ☆

Our country! in her intercourse with foreign nations may she always be in the right—but our country right or wrong!

STEPHEN DECATUR

☆ ☆ ☆

Our country, right or wrong. When right, to be kept right; when wrong, to be put right.

CARL SCHURZ

☆ ☆ ☆

CONSTITUTIONAL FREEDOM

The press shall be free to every citizen who undertakes to examine the official conduct of men acting in a public capacity, and any citizen may print freely on any subject, being responsible for the abuse of that liberty.

CONSTITUTION OF DELAWARE (1782)

☆ ☆ ☆

LIBERTY OF THE PRESS

If by the liberty of the press were understood merely the liberty of discussing the propriety of public measures and political opinions, let us have as much of it as you please; but if it means the liberty of affronting, calumniating and defaming one another, I for my part, own myself willing to part with my share of it whenever our legislators shall please so to alter the law, and shall cheerfully consent to exchange my *liberty* of abusing others for the *privilege* of not being abused myself.

BENJAMIN FRANKLIN

☆ ☆ ☆

MARTYRS

In the long, fierce struggle for freedom of opinion, the press, like the Church, counted its martyrs by thousands.

JAMES A. GARFIELD

☆ ☆ ☆

ASSUMPTION

Criticism in a free man's country is made on certain assumptions, one of which is the assumption that the government belongs to the people and is at all times subject to the people's correction and criticism.

ARCHIBALD MAC LEISH

☆ ☆ ☆

All the ills of democracy can be cured by more democracy.

ALFRED E. SMITH

☆ ☆ ☆

AMERICAN IDENTIFICATION

An American is one who loves justice
    and believes in the dignity of man.
An American is one who will fight for his
    freedom and that of his neighbor.
An American is one who will sacrifice proper-
    ty, ease, and security in order that he
    and his children may retain the rights of
    free men.
An American is one in whose heart is
    engraved the immortal second sentence of
    the Declaration of Independence.

HAROLD L. ICKES

☆ ☆ ☆

AMERICANISM

At its best, Americanism is nobody's monopoly, but a happy concentrate of some of the highest aspirations and tendencies of humanity as its best nearly everywhere at one time or another. As it seems to me, it is the highest body of idealism in the world today. It is, among other things, a movement away from primitive racism, fear and nationalism, and herd instincts and mentality; a movement toward freedom, creativeness, a universal or pan-human culture.

LOUIS ADAMIC

☆ ☆ ☆

The principal advantage of a democracy is a general elevation in the character of the people.

JAMES FENIMORE COOPER

☆ ☆ ☆

PATRIOT'S WORDS

Is life so dear or peace so sweet as to be purchased at the price of chains and slavery? Forbid it, Almighty God! I know not what course others may take; but as for me, give me liberty, or give me death!

PATRICK HENRY

IV

ONE NATION UNDER GOD

☆ ☆ ☆

I have lived, Sir, a long time, and the longer I live, the more convincing proof I see of this truth—that God governs in the affairs of men.

BENJAMIN FRANKLIN

ALTAR AT VALLEY FORGE

The sublimest figure in American history is Washington on his knees at Valley Forge.

He was in that hour and place the American personified, not depending on their own courage or goodness, but asking aid from God, their Father and Preserver.

Washington knew that morals are priceless, but he knew that morals are from within. And he knew that in that dread day when all, save courage, had forsaken the American arms, appeal must be to that Power beyond ourselves, eternal in the heavens, which after all, in every crisis of the lives of men and nations, has been their surest source of strength.

ALBERT J. BEVERIDGE

☆   ☆   ☆

Reason and experience both forbid us to expect that national morality can prevail in exclusion of religious principles.

GEORGE WASHINGTON

☆   ☆   ☆

The highest flights of charity, devotion, trust, patience, bravery, to which the wings of human nature have spread themselves, have been flown for religious ideals.

WILLIAM JAMES

☆   ☆   ☆

From FIRST INAUGURAL

In tendering this homage to the great Author of every public and private good, I assure myself that it expresses your sentiments not less than my own; nor those of my fellow citizens at large, less than either. No people can be bound to acknowledge and adore the invisible Hand, which conducts the affairs of men, more than the people of the United States. Every step by which they have advanced to the character of an independent nation seems to have been distinguished by some token of Providential agency.

GEORGE WASHINGTON

☆   ☆   ☆

THREE WEAPONS

The American pioneer faced the forest and the future with three powerful weapons in his hands: he carried an axe, a gun, and a Book.

With the axe he attacked the forests, hewed logs for his house, his school, his church.

With the gun he hunted game for his table and animal pelts for a livelihood, and protected himself against the predatory forces of the wilderness.

The Book was the center of his personal devotions, the inspiration of his institutions, and the textbook of his education.

EDWARD L. R. ELSON

☆   ☆   ☆

INNER DOMAIN

I indulge in no mere figure of speech when I say that our nation, the immortal spirit of our domain lives in us—in our hearts, and minds, and consciences. There it must find its nutriment or die. This thought, more than any other, presents to our mind the impressiveness and responsibility of American citizenship. The land we live in seems to be strong and active, but how fares the land that lives in us? Are we sure we are doing all we ought to keep it in vigor and health?

GROVER CLEVELAND

☆   ☆   ☆

NEW ENGLAND SPIRES

England grew small for them and cramped,
These Pilgrims by a dream possessed,
Who followed over alien lands
The soul's inexorable quest.
Bleak their lot and gaunt, yet still
Upon the shores they trod,
Unwavering, their steeples point
To far frontiers of God.

LESLIE SAVAGE CLARK

☆   ☆   ☆

51

FIRM BASIS

Can the liberties of a nation be thought secure, when we have removed their only firm basis, a conviction in the minds of the people that these liberties are the gift of God? That they are not to be violated but by his wrath? Indeed, I tremble for my country when I reflect that God is just; that his justice cannot sleep forever.

THOMAS JEFFERSON

☆　☆　☆

THE NEW COLOSSUS

Not like the brazen giant of Greek fame,
With conquering limbs astride from land to
　　land;
Here at our seawashed, sunset gates shall
　　stand
A mighty woman with a torch, whose flame
Is the imprisoned lightning, and her name
Mother of Exiles. From her beacon-hand
Glows world-wide welcome; her mild eyes
　　command
The air-bridged harbor that twin cities frame.
"Keep, ancient lands, your storied pomp!"
　　cries she
With silent lips. "Give me your tired, your
　　poor,
Your huddled masses yearning to breathe
　　free,
The wretched refuse of your teeming shore,
Send these, the homeless, tempest-tost to me,
I lift my lamp beside the golden door."

EMMA LAZARUS

☆　☆　☆

RELIGION IN AMERICAN LIFE

Faith in God is woven into the fabric of our national life from the beginning.

When the first settlers landed on American soil at the spot which they named Jamestown after their sovereign, they carried with them the official admonition of the London Council for Virginia that "the way to prosper is to serve and fear God, for every plantation which our heavenly Father hath not planted shall be rooted out."

When the Pilgrim Fathers set foot at Plymouth, they worshipped God "with prayer and psalm."

When William Penn established his colony of Pennsylvania, among the many expressions of his Christian concern was this exclamation: "O that thou mayst be kept faithful to the God of thy mercies and in the life of righteousness be preserved to the end!"

So from the earliest years, the name of God was known and honored. As time rolled on to bring the stirring and critical days of the Revolution, it provided the impressive picture of the American commander-in-chief on his knees in fervent prayer at Valley Forge. It gave us also his memorable prayer after his inauguration as President in which he called upon God in humble supplication for the new nation.

When later years brought violent division in the nation, we find another great figure, about to take up his presidential duties, turning to his neighbors and friends gathered to bid him farewell and saying to them: "Trusting in him who can go with me and remain with you, and be everywhere for good, let us confidently hope that all will yet be well. To his care commending you, as I hope in your prayers you will commend me, I bid you an affectionate farewell."

Instances multiply beyond number that evidence the strong religious convictions which influenced our leaders, molded our national ideals, and carried us successfully through many a crisis.

While it is true that the religious life of America had its ebbs and flow, it is also true that the undercurrents of religion were never lost and have proved to be a spiritual resource for individual and nation.

DEANE EDWARDS

☆　☆　☆

52

MESSAGE TO UNITED NATIONS DELEGATES

I propose that God should be openly and audibly invoked at the United Nations in accordance with any one of the religious faiths which are represented here. I do so in the conviction that we cannot make the United Nations into a successful instrument of God's peace without God's help, and that with his help we cannot fail.

HENRY CABOT LODGE, JR.

☆　☆　☆

Democracy is nothing but an attempt to apply the principles of the Bible to human society.

WALLACE C. SPEERS

☆　☆　☆

I do not know how a man can be an American, even if he is not a Christian, and not catch something with regard to God's purpose as to this great land.

PHILLIPS BROOKS

☆　☆　☆

From STARTING FROM PAUMANOK

I say the whole earth and all the stars in the sky are for religion's sake.
I say no man has ever yet been half devout enough,
None has ever yet adored or worship'd half enough,
None has begun to think how divine he himself is, and how certain the future is.
I say that the real and permanent grandeur of these States must be their religion.

WALT WHITMAN

☆　☆　☆

Although Christianity has never been the guarantee of a democratic state anywhere in the world, no democracy has ever thrived successfully for any period of time outside of Christian influence.

THEODORE H. WHITE

☆　☆　☆

AMERICA'S CHARACTER

Back of America's position and progress lies America's character as the factor on which our American tomorrow depends.

This means your character, and mine, and our neighbors' all over this land.

Are we willing to pull together, like a well-trained and disciplined crew, to carry out effectively the majority will of our people, as made known through our democratic processes of election and free speech?

Are we far-sighted and determined enough to make today the sacrifices necessary to safeguard America and to plan intelligently and work hard for America tomorrow?

KARL T. COMPTON

☆　☆　☆

FAREWELL

I am going home, America. Farewell.

For seventeen years I have enjoyed your hospitality, visited every one of your fifty states.

I can say I know you well. I admire and love America. It is my second home.

What I have to say now in parting is both a tribute and a warning. Never forget, America, that yours is a spiritual country.

Yes, I know that you are a practical people. Like others, I have marveled at your factories, your skyscrapers, and your arsenals. But underlying everything else is the fact that America began as a God-loving, God-fearing, God-worshipping people, knowing that there is a spark of Divine in each one of us.

It is this respect for the dignity of the human spirit which makes America invincible. May it always endure.

And so I say again in parting, thank you, America, and farewell. May God keep you always, and may you always keep God.

CARLOS P. ROMULO

☆ ☆ ☆

PRAYER

Almighty God, who didst lead our fathers to these shores that they might here lay the foundations of civil and religious liberty: bless to us the glorious heritage of faith and freedom which we have received from them.

Preserve thou the nation which was established by their prayers, their heroic deeds, and their sacrifices.

Help us to be true to the great ideals for which they stood, and may our country ever be the home of justice, liberty, and true brotherhood.

Defend it, O God, against every peril, and make it increasingly a blessing to the whole world.

☆ ☆ ☆

Our democracy in this country had its roots in religious belief, and we had to acknowledge soon after its birth that differences in religious belief are inherent in the spirit of true democracy.

ELEANOR ROOSEVELT

☆ ☆ ☆

THE NATION'S MORTAR

The whole story of America—a story worth the telling and worth the understanding—began with an idea. This idea is actually the political expression of a basic law of nature—that there is strength in diversity. According to this idea, America is a place where people can be themselves. It is a human experience rather than a purely national or cultural experience. It is built upon fabulous differences—religion, race, culture, political thinking. These differences, or pluralism, as the sociologists call it, are actually the mortar that hold the nation together.

NORMAN COUSINS

☆ ☆ ☆

From LIBERTY SONG

Then join in hand, brave Americans all!
By uniting we stand, by dividing we fall.

JOHN DICKINSON

☆ ☆ ☆

As long as we all stand up together, God will bless America. For whether God blesses America or not does not depend so much upon God as it does upon us Americans.

CARL HEALTH KOPF

☆ ☆ ☆

OUR DEEPEST PRAYERS

Before all else, we seek, upon our common labor as a nation, the favor of Almighty God. And the hopes in our hearts fashion the deepest prayers of our people.

May we pursue the right—without self-righteousness.

May we know unity—without conformity.

May we grow in strength—without pride of self.

May we, in our dealings with all people of the earth, ever speak the truth and serve justice.

May the light of freedom, coming to all darkened lands, flame brightly—until at last the darkness is no more.

May the turbulence of our age yield to a true time of peace, when men and nations shall share a life that honors the dignity of each, the brotherhood of all.

DWIGHT D. EISENHOWER

☆ ☆ ☆

The destiny of the world is in the hands of those statesmen who can interpret faithfully the commands of the Almighty.

DAVID LAWRENCE

☆ ☆ ☆

It is the government of all; its powers are delegated by all; it represents all and acts for all.

JOHN MARSHALL

☆ ☆ ☆

HE LOST A WAR AND WON IMMORTALITY

Even among the free, it is not always easy to live together. There came a time, less than a hundred years ago, when the people of this country disagreed so bitterly among themselves that some of them felt they could not go on living with the rest.

A test of arms was made to decide whether Americans should remain one nation or become two. The armies of those who believed in two nations were led by a man named Robert E. Lee.

What about Lee? What kind of man was he who nearly split the history of the United States down the middle and made two separate books of it?

They say you had to see him to believe that a man so fine could exist. He was handsome. He was clever. He was brave. He was gentle. He was generous and charming, noble and modest, admired and beloved. He had never failed at anything in his upright soldier's life. He was a born winner, this Robert E. Lee. Except for once. In the greatest contest of his life, in the war between the South and the North, Robert E. Lee lost.

Now there were men who came with smouldering eyes to Lee and said: "Let's not accept this result as final. Let's keep our anger alive. Let's be grim and unconvinced, and wear our bitterness like a medal. You can be our leader in this."

But Lee shook his head at those men. "Abandon your animosities," he said, "and make your sons Americans."

And what did he do himself when his war was lost? He took a job as president of a tiny college, with forty students and four professors, at a salary of $1500 a year. He had commanded thousands of young men in battle. Now he wanted to prepare a few hundred of them for the duties of peace. So the countrymen of Robert E. Lee saw how a born winner loses, and it seemed to them that in defeat he won his most lasting victory.

There is an art of losing, and Robert E. Lee is its finest teacher. In a democracy, where opposing viewpoints regularly meet for a test of ballots, it is good for all of us to know how to lose occasionally, how to yield peacefully, for the sake of freedom. Lee is our master in this. The man who fought against the Union showed us what unity means.

LOUIS REDMOND

☆ ☆ ☆

Let us be true to our democratic ideals, not by the utterance of cheap platitudes, not by windy oratory, but by living in such a manner as to show that democracy can be efficient in promoting the public welfare during periods of peace and efficient in securing national freedom in time of war.

THEODORE ROOSEVELT

☆ ☆ ☆

From PROFILES IN COURAGE

Not only do the problems of courage and conscience concern every officeholder in our land, however humble or mighty, and to whomever he may be responsible—voters, a legislature, a political machine or a party organization. They concern as well every voter in our land—and they concern those who do not vote, those who take no interest in Government, those who have only disdain for the politician and his profession. They concern everyone who has ever complained about corruption in high places, and everyone who has ever insisted that his representative abide by his wishes. For, in a democracy, every citizen . . . "holds office"; every one of us is in a position of responsibility; and, in the final analysis, the kind of government we get depends upon how we fulfill these responsibilities.

JOHN F. KENNEDY

☆ ☆ ☆

America is another name for opportunity. Our whole history appears like a last effort of divine Providence in behalf of the human race.

RALPH WALDO EMERSON

☆ ☆ ☆

WHO IS THE AMERICAN?

He hears an airplane, and if he does look up at all, he does so out of curiosity, not fear. He comes home through streets well lighted at night, not dimly in blue. He reads his paper and knows that what it says is not concocted by some bureau, but represents an honest effort to present the truth.

He converses with friends and strangers, expressing freely his opinion on any topic. He does not expect his mail to be opened, or his telephone tapped. He doesn't report his change of address to the police.

He thinks of his neighbors across the international borders as though they were across state lines, rather than foreigners; and does not feel that matters of difference between the governments need lead to war.

He worships God in the fashion of his choice.

He has his problems, his troubles, his uncertainties, but they are not overshadowed by the imminence of battle and sudden death. He is a fortunate man.

He is an American.

THE NEW YORK SUN

☆ ☆ ☆

Only if the religious forces have the courage and the intelligence to insist that America keep its purposes clean and clear will religious values be enabled to play an active role in the building of the new world.

WENDELL WILLKIE

☆ ☆ ☆

From REPLY TO HAYNE
(JANUARY 27, 1830)

When my eyes shall be turned to behold for the last time the sun in heaven, may I not see him shining on the broken and dishonored fragments of a once glorious Union; on states dissevered, discordant, belligerent; on a land rent with civil feuds, or drenched, it may be, in fraternal blood! Let their last feeble and lingering glance rather behold the gorgeous ensign of the Republic, now known and honored throughout the earth, still full high advanced, its arms and trophies streaming in their original lustre, not a stripe erased or polluted, not a single star obscured, bearing for its motto no such miserable interrogatory as "What is all this worth?" nor those other words of delusion and folly, "Liberty first and Union afterwards"; but everywhere, spread all over in characters of living light, blazing on all its ample folds, as they float over the sea and over the land, and in every wind under the whole heavens, that other sentiment, dear to every true American heart—Liberty and Union, now and forever, one and inseparable!

DANIEL WEBSTER

☆ ☆ ☆

NATIONAL CHARACTER

Our national future depends upon our national character; that is, whether it is spiritually or materially minded.

ROGER W. BABSON

☆ ☆ ☆

GUARANTOR OF FREEDOM

Freedom is a need of the soul, and nothing else. It is in striving toward God that the soul strives continually after a condition of freedom. God alone is the inciter and guarantor of freedom. He is the only guarantor.

WHITTAKER CHAMBERS

☆ ☆ ☆

America, we must remember, is no more than the sum of ourselves.

JOHN D. ROCKEFELLER 3rd

☆　☆　☆

LIFT EVERY VOICE AND SING

Lift every voice and sing, till earth and
    heaven ring,
Ring with the harmonies of liberty;
Let our rejoicing rise, high·as the
    list'ning skies,
Let it resound loud as the rolling sea.

Sing a song full of the faith that the dark
    past has taught us.
Sing a song full of the hope that the present
    has brought us;
Facing the rising sun of our new day begun,
Let us march on till victory is won.

Stony the road we trod, bitter the
    chastening rod,
Felt in the days when hope unborn had died;
Yet with a steady beat, have not our weary
    feet
Come to the place for which our fathers
    sighed?

We have come over a way that with tears has
    been watered;
We have come, treading our path through
    the flood of the slaughtered;
Out from the gloomy past, 'til now we
    stand at last
Where the white gleam of our bright star
    is cast.

God of our weary years, God of our
    silent tears,
Thou who hast brought us thus far on
    the way;
Thou who hast by thy might led us into
    the light,
Keep us forever in thy path, we pray.

Lest our feet stray from the places, our
    God, where we met thee,
Lest, our hearts, drunk with the wine of the
    world, we forget thee;
Shadowed beneath thy hand, may we forever
    stand,
True to our God, true to our native land.

JAMES WELDON JOHNSON

☆　☆　☆

PROMISED LAND

In the history of religion in the United States, surely no story is more astounding than that of the Mormons, or, as they style themselves, the Church of Jesus Christ of Latter-day Saints.

Their chronicle has a Biblical ring, for it contains not only a revelation and a martyred prophet but also a pilgrimage through a wilderness and a discovery, after long sufferings, of a promised land.

It starts with a few disciples, then a few score; today it reckons its numbers close to two millions, many of them beyond the seas, with fresh converts added daily.

Yet all this is the work of barely a century and a third—as if the whole Old Testament could be crowded into the span of but four or five begats, and Moses were the contemporary of Abraham Lincoln, Ralph Waldo Emerson, and Mark Twain.

AMERICAN HERITAGE

☆　☆　☆

There are no points of the compass on the chart of true patriotism.

ROBERT C. WINTHROP

☆　☆　☆

STRENGTH

That government is the strongest of which every man feels himself a part.

THOMAS JEFFERSON

☆　☆　☆

58

RECIPE

Take a cup of Choctaw and add Frenchmen:
  aventuriers de bois and Acadian refugees
  from Nova Scotia
Blend in a Mississippi Bubble, a sprinkling
  of fugitives from justice, and a few
  filles de joie
Now sift in Catalans, Spanish planters,
  gens de couleur, and a large *gombò negre*
Make a *Code Noir* and some Quadroon Balls
Stir together gently, adding Dalmatian
  oystermen, Filipino shrimpers, Germans,
  and "Kaintucks" (often rather tough)
Add a pinch of pirates
Simmer slowly under six flags
Serves most of southern Louisiana

AMERICAN HERITAGE

☆　☆　☆

1776–1876

The whole year has been so much of a Fourth of July in its proud and exulting feeling that the return of the very day itself seems already to have been partly celebrated. But the emotion with which it is greeted must still be exceptional and immense. That little assembly of brave and patriotic men in the Philadelphia hall will be the chief figure in the national imagination on this day, and great for their indomitable courage will be the inspiration of the hour. The celebration upon the very spot consecrated by the great event of a hundred years ago cannot fail to be as touching as it will be imposing. And the whole land will shine and sing and shout with the fullness of a great joy. The President has wisely recommended a universal observance of the day.

The act which it commemorates grew naturally out of the character and training of the race from which our fathers chiefly sprang. The Declaration of Independence was the offspring of the Magna Charta, and Magna Charta grew in the old Teutonic traditions from which English political civilization emerged. There is nothing in English history more English than the American Declaration of Independence. New England defended old England against herself; and Sam Adams and James Otis and Patrick Henry were more English than the entire English ministry. The Declaration was but an extension of that assertion of individual independence which is instinctive in the English race. It can stand alone and go alone; and it will stand and go alone. The proof is America and England. And this anniversary shows what the political genius of a race has accomplished in a century.

The day's celebration will, we hope, add much to our historical material. It is a day on which every community, especially those that can go back to the Revolutionary epoch, will feel its own importance, and gladly recount its own history. And every where the one great lesson will be enforced, that it was fidelity to an idea, loyalty to a sentiment, trust in human nature and in the general intelligence and good sense, which founded the nation and has made it what this day beholds.

HARPER'S WEEKLY (JULY 15, 1876)

☆　☆　☆

PRESIDENTIAL OATH

I do solemnly swear (or affirm) that I will faithfully execute the office of President of the United States, and will, to the best of my ability, preserve, protect, and defend the Constitution of the United States.

☆　☆　☆

THE DAWN

The quiet determination of humble faith is the real secret of American strength. With this faith, the dark clouds of the moment will indeed be the darkness before the dawn, the dawn of a new future of peace, of human brotherhood, and of respect for the dignity of all men.

RICHARD M. NIXON

☆ ☆ ☆

From LISTEN TO THE PEOPLE
(INDEPENDENCE DAY, 1941)

Our voice is not one voice but many voices.
Not one man's, not the greatest, but the peo-
ple's.
The blue sky and the forty-eight States of the
people.
Many in easy times but one in a pinch
And that's what some folks forget.
Our voice is all the objectors and dissenters
And they sink and are lost in the
groundswell of the people,
Once the people rouse, once the people wake
and listen.

*

We are the people. Listen to us now.

Says you we're puny? We built Boulder Dam.
We built Grand Coulee and the T.V.A.
We built them out of freedom and our sweat.

Says you we're faint of heart and little of
mind?
We poured like wheat through the gaps of
the Appalachians.
We made the seas of wheat, the seas of corn.
We made five States a sea of wheat and corn.

*

We lost our way for a while but we've
found our way.
We know it and we'll hold it and we'll keep it.
We'll tell it to the world. We're saying it.

Freedom to speak and pray.
Freedom from want and fear.
That's what we're building.
Now and here and now.

STEPHEN VINCENT BENÉT

☆ ☆ ☆

'Tis not in numbers but in unity that our
great strength lies.

THOMAS PAINE

☆ ☆ ☆

MEN AND GOVERNMENTS

Governments, like clocks, go from the motion
men give them; and as governments are
made and moved by men, so by them they are
ruined too. Governments rather depend
upon men, than men upon governments. If
men be bad, let the government be never so
good, they will endeavor to warp and spoil it
to their turn.

WILLIAM PENN

☆ ☆ ☆

TEN TESTS OF AN AMERICAN

1. He is loyal. This is his country.
2. He is patriotic. He recognizes the debt
he owes for our institutions.
3. He stands for fair play. He will tolerate
no injustice, no force, no coercion. Believing
in fair play, he demands it from others.
4. He is square. He wants nothing that is
not his own. Unto each man his due.
5. He loves liberty. Liberty breathes life.
He is willing to die for liberty.
6. He respects the flag. Not because others
are watching, but because it is the symbol of
the sacrifice, the love and the devotion to liberty of his forebears.
7. He hates tyranny, whether revealed in
one-man despotism or in the mob. It is the
active enemy of his freedom.
8. He demands law and order. All security,
whether of persons or of property, depends
upon it.
9. He respects property. It represents the
labor and skill of others, and he demands the
same consideration for it from them.
10. He works. He earns his bread. He has
respect only for those who do the same.

SUNSHINE MAGAZINE

☆ ☆ ☆

60

V

HOME OF THE BRAVE

☆　☆　☆

The cause of liberty animated my youthful days; it has engaged the zealous attention of my maturer years; it will command my best efforts in its support so long as I shall be permitted to live.

JAMES MONROE

Under God we are determined that where-
soever, whensoever, or howsoever we shall be
called to make our exit, we will die free men.

JOSIAH QUINCY

☆   ☆   ☆

From THE POEM OF BUNKER HILL
Here on this spot was born a nation that
     will be
     Adept in all the humanities. Spreading
     in circles, as when
A pebble is thrown into a morning lake,
     Its concepts will cover a continent with
     a vision of dignity
At last made real. Here a race of men will
     evolve
     That will instruct the world in justice
     and in love.
A race of men to whom the entire world is
     a religion,
     Whose vessels, laden with much more than
     cargoes,
Will pass through the seven oceans, bearing
     with them
     The beliefs of all our countries, all our
     hearts.

Let us now honor, and throughout all time,
     The men who died upon this hill, the men
Who began to make us possible. The sun has
     gone down again,
     But it will rise tomorrow with a new
     brightness,
That will be ours. O under it let us build
     Our desires into events. O let us proceed
     toward wisdom,
And find in ourselves the implicit order
     of life,
     That, swaying beneath the storms that are
     always waiting to shake us,
We may still find in the lives of our heroes
     the mirror of ourselves,
     And see in their deaths the power of our
     defenses.

HARRY PETER MCNAB BROWN, JR.

☆   ☆   ☆

INSCRIPTION ON LEXINGTON
GREEN
Line of the Minute Men
April 19, 1775
Stand your ground
Don't fire unless fired upon
But if they mean to have a war
Let it begin here.

☆   ☆   ☆

I for one will never concede that we cannot
do as much in defense of our freedoms as any
enemy may be doing to destroy them.

BERNARD M. BARUCH

☆   ☆   ☆

From AN ODE FOR THE FOURTH
OF JULY, 1876
God of our fathers, thou who wast,
Art, and shalt be when those eye-wise who
     flout
Thy secret presence shall be lost
In the great light that dazzles them to
     doubt,
We, sprung from loins of stalwart men
Whose strength was in their trust
That thou wouldst make thy dwelling in their
     dust
And walk with those a fellow-citizen
Who build a city of the just,
We, who believe Life's bases rest
Beyond the probe of chemic test,
Still, like our fathers, feel thee near,
Sure that, while lasts the immutable decree,
The land to Human Nature dear
Shall not be unbeloved of thee.

JAMES RUSSELL LOWELL

☆   ☆   ☆

One man with courage makes a majority.

ANDREW JACKSON

☆   ☆   ☆

RECOLLECTIONS OF THE BOSTON TEA PARTY

I dressed myself in the costume of an Indian, equipped with a small hatchet, which I and my associates denominated the tomahawk, with which, and a club, after having painted my face and hands with coal dust in the shop of a blacksmith, I repaired to Griffin's wharf, where the ships lay that contained the tea. When I first appeared in the street after being thus disguised, I fell in with many who were dressed, equipped and painted as I was, and who fell in with me and marched in order to the place of our destination.

When we arrived at the wharf, there were three of our number who assumed an authority to direct our operations, to which we readily submitted. They divided us into three parties, for the purpose of boarding the three ships which contained the tea at the same time. The name of him who commanded the division to which I was assigned was Leonard Pitt. The names of the other commanders I never knew. We were immediately ordered by the respective commanders to board all the ships at the same time, which we promptly obeyed. The commander of the division to which I belonged, as soon as we were on board the ship, appointed me boatswain, and ordered me to go to the captain and demand of him the keys to the hatches and a dozen candles. I made the demand accordingly, and the captain promptly replied, and delivered the articles; but requested me at the same time to do no damage to the ship or rigging. We then were ordered by our commander to open the hatches and take out all the chests of tea and throw them overboard, and we immediately proceeded to execute his orders, first cutting and splitting the chests with our tomahawks, so as thoroughly to expose them to the effects of the water.

In about three hours from the time we went on board, we had thus broken and thrown overboard every tea chest to be found in the ship, while those in the other ships were disposing of the tea in the same way, at the same time. We were surrounded by British armed ships, but no attempt was made to resist us.

We then quietly retired to our several places of residence, without having any conversation with each other, or taking any measures to discover who were our associates; nor do I recollect of our having had the knowledge of the name of a single individual concerned in that affair, except that of Leonard Pitt, the commander of my division, whom I have mentioned. There appeared to be an understanding that each individual should volunteer his services, keep his own secret, and risk the consequence for himself. No disorder took place during that transaction, and it was observed at that time that the stillest night ensued that Boston had enjoyed for many months.

GEORGE R. T. HEWES

☆　☆　☆

Every drop of blood in me holds a heritage of patriotism.

ELIAS LIEBERMAN

☆　☆　☆

CALL TO SACRIFICE

We must be willing, individually and as a nation, to accept whatever sacrifices may be required of us. A people that values its privileges above its principles soon loses both.

DWIGHT D. EISENHOWER

☆　☆　☆

LIBERTY AND COURAGE

Those who won our independence believed liberty to be the secret of happiness and courage to be the secret of liberty.

LOUIS D. BRANDEIS

☆　☆　☆

REPORT ON THE MINUTE MEN

In the obedience to your Excellency's commands, I marched on the evening of the 18th inst. with the corps of grenadiers and light infantry for Concord, to execute your Excellency's orders with respect to destroying all ammunition, artillery, tents, &c, collected there.

I think it proper to observe, that when I had got some miles on the march from Boston, I detached six light infantry companies to march with all expedition to seize the two bridges on different roads beyond Concord. On these companies' arrival at Lexington, I understand, from the report of Major Pitcairn, who was with them, and from many officers, that they found on a green close to the road a body of the country people drawn up in military order, with arms and accoutrement, and, as appeared after, loaded.

LIEUTENANT COLONEL SMITH
TO GOVERNOR GAGE, APRIL 22, 1775

☆　☆　☆

SHOT HEARD ROUND THE WORLD

Lexington and Concord may argue for another hundred years about where the shot heard round the world was actually fired, but to the town of Salem, over on the Massachusetts coast, the question will remain largely academic. The point of the discussion, after all, is where the War of Independence began, and Salem has her own claims to the honor. It was at Salem's North River Bridge, two months before the clashes at Lexington and Concord, that British troops first met armed American resistance—and retreated. Although no shots were fired at the North Bridge (not to be confused with the Concord landmark of the same name), at least one bayonet was brought into play, and the first American blood was shed.

ERIC W. BARNES

☆　☆　☆

Those who expect to reap the blessings of freedom must, like men, undergo the fatigues of supporting it.

THOMAS PAINE

☆　☆　☆

Loyalty means nothing unless it has at its heart the absolute principle of self-sacrifice. Loyalty means that you ought to be ready to sacrifice every interest that you have, and your life itself, if your country calls upon you to do so, and that is the sort of loyalty which ought to be inculcated into these newcomers, that they are not to be loyal only so long as they are pleased, but that, having once entered into this sacred relationship, they are bound to be loyal whether they are pleased or not; and that loyalty which is merely self-pleasing is only self-indulgence and selfishness. No man has ever risen to the real stature of spiritual manhood until he has found that it is finer to serve somebody else than it is to serve himself.

WOODROW WILSON

☆　☆　☆

From LEXINGTON

Swift as their summons came they left
　The plow mid-furrow standing still,
　The half-ground corn grist in the mill,
The spade in earth, the axe in cleft.

They went where duty seemed to call,
　They scarcely asked the reason why;
　They only knew they could but die,
And death was not the worst of all!

Of man for man the sacrifice,
　All that was theirs to give, they gave.
　The flowers that blossomed from their
　　grave
Have sown themselves beneath all skies.

JOHN GREENLEAF WHITTIER

☆　☆　☆

65

NATHAN HALE

One hero dies,—a thousand new ones rise,
As flowers are sown where perfect blossoms
    fall,—
Then quite unknown,—the name of Hale
    now cries
Where duty sounds her silent call;
With head erect he moves, and stately pace,
To meet an awful doom,—no ribald jest
Brings scorn or hate to that exalted face,
His thoughts are far away, poised and at
    rest;
Now on the scaffold see him turn and bid
Farewell to home and all his heart holds
    dear,
Majestic presence,—all men's weakness hid,
And all his strength in that one hour made
    clear,—
"I have one last regret,—that is to give
But one poor life, that my own land may
    live!"

WILLIAM ORDWAY PARTRIDGE

☆   ☆   ☆

CONCERNING NATHAN HALE

I can now in imagination see his person &
hear his voice—his person I should say was a
little above the common stature in height, his
shoulders of a moderate breadth, his limbs
strait & very plump: regular features—very
fair skin—blue eyes—flaxen or very light hair
which was always kept short—his eyebrows a
shade darker than his hair & his voice rather
sharp or piercing—his bodily agility was remarkable. I have seen him follow a football &
kick it over the tops of the trees in the Bowery
at New York, (an exercise which he was fond
of)—his mental powers seemed to be above
the common sort—his mind of a sedate and
sober cast, & he was undoubtedly Pious; for it
was remark'd that when any of the soldiers of
his company were sick he always visited them
& usually Prayed for & with them in their
sickness.

ELISHA BOSTWICK

☆   ☆   ☆

PATRIOTS' WORDS

SIGNING THE DECLARATION
There, I guess King George will be able to
read that.

JOHN HANCOCK (July 4, 1776)

LAST WORDS
I only regret that I have but one life to lose
for my country.

NATHAN HALE (September 22, 1776)

MESSAGE TO HIS COMMANDERS
Put none but Americans on guard tonight.

GEORGE WASHINGTON (April 30, 1777)

WHEN HIS SHIP WAS LOST
I have not yet begun to fight.

JOHN PAUL JONES (September 23, 1779)

REPLY TO THE BRITISH
We give up the fort when there's not a man
left to defend it.

GEORGE CROGHAN (August 1, 1813)

CIVIL WAR SENTIMENT
I hope for success, shall do all in my power to
secure it, and trust to God for the rest.

DAVID GLASGOW FARRAGUT

☆   ☆   ☆

AMERICANS IN PARIS
Lafayette, we are here.

C. E. STANTON (July 4, 1917)

AT PEARL HARBOR
Praise the Lord and pass the ammunition.

HOWELL M. FORGY (December 7, 1941)

MOTTO
The difficult we do immediately. The impossible takes a little longer.

U.S. ARMY CORPS OF ENGINEERS

WEST POINT CADETS PRAYER

O God, our Father, thou Searcher of men's hearts, help us to draw near to thee in sincerity and truth. May our religion be filled with gladness and may our worship of thee be natural.

Strengthen and increase our admiration for honest dealing and clean thinking, and suffer not our hatred of hypocrisy and pretense ever to diminish.

Encourage us in our endeavor to live above the common level of life.

Make us to choose the harder right instead of the easier wrong, and never to be content with a half truth when the whole can be won.

Endow us with courage that is born of loyalty to all that is noble and worthy, that scorns to compromise with vice and injustice and knows no fear when truth and right are in jeopardy.

Guard us against flippancy and irreverence in the sacred things of life.

Grant us new ties of friendship and new opportunities of service.

Kindle our hearts in fellowship with those of a cheerful countenance, and soften our hearts with sympathy for those who sorrow and suffer.

Help us to maintain the honor of the Corps untarnished and unsullied and to show forth in our lives the ideals of West Point in doing our duty to thee and to our Country.

All of which we ask in the name of the Great Friend and Master of men.

CLAYTON E. WHEAT

☆   ☆   ☆

We would rather die on our feet than live on our knees.

FRANKLIN D. ROOSEVELT

☆   ☆   ☆

We are not to expect to be translated from despotism to liberty in a featherbed.

THOMAS JEFFERSON

☆   ☆   ☆

TRIBUTE TO F.D.R.

Greatness is not mortal. The qualities which the great have to give, they give perpetually. Their gifts are taken into the pattern of life, and they appear thereafter in the fabric of the lives of nations, renewing themselves as the leaves of the trees are renewed by the seasons.

ROBERT TROUT

☆   ☆   ☆

The boisterous sea of liberty is never without a wave.

THOMAS JEFFERSON

☆   ☆   ☆

America triumphant!
Brave land of pioneers!
On mountain peak and prairie
Their winding trail appears.
The wilderness is planted;
The deserts bloom and sing;
On coast and plain the cities
Their smoky banners fling.

America triumphant!
Dear homeland of the free!
Thy sons have fought and fallen,
To win release for thee.
They broke the chains of empire;
They smote the wrongs of state;
And lies of law and custom
They blasted with their hate.

America, America!
Triumphant thou shalt be!
Thy hills and vales shall echo
The shouts of liberty.
Thy bards shall sing thy glory,
Thy prophets tell thy praise,
And all thy sons and daughters
Acclaim thy golden days.

JOHN HAYNES HOLMES

☆ ☆ ☆

FAREWELL TO THE ARMY OF NORTHERN VIRGINIA

After four years of arduous service, marked by unsurpassed courage and fortitude, the Army of Northern Virginia has been compelled to yield to overwhelming numbers and resources.

I need not tell the survivors of so many hard-fought battles who have remained steadfast to the last that I have consented to this result from no distrust of them; but feeling that valor and devotion could accomplish nothing that could compensate for the loss that would have attended the continuance of the contest, I determined to avoid the useless sacrifice of those whose past services have endeared them to their countrymen. By the terms of the agreement, officers and men can return to their homes and remain until exchanged.

You may take with you the satisfaction that proceeds from the consciousness of duty faithfully performed, and I earnestly pray that a merciful God will extend to you his blessing and protection.

With an unceasing admiration of your constancy and devotion to your country, and a grateful remembrance of your kind and generous consideration of myself, I bid you all an affectionate farewell.

ROBERT E. LEE

☆ ☆ ☆

THE CHARACTER OF LEE

He possessed every virtue of the great commanders, without their vices. He was a foe without hate; a friend without treachery; a private citizen without wrong; a neighbor without reproach; a Christian without hypocrisy, and a man without guilt.

He was a Caesar without his ambition; a Frederick without his tyranny; a Napoleon without his selfishness; and a Washington without his reward.

He was obedient to authority as a servant, and loyal in authority as a true king.

He was gentle as a woman in life; modest and pure as a virgin in thought; watchful as a Roman vestal in duty; submissive to law as Socrates, and grand in battle as Achilles.

JOHN WILLIAM JONES

☆ ☆ ☆

ROBERT E. LEE

The man was loved, the man was idolized,
The man had every just and noble gift.
He took great burdens and he bore them
   well,
Believed in God but did not preach too much,
Believed and followed duty first and last
With marvellous consistency and force,
Was a great victor, in defeat as great,
No more, no less, always himself in both,
Could make men die for him but saved his
   men
Whenever he could save them—was most
   kind
But was not disobeyed—was a good father,
A loving husband, a considerate friend.

STEPHEN VINCENT BENÉT
From JOHN BROWN'S BODY

☆ ☆ ☆

If it were my destiny to die for the cause of liberty, I would die upon the tomb of the Union, the American flag as my winding sheet.

ANDREW JOHNSON

☆ ☆ ☆

ALWAYS THE BRAVE

Every great crisis of human history is a pass of Thermopylae, and there is always a Leonidas and his three hundred to die in it, if they cannot conquer.

GEORGE WILLIAM CURTIS

☆ ☆ ☆

69

BEYOND THE HORIZON

Beyond the horizon
America waited—
A land of forests and mighty rivers
A land of prairies and towering mountains
An untamed land—

America waited
The first of Europe's peoples
Brave enough to sail across endless seas
　　for new freedoms
Strong enough to carve out new homes from
　　the wilderness
Determined enough to build new lives on
　　new frontiers of land
Beyond the horizon.

They reached, too, for new frontiers of the
　　mind.
They wrote:
　　"We hold these truths . . . that all men
　　are created equal . . .
　　They are endowed by their Creator with certain
　　　unalienable rights . . .
　　　Life . . . Liberty . . . Pursuit of Happi-
　　ness."
And they fought and died to make safe that
　　new frontier of mind—that new concept
　　of human dignity—
For their right to march on
Beyond the horizon.

With their freedom won
They pushed westward, saying:
"When you see the smoke of your neighbor's
　　chimney, it's time to move on."
Yes, on into the setting sun—
In prairie schooners 'cross the plains
On sailing ships 'round the Horn
On to new frontiers of land
Beyond the horizon.

But when they reached the Pacific, some
　　cried:
"Now—no new land to find.

No more new horizons."
Yet, in others' minds sprang still newer
　　frontiers—
The harvester to cut prairie grain
The steamboat to ply the rivers
Power looms to weave cloth for clothes
New frontiers—of test tube and machine—of
　　technology
And Americans found new strength
Beyond the horizon.

From Europe's old, tired nations
Came others—new pioneers—
And read on Liberty's Statue
"Give me your tired, your poor, your
　　huddled
　　　masses yearning to
　　　breathe free. . . .
　　　I lift my lamp beside the golden door."
And in the hearts of new frontiersmen
Was kindled the spark of freedom—of the
　　chance to build
Beyond the horizon.

And America grew strong—
Outstripped in material wealth the whole of
　　the Old World.
Skyscrapers reached high into the clouds
Machines echoed the beat of ocean waves
Power of rushing rivers and glittering oil
　　was harnessed—to do her people's
　　bidding.
New drugs saved lives
New paring knives sold for a dime each
New opportunity to move ahead
For a people who looked
Beyond the horizon.

But freedom was never cheap—never sure
And Americans sweated and fought and died
　　as its price.
In muddy trenches of the Argonne
In steeping jungles of the Philippines
They sweated and fought and died
To ensure their nation's right—the right of

70

their children yet unborn—
To look and to travel as free men
Beyond the horizon.

Yet today some cry:
  "There are no new frontiers now."
  "We've expanded to the limit."
  "Let's divide everything—not try to mul-
    tiply it."
  "Let the Government plan—blueprint—or-
    ganize everything."
While mourning those who died for freedom,
  they shout:
  "Let others tell us what to do."
  "There are no new horizons now."

Have they forgotten so soon?
Will we trade our success for failure?
Will we sell our birthrights
  —Of opportunity—of human dignity
For a mess of pottage—
  —A promise of Utopia from foreign lands?
  —A twisted phrase like "common man"?
  —A ball and chain—"gilt-edged security"?

Or will we have a new birth of freedom
Will we keep high the torch—for the tired,
  the poor, the huddled masses yearning
  to breathe free.
Will we know that our frontiers of mind and
  heart are endless
That our stars—freedom, opportunity,
  faith—are ever constant
That our sun, the future unlimited, lies
Beyond the horizon.

THOMAS M. WOLFF

☆   ☆   ☆

FROM THE ALAMO
FEBRUARY 24, 1836
I am besieged by a thousand or more of the
Mexicans under Santa Anna. I have sustained
a continual bombardment and cannonade for
twenty-four hours and have not lost a man.
  The enemy has demanded a surrender at
discretion; otherwise the garrison are to be
put to the sword if the fort is taken. I have
answered the demand with a cannon shot,
and our flag still waves proudly from the
walls.
  I shall never surrender or retreat.
  Then, I call on you in the name of liberty,
of patriotism, and everything dear to the
American character, to come to our aid with
all dispatch. The enemy is receiving reinforcements daily and will no doubt increase
to three or four thousand in four or five days.
  If this call is neglected, I am determined to
sustain myself as long as possible and die like
a soldier who never forgets what is due to his
own honor and that of our country. Victory
or death.

WILLIAM BARRET TRAVIS

☆   ☆   ☆

ALAMO INSCRIPTION
In memory of the heroes who sacrificed their
lives at the Alamo, March 6, 1836, in the defense of Texas. They chose never to surrender nor retreat. These brave hearts, with
flag still proudly waving, perished in the
flames of immortality that their high sacrifice
might lead to the founding of this Texas.
From the fire that burned their bodies rose
the eternal spirit of the sublime, heroic sacrifice which gave birth to an empire state.

SAN ANTONIO, TEXAS

☆   ☆   ☆

That patriotism, which, catching its inspiration from the immortal God, animates and
prompts to deeds of self-sacrifice, of valor, of
devotion, and of death itself—that is public
virtue, that is the sublimest of all public virtues.

HENRY CLAY

☆   ☆   ☆

Never take counsel of your fears.

"STONEWALL" JACKSON

71

☆ ☆ ☆

BATTLE HYMN OF THE REPUBLIC

Mine eyes have seen the glory of the
    coming of the Lord;
He is trampling out the vintage where the
    grapes of wrath are stored;
He hath loosed the fateful lightning of
    his terrible swift sword:
    His truth is marching on.

I have seen him in the watch-fires of a
    hundred circling camps;
They have builded him an altar in the
    evening dews and damps;
I can read his righteous sentence by the
    dim and flaring lamps;
    His day is marching on.

I have read a fiery gospel, writ in
    burnished rows of steel:
"As ye deal with my contemners, so with you
    my grace shall deal;
Let the Hero, born of woman, crush the
    serpent with his heel,
    Since God is marching on."

He has sounded forth the trumpet that shall
    never call retreat;
He is sifting out the hearts of men before
    his judgment-seat;
Oh, be swift, my soul, to answer him!
    be jubilant, my feet!
    Our God is marching on.

In the beauty of the lilies Christ was
    born across the sea,
With a glory in his bosom that transfigures
    you and me:
As he died to make men holy, let us die to
    make men free,
    While God is marching on.

JULIA WARD HOWE

☆ ☆ ☆

There is nothing wrong with America that
the faith, love of freedom, intelligence, and
energy of her citizens cannot cure.

DWIGHT D. EISENHOWER

☆ ☆ ☆

D-DAY ORDER
(JUNE 6, 1944)

Soldiers, sailors, and airmen of the Allied
expeditionary force: You are about to embark upon a great crusade toward which we
have striven these many months. The eyes of
the world are upon you. The hopes and
prayers of liberty-loving peoples everywhere
march with you.

You will bring about the destruction of the
German war machine, the elimination of Nazi
tyranny over the oppressed peoples of Europe, and security for ourselves in a free
world.

Your task will not be an easy one. Your
enemy is well trained, well equipped, and
battle-hardened. He will fight savagely.

But this is the year 1944. Much has happened since the Nazi triumphs of 1940-41.

The United Nations have inflicted upon
the Germans great defeat in open battle man
to man. Our air offensive has seriously re-
duced their strength in the air and their capacity to wage war on the ground.

Our home fronts have given us an overwhelming superiority in weapons and
munitions of war and placed at our disposal
great reserves of trained fighting men.

The tide has turned.

The free men of the world are marching
together to victory. I have full confidence in
your courage, devotion to duty, and skill in
battle.

We will accept nothing less than full victory.

Good luck, and let us all beseech the blessings of Almighty God upon this great and
noble undertaking.

DWIGHT D. EISENHOWER

☆ ☆ ☆

LETTER FROM A NAVY PILOT
BATTLE OF MIDWAY

The Fates have been kind to me. When you hear people saying harsh things about American youth, you will know how wrong they all are. So many times that now they have become commonplace, I've seen incidents that make me know that we were never soft, never weak.

Many of my friends are now dead. To a man, each died with a nonchalance that each would have denied was courage, but simply called a lack of fear and forgot the triumph. If anything great or good has been born of this war, it should be valued in the youth of our country, who were never trained for war, who almost never believed in war, but who have, from some hidden source, brought forth a gallantry which is homespun, it is so real.

Out here between the spaceless sea and sky, American youth has found itself, and given of itself, so that a spark may catch, burst into flame, and burn high. If our country takes these sacrifices with indifference it will be the cruelest ingratitude the world has ever known.

You will, I know, do all in your power to help others keep the faith. My luck can't last much longer. But the flame goes on and only that is important.

READER'S DIGEST

☆ ☆ ☆

My first recollection is that of a bugle call.

DOUGLAS MAC ARTHUR

☆ ☆ ☆

The inescapable price of liberty is an ability to preserve it from destruction.

DOUGLAS MAC ARTHUR

☆ ☆ ☆

MESSAGE TO UNIT COMMANDERS

Help is on the way from the United States. Thousands of troops and hundreds of planes are being dispatched. The exact time of arrival of reinforcements is unknown as they will have to fight their way through Japanese attempts against them. It is imperative that our troops hold until these reinforcements arrive.

No further retreat is possible. We have more troops in Bataan than the Japanese have thrown against us; our supplies are ample; a determined defense will defeat the enemy's attack.

It is a question now of courage and determination. Men who run will merely be destroyed but men who fight will save themselves and their country.

I call upon every soldier in Bataan to fight in his assigned position, resisting every attack. This is the only road to salvation. If we fight we will win; if we retreat we will be destroyed.

DOUGLAS MAC ARTHUR

☆ ☆ ☆

AN AMERICAN WITHOUT
RESERVE

I was born an American; I live an American; I shall die an American; and I intend to perform the duties incumbent upon me in that character to the end of my career. I mean to do this with absolute disregard of personal consequences.

What are the personal consequences? What is the individual man, with all the good or evil that may betide him, in comparison with the good or evil which may befall a great country, and in the midst of great transactions which concern that country's fate?

Let the consequences be what they will, I am careless. No man can suffer too much, and no man can fall too soon, if he suffer, or if he fall, in the defense of the liberties and constitution of his country.

DANIEL WEBSTER

☆ ☆ ☆

I AM AN AMERICAN
I
I am an American.
My father belongs to the Sons of the
    Revolution;
My mother, to the Colonial Dames.
One of my ancestors pitched tea overboard in
    Boston Harbor;
Another stood his ground with Warren;
Another hungered with Washington at
    Valley Forge.
My forefathers were America in the making:
They spoke in her council halls;
They died on her battlefields;
They commanded her ships;
They cleared her forests.
Dawns reddened and paled.
Stanch hearts of mine beat fast at each new
    star
In the nation's flag.
Keen eyes of mine foresaw her greater glory:
The sweep of her seas,
The plenty of her plains,
The man-hives in her billion-wired cities.
Every drop of blood in me holds a heritage
    of patriotism.
I am proud of my past.
I am an American.

II

I am an American.
My father was an atom of dust,
My mother a straw in the wind,
To his serene majesty.
One of my ancestors died in the mines of
    Siberia;
Another was crippled for life by twenty
    blows of the knout;
Another was killed defending his home
    during the massacres.
The history of my ancestors is a trail of
    blood

To the palace gate of the Great White Czar.
But then the dream came—
The dream of America.
In the light of the Liberty torch
The atom of dust became a man
And the straw in the wind became a woman
For the first time.
"See," said my father, pointing to the flag
    that fluttered near,
"That flag of stars and stripes is yours;
It is the emblem of the promised land,
It means, my son, the hope of humanity.
Live for it—die for it!"
Under the open sky of my new country I
    swore to do so;
And every drop of blood in me will keep that
    vow.
I am proud of my future.
I am an American.

ELIAS LIEBERMAN

☆ ☆ ☆

GUIDE
Honest conviction is my courage; the Constitution is my guide.

ANDREW JOHNSON

☆ ☆ ☆

From THE MORAL WARFARE
Our fathers to their graves have gone;
Their strife is past,—their triumph won;
But sterner trials wait the race
Which rises in their honored place,—
A moral warfare with the crime
And folly of an evil time.

So let it be. In God's own might
We gird us for the coming fight,
And, strong in him whose cause is ours
In conflict with unholy powers,
We grasp the weapons he has given,—
The Light, the Truth, and Love of Heaven.

JOHN GREENLEAF WHITTIER

☆ ☆ ☆

VI

THEIR LAST FULL
MEASURE OF DEVOTION

☆　☆　☆

*A nation reveals itself not only by the men it produces but
also by the men it honors, the men it remembers.*

JOHN F. KENNEDY

TRIBUTE

These heroes are dead. They died for liberty—they died for us. They are at rest. They sleep in the land they made free, under the flag they rendered stainless, under the solemn pines, the sad hemlocks, the tearful willows, the embracing vines. They sleep beneath the shadow of the clouds, careless alike of sunshine or storm, each in the windowless palace of rest. Earth may run red with other wars—they are at peace. In the midst of battles, in the roar of conflicts, they found the serenity of death.

ROBERT G. INGERSOLL

☆　☆　☆

From CHARLES SUMNER

So when a great man dies,
　For years beyond our ken,
The light he leaves behind him lies
　Upon the paths of men.

HENRY WADSWORTH LONGFELLOW

☆　☆　☆

ETERNAL SIGNIFICANCE

If a soldier dies merely through the hazards of war, that is one thing. But if he dies for a cause to which his country has linked its destiny, such as human freedom or the maintenance of justice, he has linked himself to a cause which is great and glorious.

If that cause is eternal, an eternal significance is given to his dying. But if not, his attachment to it gives him the distinction of a patriot and a hero, but not necessarily that of a saint.

To die for justice, for freedom, links a man to something different from mere devotion to a flag. Justice is not temporal, it is eternal. In dying for it, one gives significance to his final act.

JOHN GARDNER

☆　☆　☆

INSCRIPTION

Here rests in honored glory an American soldier known but to God.

TOMB OF THE UNKNOWN SOLDIER
ARLINGTON NATIONAL CEMETERY

☆　☆　☆

TOMB OF THE UNKNOWN SOLDIER

Echoes cleave the stillness where he sleeps;
The bark of guns, the bullets' angry whine
　Resound upon his home
　Of his last loneliness.

No name is carved upon the stone, no date
Of birth or death; but silvered angels stand
　Upon the wind, and weep
　Their tears of penitence.

Cold songs of snow, and sharp-sweet tears
　of spring
Here consecrate this one who sleeps alone;
　A nation's pride is couched
　In grief, upon his breast.

LEILA PIER KING

☆　☆　☆

The body of the Unknown Soldier has come home, but his spirit will wander with that of his brothers. There will be no rest for his soul until the great democracy of death has been translated into the unity of life.

HEYWOOD BROUN

☆　☆　☆

MEMORIAL FOUNTAIN PLAQUE

Dedicated in memory of
John Honeyman
who served Washington and
the Continental Army
as a spy.
Drink of the fount of liberty.
Let posterity inherit freedom.

WASHINGTON CROSSING STATE
PARK, NEW JERSEY

☆　☆　☆

TOMB OF THE UNKNOWN REVOLUTIONARY SOLDIER

Here lies a soldier of
The Revolution whose identity
Is known but to God.
His was an idealism
That recognized a Supreme
Being, that planted
Religious liberty on our
Shores, that overthrew
Despotism, that established
A people's government,
That wrote a Constitution
Setting metes and bounds
Of delegated authority,
That fixed a standard of
Value upon men above
Gold and lifted high the
Torch of civil liberty
Along the pathway of
Mankind.
In ourselves his soul
Exists as part of ours,
His memory's mansion.

ALEXANDRIA, VIRGINIA
(WRITTEN BY WILLIAM TYLER PAGE)

☆　☆　☆

TRIBUTE TO THEODORE ROOSEVELT

There was no hour down to the end when he would not turn aside from everything else to preach the doctrine of Americanism, of the principles and the faith upon which American government rested, and which all true Americans should wear in their heart of hearts.

He was a great patriot, a great man, above all, a great American.

His country was the ruling, mastering passion of his life from the beginning even unto the end.

HENRY CABOT LODGE

☆　☆　☆

EPITAPH

Elisha Brown
of Boston
who in Octr 1769 during 17 days
inspired with
a generous Zeal for the LAWS
bravely & successfully
opposed a whole British Regt
in their violent attempt
to FORCE him from his
legal habitation
Happy Citizen when call'd singly
to be a Barrier to the Liberties
of a Continent.

OLD GRANARY BURYING GROUND
BOSTON, MASSACHUSETTS

☆　☆　☆

LETTER TO BENJAMIN FRANKLIN

If to be venerated for benevolence, if to be admired for talents, if to be esteemed for patriotism, if to be beloved for philanthropy, can gratify the human mind, you must have the pleasing consolation to know that you have not lived in vain. And I flatter myself that it will not be ranked among the least grateful occurrences of your life to be assured that, so long as I retain my memory, you will be thought on with respect, veneration, and affection by your sincere friend.

GEORGE WASHINGTON

☆　☆　☆

LIVING MEMORIES

I think it is a noble and pious thing to do whatever we may by written word and moulded bronze and sculptured stone to keep our memories, our reverence, and our love alive and to hand them on to new generations all too ready to forget.

OLIVER WENDELL HOLMES, JR.

☆　☆　☆

DANIEL WEBSTER SPEAKS
AT BUNKER HILL

The first time I ever saw Mr. Webster was on the 17th of June, 1825, at the laying of the corner-stone of the Bunker Hill Monument. I shall never forget his appearance as he strode across the open area, encircled by some fifty thousand persons—men and women—waiting for the "Orator of the Day," nor the shout that simultaneously burst forth, as he was recognized, carrying up to the skies the name of "Webster!" "Webster!" "Webster!"

It was one of those lovely days in June, when the sun is bright, the air clear, and the breath of nature so sweet and pure as to fill every bosom with a grateful joy in the mere consciousness of existence. There were present long files of soldiers in their holiday attire; there were many associations, with their mottoed banners; there were lodges and grand lodges, in white aprons and blue scarfs; there were miles of citizens from the towns and the country round about; there were two hundred gray-haired men, remnants of the days of the Revolution.

Mr. Webster was in the very zenith of his fame and of his powers.

There was a grandeur in his form, an intelligence in his deep dark eye, a loftiness in his expansive brow, a significance in his arched lip, altogether beyond those of any other human being I ever saw. And these, on the occasion to which I allude, had their full expression and interpretation.

When he came to address the few scarred and time-worn veterans—some forty in number—who had shared in the bloody scene which all had now gathered to commemorate, he paused a moment, and, as he uttered the words "Venerable men," his voice trembled, and I could see a cloud pass over the sea of faces that turned upon the speaker.

He said: "Our poor work may perish, but thine shall endure: this monument may moulder away, the solid ground it rests upon may sink down to the level of the sea; but thy memory shall not fail. Wherever among men a heart shall be found that beats to the transports of patriotism and liberty, its aspirations shall claim kindred with thy spirit!"

I have never seen such an effect, from a single passage. Lifted as by inspiration, every breast seemed now to expand, every gaze to turn above, every face to beam with a holy yet exulting enthusiasm. It was the omnipotence of eloquence, which, like the agitated sea, carries a host upon its waves, sinking and swelling with its irresistible undulations.

SAMUEL GRISWOLD GOODRICH

☆   ☆   ☆

The dead do not need us, but forever and forever more we need them.

JAMES A. GARFIELD

☆   ☆   ☆

CONCORD HYMN

By the rude bridge that arched the flood,
    Their flag to April's breeze unfurled,
Here once the embattled farmers stood,
    And fired the shot heard round the world.

The foe long since in silence slept;
    Alike the conqueror silent sleeps;
And Time the ruined bridge has swept
    Down the dark stream which seaward
        creeps.

On this green bank, by this soft stream,
    We set to-day a votive stone;
That memory may their deed redeem,
    When, like our sires, our sons are gone,

Spirit, that made those heroes dare
    To die, and leave their children free,
Bid Time and Nature gently spare
    The shaft we raise to them and thee.

RALPH WALDO EMERSON

☆   ☆   ☆

☆   ☆   ☆

LETTER TO MRS. BIXBY

Dear Madam: I have been shown in the files of the War Department a statement of the Adjutant-General of Massachusetts that you are the mother of five sons who have died gloriously on the field of battle. I feel how weak and fruitless must be any words of mine which should attempt to beguile you from the grief of a loss so overwhelming. But I cannot refrain from tendering to you the consolation that may be found in the thanks of the Republic they died to save. I pray that our heavenly Father may assuage the anguish of your bereavement, and leave you only the cherished memory of the loved and lost, and the solemn pride that must be yours to have laid so costly a sacrifice upon the altar of freedom.

ABRAHAM LINCOLN

☆   ☆   ☆

THE GETTYSBURG ADDRESS
(NOVEMBER 19, 1863)

Fourscore and seven years ago our fathers brought forth on this continent a new nation, conceived in liberty, and dedicated to the proposition that all men are created equal.

Now we are engaged in a great civil war, testing whether that nation, or any nation so conceived and so dedicated, can long endure. We are met on a great battlefield of that war. We have come to dedicate a portion of that field as a final resting-place for those who here gave their lives that that nation might live. It is altogether fitting and proper that we should do this.

But in a larger sense we cannot dedicate, we cannot consecrate, we cannot hallow this ground. The brave men, living and dead, who struggled here have consecrated it, far above our poor power to add or detract. The world will little note, nor long remember, what we say here, but it can never forget what they did here. It is for us the living, rather, to be dedicated here to the unfinished work which they who fought here have thus far so nobly advanced.

It is rather for us to be here dedicated to the great task remaining before us, that from these honored dead we take increased devotion to that cause for which they gave the last full measure of devotion; that we here highly resolve that these dead shall not have died in vain—that this nation, under God, shall have a new birth of freedom—and that government of the people, by the people, for the people, shall not perish from the earth.

ABRAHAM LINCOLN

☆   ☆   ☆

From THE BLUE AND THE GRAY

No more shall the war-cry sever,
Or the winding river be red;
They banish our anger forever
When they laurel the graves of our dead!
Under the sod and the dew
Waiting the Judgment Day:
Love and tears for the Blue,
Tears and love for the Gray.

FRANCIS MILES FINCH

☆   ☆   ☆

From THE BIVOUAC OF THE DEAD

The muffled drum's sad roll has beat
    The soldier's last tattoo;
No more on life's parade shall meet
    The brave and fallen few.
On fame's eternal camping-ground
    Their silent tents are spread,
And glory guards, with solemn round,
    The bivouac of the dead.

THEODORE O'HARA

☆   ☆   ☆

We are fit to entertain great hopes only as we cherish great memories.

GEORGE S. GORDON

☆   ☆   ☆

80

☆ ☆ ☆

INSCRIPTION TO GENERAL BARNARD ELLIOTT BEE

Just before his death,
To rally his scattered troops,
He gave the command:
"Form, form, there stands Jackson
Like a stone wall;
Rally behind the Virginians."

MANASSAS NATIONAL BATTLE-
FIELD PARK, VIRGINIA

☆ ☆ ☆

REFLECTIONS ON GETTYSBURG

Gettysburg today is a place where gallant spirits still tell their story of high sacrifice and undying devotion. There is a cemetery, there are gentle ridges rolling unbroken toward the sunset, and here and there one can find spots where everything that is significant in the American dream speaks to today's world with an undying voice.

Yet the battle was here and its presence is felt, and you cannot visit the place without feeling the echoes of what was once a proving ground for everything America believes in.

For Gettysburg was where we Americans came to grips with ourselves. On these Pennsylvania hills, fate once asked men of our flesh: Do you really mean it? Are you just coasting, or is the vision this land gave you something you are willing to die for? They died on these hills and fields in fantastic numbers, and the dying was not easy, but young men who would have preferred to live did die and this open, sunlit country remembers them, Northerners and Southerners alike.

We are a young country with the future still ahead of us, but we do have our shrines and Gettysburg is one of the greatest of them. It is great because it once brought us face to face with certain fundamentals. These still live with us; we passed one test, and by the story which the passing of that test tells us, we do not need to be afraid of anything that can happen in the future. The America of today was beaten into form on what are now the quiet, dreamy fields around this hilltop town in Pennsylvania.

BRUCE CATTON

☆ ☆ ☆

OUR TRIBUTE

There is no greater tribute we could pay to America's war dead than to find the road to peace.

RICHARD M. NIXON

☆ ☆ ☆

ODE TO THE CONFEDERATE DEAD IN MAGNOLIA CEMETERY

Sleep sweetly in your humble graves,
Sleep, martyrs of a fallen cause;
Though yet no marble column craves
The pilgrim here to pause.

In seeds of laurels in the earth
The garlands of your fame are sown;
And somewhere, waiting for its birth,
The shaft is in the stone!

Meanwhile, your sisters for the years
Which hold in trust your storied tombs,
Bring all they now can give you —tears,
And these memorial blooms.

Small tributes! but your shades will smile
More proudly on those wreaths today,
As when some cannon-moulded pile
Shall overlook this Bay.

Stoop, angels, hither from the skies!
There is no holier spot of ground
Than where defeated valor lies,
By mourning beauty crowned!

HENRY TIMROD

☆ ☆ ☆

TWENTY-FIFTH ANNIVERSARY

The reunion of the Blue and the Gray at Gettysburg was one of the most significant and interesting events since the war. There have been similar meetings of the old Confederate and Union soldiers before this year. But the meeting, upon the twenty-fifth anniversary of the battle, of the two armies by which the battle was fought to shake hands in perfect amity as peacefully cooperating citizens of a common country is one of the most memorable incidents in history, and gave to the occasion a charm that can never be forgotten.

The points of interest upon such a field are innumerable. Every army corps and division and regiment and company has its spots of peculiar association; and a battle of three days, drifting over a large space, and touching every part of it, invests the whole territory with a glamour of heroism and romantic recollection. The story of Gettysburg is one of the most interesting narratives of battle. The courage and persistence displayed upon both sides leave in those respects nothing to be concealed. Both sides may be equally proud of their bravery, and feel a certain American satisfaction in the terrible story.

HARPER'S WEEKLY (1888)

☆   ☆   ☆

They gave their safety for our own;
   For us they fought and bled and died;
Drained sorrow's cup, took on themselves
   The anguish of the Crucified;
Bought our slow ease with pierced hands,
   Our laughter with their piteous cries;
Our singing with pale silenced lips,
   Our wonder with their blinded eyes.

Their names are writ on every flower,
   On every tree their sign is set.
Birds are their words; by day and night
   The very stones cry out our debt.
We will keep faith! Our hands take up

The charge their dying hands let fall—
And in an everlasting peace
   We build their proud memorial.

ADA JACKSON

☆   ☆   ☆

BY THE SCULPTOR OF THE MOUNT RUSHMORE MEMORIAL

I want somewhere in America . . .
a few feet of stone that bears witness . . .
of the great things we accomplished as a
   nation . . .
placed so high it won't pay to pull it down
   for lesser purposes . . .
carved high, as close to heaven as we can . . .
Then breathe a prayer that these records
   will endure . . .
until the wind and the rain alone . . .
shall wash them away.

GUTZON BORGLUM

☆   ☆   ☆

THE PEACEMAKER

Upon his will he binds a radiant chain,
   For Freedom's sake he is no longer free,
   It is his task, the slave of Liberty,
With his own blood to wipe away a stain.
That pain may cease, he yields his flesh to
   pain.
   To banish war, he must a warrior be,
   He dwells in Night, eternal Dawn to see,
And gladly dies, abundant life to gain.

What matters Death, if Freedom be not dead?
   No flags are free, if Freedom's flag be
   furled.
Who fights for Freedom, goes with joyful
   tread
   To meet the fires of Hell against him
   hurled,
And has for captain Him whose thorn-
   wreathed head
   Smiles from the Cross upon a conquered
   world.

JOYCE KILMER

EYES OF GRANITE

It's right to have a statue in the park,
Where swords and anchors guard the pledge
    in stone;
I come here often in the evening's dark,
And find a courage stronger than my own.

The Cannoneer is looking to the south;
There to the north, the Cavalry's at rest;
The Rifle's east, with sternness on his
    mouth;
And on my side the Sailor, facing west.

They've stood here long before my father's
    time,
While I've grown up beneath their sleepless
    gaze,
And now my sons are men, and theirs will
    climb
Upon this shaft on flag-filled holidays.

Mankind must live, and love, more Godly-
    wise,
Under the plea ingrained in granite eyes.

RALPH W. SEAGER

MEMORIAL DAY IN MAINE

At that time, in the eighteen nineties and at
the turn of the century, New England villages
and small towns, and many outside New England as well, provided they were north of
Mason and Dixon's line, observed this sacred
day after a carefully prescribed manner; and
ours was no exception to the rule.

In the morning all graves in the village
cemetery, which during the preceding week
had been mown and clipped by our sexton,
were decorated by the families concerned
with potted plants and with jars and vases of
flowers; and small American flags were set
upright by our town authorities on those
which marked the resting place of soldiers,
whether of the Revolutionary or of the Civil
War.

At precisely two o'clock in the afternoon a
long procession marched from our town hall
on the green toward the cemetery one half
mile distant above our small, quiet harbor.

Our village band headed the line of march,
erect and spruce in gold-laced green uni-
forms, which upon its original formation had
been eagerly provided by local contributions.

Its few members played their fifes, cornets,
trumpets, and drums with marked dignity,
martial music being the order before the procession entered the cemetery, when muffled
drumbeats superseded it.

Directly behind the band rode our one cavalry officer, Captain Augustus Stevens. He
wore a broad-brimmed hat with a faded gold
cord and in his free right hand held aloft a
flashing sword. He was an imposing figure,
who each year sent a chill down my back; and
although his horse was hardly of the mettle of
those which charged at Gettysburg, he, too,
seemed to us magnificent as his hoofs sent up
whirls of dust from the country road. . . .

Children completed the line of march:
scores of children; boys in tight knee pants
and white blouses, girls in summer frocks of
gingham or percale, all awe-struck and silent.

Each child carried a bouquet of flowers
—lilacs and apple blossoms if the spring was
early enough, violets and wild cherry if it was
slow in coming—to place upon the graves of
our honored dead when once the procession
with a final roll of drumbeats should halt in
the cemetery and the signal should be given.

MARY ELLEN CHASE

84

VII

THY ROCKS AND RILLS, THY WOODS AND TEMPLED HILLS

☆　☆　☆

*This country and this people seem
to have been made for each other.*

JOHN JAY

THE GIFT OUTRIGHT

The land was ours before we were the land's.
She was our land more than a hundred years
Before we were her people. She was ours
In Massachusetts, in Virginia,
But we were England's, still colonials,
Possessing what we still were unpossessed by,
Possessed by what we now no more possessed.
Something we were withholding made us
      weak
Until we found it was ourselves
We were withholding from our land of living,
And forthwith found salvation in surrender.
Such as we were we gave ourselves outright
(The deed of gift was many deeds of war)
To the land vaguely realizing westward,
But still unstoried, artless, unenhanced,
Such as she was, such as she would become.

                                    ROBERT FROST

☆   ☆   ☆

My God! how little do my countrymen know
what precious blessings they are in possession
of, and which no other people on earth
enjoy!

                                    THOMAS JEFFERSON

☆   ☆   ☆

In both the northern and southern hemi-
spheres of the New World, Nature has not
only outlined her works on a larger scale, but
has painted the whole picture with brighter
and more costly colors than she used in delin-
eating and in beautifying the Old World. The
heavens of America appear infinitely higher,
the sky is bluer, the air is fresher, the cold is
intenser, the moon looks larger, the stars are
brighter, the thunder is louder, the lightning
is vivider, the wind is stronger, the rain is
heavier, the mountains are higher, the rivers
longer, the forests bigger, the plains broader.

                                    FRANCIS HEAD

☆   ☆   ☆

The forests of America, however slighted by
man, must have been a great delight to God,
for they were the best he ever planted.

                                    JOHN MUIR

☆   ☆   ☆

AMERICA THE BEAUTIFUL

O beautiful for spacious skies,
    For amber waves of grain,
For purple mountain majesties
    Above the fruited plain!
America! America!
    God shed His grace on thee,
And crown thy good with brotherhood,
    From sea to shining sea!

O beautiful for pilgrim feet,
    Whose stern, impassioned stress
A thoroughfare for freedom beat
    Across the wilderness!
America! America!
    God mend thine every flaw,
Confirm thy soul in self-control,
    Thy liberty in law!

O beautiful for heroes proved
    In liberating strife,
Who more than self their country loved,
    And mercy more than life!
America! America!
    May God thy gold refine,
Till all success be nobleness,
    And every gain divine!

O beautiful for patriot dream
    That sees beyond the years
Thine alabaster cities gleam
    Undimmed by human tears!
America! America!
    God shed His grace on thee,
And crown thy good with brotherhood,
    From sea to shining sea!

                                    KATHARINE LEE BATES

☆   ☆   ☆

PRAIRIE COUNTRY

Trees have their own significance on the prairie. When they stand solitary—a big oak outlined against the sunset or a wild plum in bloom on a pasture slope—or when they stand in groves, seen across the swell of plowed fields, a thick dark brushwork on the rim of the world—always they gain meaning because of the prairie setting. To go from the prevailing big openness of air and sky and sunlight into the coolness, depth, and mystery of the woods, where all kinds of wild things grow haphazard instead of in the neat, planned rows of the worked land, is to savor the natural variety of the prairie country.

RUTH SUCKOW

☆　☆　☆

NATURE'S MASTERPIECE

The Big Tree (*Sequoia gigantea*) is nature's forest masterpiece, and, as far as I know, the greatest of living things. It belongs to an ancient stock, as its remains in old rocks show, and has a strange air of other days about it, a thoroughbred look inherited from the long ago, the auld lang syne of the trees.

The Pacific coast in general is the paradise of conifers. Here nearly all of them are giants, and display a beauty and magnificence unknown elsewhere. The climate is mild, the ground never freezes, and moisture and sunshine abound all the year.

Nevertheless, it is not easy to account for the colossal size of the sequoias. The largest are about three hundred feet high and thirty feet in diameter. Who of all the dwellers of the plains and prairies and fertile home forests of round-headed oak and maple, hickory and elm, ever dreamed that earth could bear such growths?

Sequoias are trees that the familiar pines and firs seem to know nothing about, lonely, silent, serene, with a physiognomy almost godlike, and so old that thousands of them still living had already counted their years by tens of centuries when Columbus set sail from Spain, and were in the vigor of youth or middle age when the star led the Chaldean sages to the infant Saviour's cradle. As far as man is concerned, they are the same yesterday, today, and forever, emblems of permanence.

JOHN MUIR

☆　☆　☆

From JOHNNY APPLESEED'S SONG

Walking lonesome through the feathered
 forest,
in buckskin breeches ragged to my knees,
my knapsack filled with appleseeds, I
 wander,
singing of apple trees.

Thundering westward roll the covered
 wagons
over the Alleghenies toward the plains;
westward I sow my dreams of apple orchards
blowing in April rains.

*

O wide America, where covered wagons
roll to the west, whose great heart fights
 and bleeds,
see, I come singing into your wilderness
sowing my appleseeds!

Walking barefoot through the Indian forest,
my red-brown seeds alive in my firm brown
 hand,
westward I sow my dreams of apple blossoms
white over wild sweet land!

FRANCES FROST

☆　☆　☆

HALL OF FAME INSCRIPTION

Every formula which expresses a law of nature is a hymn of praise to God.

MARIA MITCHELL

☆　☆　☆

88

From CONNECTICUT

They love their land, because it is their
  own,
    And scorn to give aught other reason why;
Would shake hands with a king upon his
  throne,
    And think it kindness to his majesty.

FITZ-GREENE HALLECK

☆   ☆   ☆

NEW ENGLAND PERSPECTIVES

New England, I sometimes think, is my walled-in house and garden. I am not sure of all the rooms in the house save that Massachusetts is most certainly my library, Maine my bedroom opening on the sea, Boston my Bulfinch dining room, Connecticut and Rhode Island my guest rooms, New Hampshire my front porch, and Vermont my ample garden. My bouldered walls are the Atlantic, the Empire State, Quebec, New Brunswick. From almost any vantage point, at almost any window, I can look at once upon the summer dunes and beaches southward from the Cape, hear the foundry hammers in the surf below the northern rocks, stare level as the sun's ray into the green wilderness of New Brunswick across the noble St. John, or north and down upon the peneplain of the St. Lawrence, or west and over beyond the Catskills and the Adirondacks to the vast reach of Parkman's America whence the wagons, the canal barge, glistening irons, and the vapor trails each in their turn and after him have borne away what New England of herself could spare.

DAVID MC CORD

☆   ☆   ☆

PERSONAL PREFERENCE

New England has a harsh climate, a barren soil, a rough and stormy coast, and yet we love it, even with a love passing that of dwellers in more favored regions.

HENRY CABOT LODGE

☆   ☆   ☆

FAVORED SITUATION

To Americans I hardly need to say, "Westward the star of empire takes its way." As a true patriot, I should be ashamed to think that Adam in paradise was more favorably situated on the whole than the backwoodsman in this country.

HENRY DAVID THOREAU

☆   ☆   ☆

THE COVERED BRIDGE

For a hundred and fifty years, the covered bridge has been an old American landmark. Today it is becoming increasingly difficult to find even one, but only fifty years ago the traveler encountered countless numbers of them—at cities, villages, and country crossings from Maine to Georgia and west to California.

The village bridge of the past century was the meeting place of town and country. In its dim interior men argued crops and politics while their womenfolk exchanged gossip and recipes and their children exclaimed over the gaudy circus posters that hung in the bridge long after the show had left town.

Out in the countryside a covered bridge was a good place to save a load of hay in a sudden summer shower. Farm boys found favorite fishing spots in its shade. It seemed as though a high-spirited mare could actually read the signs that were posted prominently over the bridge portals: "Five Dollars Fine for Riding or Driving Faster Than a Walk on This Bridge!"; for often as not she would automatically slow to a sedate pace on coming in sight of the cool, timbered passageway. For years the covered bridge was the country cousin to the city amusement park's Tunnel of Love. The longer the bridge, the better. Just ask grandpa why they called them "kissin' bridges."

RICHARD SANDERS ALLEN

☆ ☆ ☆

From DIARY IN AMERICA (1839)

America is a wonderful country, endowed by the Omnipotent with natural advantages which no other can boast of; and the mind can hardly calculate upon the degree of perfection and power to which, whether the States are eventually separated or not, it may in the course of two centuries arrive.

At present all is energy and enterprise; every thing is in a state of transition, but of rapid improvement—so rapid, indeed, that those who would describe America now would have to correct all in the short space of ten years; for ten years in America is almost equal to a century in the old continent.

Now, you may pass through a wild forest, where the elk browses and the panther howls. In ten years, that very forest, with its denizens, will, most likely, have disappeared, and in their place you will find towns with thousands of inhabitants; with arts, manufactures, and machinery, all in full activity.

FREDERICK MARRYAT

☆ ☆ ☆

From NIAGARA

Flow on, forever, in thy glorious robe
Of terror and of beauty. Yea, flow on
Unfathomed and resistless. God hath set
His rainbow on thy forehead: and the cloud
Mantled around thy feet. And he doth give
Thy voice of thunder power to speak of him
Eternally—bidding the lip of man
Keep silence—and upon thine altar pour
Incense of awe-struck praise.

LYDIA H. SIGOURNEY

☆ ☆ ☆

The land belongs to the future. We come and go, but the land is always here.

WILLA CATHER

☆ ☆ ☆

THE THUNDERING WATER

Right from the beginning Niagara Falls has been the big showpiece. Once the United States had begun, visitors who wanted to see what the country was like went to Niagara first of all, and probably they were quite right.

This stupendous cataract is beautiful, romantic, overpowering, and somehow rather frightening; it can charm you and it can also kill you, and if its filmy mists are enchanting, the violence that makes the mists is something to think twice about.

Altogether, this foremost of America's wonders is perfectly representative of the nation that has made it a tourist trap, a haven for the newly married, a prime source of electric power, and a rendezvous for any number of wacky daredevils.

You can do just about anything with Niagara Falls except ignore it.

BRUCE CATTON

☆ ☆ ☆

THE BALD EAGLE

The figure of this noble bird is well known throughout the civilized world, emblazoned as it is on our national standard, which waves in the breeze of every clime, bearing to distant lands the remembrance of a great people living in a state of peaceful freedom. May that peaceful freedom last for ever! The great strength, daring and cool courage of the White-headed Eagle, joined to his unequalled power of flight, render him highly conspicuous among his brethren. To these qualities did he add a generous disposition towards others, he might be looked up to as a model of nobility. The ferocious, overbearing and tyrannical temper which is ever and anon displaying itself in his actions, is, nevertheless, best adapted to his state, and was wisely given him by the Creator to enable him to perform the office assigned to him.

JOHN JAMES AUDUBON

☆ ☆ ☆

JOHN JAMES AUDUBON: AMERICAN WOODSMAN

He had roamed the length and breadth of the American borderland with all the freedom of the wild creatures he knew so well and recorded so faithfully. He had talked with Daniel Boone. He had hunted and camped with Indians along the frontier; he knew their ways and may have spoken their language. He had traveled by ark and keelboat with the rough rivermen of the western waterways, and he could speak their language eloquently.

MARSHALL B. DAVIDSON

☆ ☆ ☆

Mountains are earth's undecaying monuments.

NATHANIEL HAWTHORNE

☆ ☆ ☆

MAP OF MY COUNTRY

Every now and then, when the world grows
 dull,
And the edge of sunshine or the song of a
 bird
Frays away to the shadow of a dream,
I take a map, a map, perhaps, of my state,
One of my states—New York of the glorious
 hills,
Or Pennsylvania of the shaggy woods,
Or great high-shouldered, blue-eyed Minne-
 sota,
Or swart New Jersey, the commuters' pocket,
Or cramped and memory-riddled Massachu-
 setts,
Or the enigmatic steppes of the Dakotas,
Or California of the laughing sunshine—
They are all my states, and I have loved them
 all,
Worked, sweated, hated, and taken joy in
 them.
I know their streets, their roads, and the
 ways between

The great green stretches south of the Great
 Lakes,
The hills, and dunes, and plains, and sunny
 crossroads,
Remember the turns, the heartfelt run of the
 land,
The weeds beside the road, the meadow
 larks,
The waiting houses, the whispering cry of
 rain,
Lakes in the sunlight, and darkness over the
 land.
And I see roads I have not yet come to
 travel—
But I know they, too, are good, and I shall
 be there
Some day, all in good time, for this is my
 home,
This is America, my own country.

ALLEN E. WOODALL

☆ ☆ ☆

From AMERICAN LETTER

We dwell
On the half earth, on the open curve of a
 continent.
Sea is divided from sea by the day-fall. The
 dawn
Rides the low east with us many hours;
First are the capes, then are the shorelands,
 now
The blue Appalachians faint as the day rise;
The willows shudder with light on the long
 Ohio:
The Lakes scatter the low sun: the prairies
Slide out of the dark: in the eddy of clean
 air
The smoke goes up from the high plains of
 Wyoming:
The steep Sierras rise: the struck foam
Flames at the wind's heel on the far Pacific.
Already the noon leans to the eastern cliff:
The elms darken the door and the dust-heavy
 lilacs.

ARCHIBALD MAC LEISH

☆ ☆ ☆

A SENATOR CHAMPIONS THE MARIGOLD

When spring comes, there will be flowers. We shall be delighted with the earlier flowers —the tulips, the daffodils, the redbud, and the dogwood blossoms. A little later will come all the delightful annual flowers, which nature compels us to cultivate every year, but leaves a residue of seed which makes them almost perpetual. They will include the humble but beautiful petunia, the zinnia and the calendula, and also the marigold.

Two or three years ago, I introduced a joint resolution to make the marigold the national flower. That stirred quite a controversy; and, as a result, the corn tassel and the rose and other flowers were advanced as candidates of our national floral emblem.

But I still find myself wedded to the marigold—robust, rugged, bright, stately, single-colored and multicolored, somehow able to resist the onslaught of insects; it takes in its stride extreme changes in temperature, and fights back the scorching sun in summer and the chill of early spring evenings.

What a flower the marigold is! I am looking forward to the time when these gay flowers will salute and intrigue our sense of beauty.

So once more I find myself impelled to introduce a joint resolution to make the American marigold—its botanical name is Tagetes erecta—the national flower of our country.

EVERETT MC KINLEY DIRKSEN

☆ ☆ ☆

STATE FLOWERS

Alabama: Camellia.
Alaska: Blue forget-me-not.
Arizona: Saguaro cactus.
Arkansas: Apple blossom.
California: Golden poppy.
Colorado: Rocky Mountain columbine.
Connecticut: Mountain laurel.
Delaware: Peach blossom.
Florida: Orange blossom.
Georgia: Cherokee rose.
Hawaii: Hibiscus.
Idaho: Syringa.
Illinois: Native violet.
Indiana: Peony.
Iowa: Wild rose.
Kansas: Native sunflower.
Kentucky: Goldenrod.
Louisiana: Magnolia.
Maine: Pine cone and tassel.
Maryland: Black-eyed Susan.
Massachusetts: Mayflower.
Michigan: Apple blossom.
Minnesota: Pink and white lady's slipper.
Mississippi: Magnolia.
Missouri: Hawthorn.
Montana: Bitterroot.
Nebraska: Goldenrod.
Nevada: Sagebrush.
New Hampshire: Purple lilac.
New Jersey: Purple violet.
New Mexico: Yucca.
New York: Rose.
North Carolina: Dogwood.
North Dakota: Wild prairie rose.
Ohio: Scarlet carnation.
Oklahoma: Mistletoe.
Oregon: Oregon grape.
Pennsylvania: Mountain laurel.
Rhode Island: Violet.
South Carolina: Yellow jessamine.
South Dakota: Pasque flower.
Tennessee: Iris.
Texas: Bluebonnet.
Utah: Sego lily.
Vermont: Red clover.
Virginia: Dogwood.
Washington: Western rhododendron.
West Virginia: Big rhododendron.
Wisconsin: Wood violet.
Wyoming: Indian paint brush.

☆ ☆ ☆

From DAWN AT SAN DIEGO
Behold! the Holy Grail is found,
Found in each poppy's cup of gold;
And God walks with us as of old.
Behold! the burning bush still burns
For man, whichever way he turns;
And all God's earth is holy ground.

JOAQUIN MILLER

☆ ☆ ☆

OPEN COUNTRY
Of all places in the world where life can be lived to its fullest and freest, where it can be met in its greatest variety and beauty, there is none to equal the open country or the country town.

RAY STANNARD BAKER

☆ ☆ ☆

I consider it the best part of an education to have been born and brought up in the country.

AMOS BRONSON ALCOTT

☆ ☆ ☆

THREAT
To waste, to destroy, our natural resources, to skin and exhaust the land instead of using it so as to increase its usefulness, will result in undermining in the days of our children the very prosperity which we ought by right to hand down to them amplified and developed.

THEODORE ROOSEVELT

☆ ☆ ☆

REVELATION
The Grand Canyon is a sort of landscape Day of Judgment. It is not a show place, a beauty spot, but a revelation.

The Colorado River, which is powerful, turbulent, and so thick with silt that it is like a saw, made with the help of the erosive forces of rain, frost, and wind, and some strange geological accidents; and all these together have been hard at work on it for the last seven or eight million years.

It is the largest of the eighteen canyons of the Colorado River, is over two miles long, has an average width of twelve miles, and is a good mile deep.

It is the world's supreme example of erosion. But this is not what it really is.

It is, I repeat, a revelation.

The Colorado River made it, but you feel when you are there that God gave the Colorado River its instructions. It is all Beethoven's nine symphonies in stone and magic light. Even to remember that it is still there lifts up the heart.

If I were an American, I should make my remembrance of it the final test of men, art, and policies. I should ask myself: Is this good enough to exist in the same country as the Canyon?

J. B. PRIESTLEY

☆ ☆ ☆

FISHING
Fishing is much more than fish; it is the vitalizing lure to outdoor life. It is the great occasion when we may return to the fine simplicity of our forebears.

HERBERT HOOVER

☆ ☆ ☆

RELATIONSHIP
Any relation to the land, the habit of tilling it, or mining it, or even hunting on it, generates the feeling of patriotism.

RALPH WALDO EMERSON

☆ ☆ ☆

LAWS OF NATURE
There is nothing in the laws of nature or the nature of man to require that a state which is big and vital and productive must also be mundane and dirty and ugly.

NELSON A. ROCKEFELLER

VIII

EQUAL JUSTICE
UNDER LAW

☆　　☆　　☆

*Liberty, the precious boon of Heaven, is meek and reasonable.
She admits that she belongs to all—to the high and the low, the
rich and the poor, the black and the white—and that she belongs
to them all equally.*

GERRIT SMITH

INSCRIPTION

Justice is founded in the rights bestowed by nature upon man. Liberty is maintained in the security of justice.

DEPARTMENT OF JUSTICE
WASHINGTON, D.C.

☆ ☆ ☆

Law can offer us a moral precept. To the extent that laws are founded on morality and on logic, they can lead men's hearts and minds. But this aspect of law can have meaning only to the extent that the constituents of law are moral and are rational.

ROBERT F. KENNEDY

☆ ☆ ☆

PROMISE OF AMERICA

. . . to every man his chance—to every man, regardless of his birth, his shining, golden opportunity—to every man the right to live, to work, to be himself, and to become whatever thing his manhood and his vision can combine to make him—this, seeker, is the promise of America.

THOMAS WOLFE

☆ ☆ ☆

The Constitution of the United States is the result of the collected wisdom of our country.

THOMAS JEFFERSON

☆ ☆ ☆

From THE DECLARATION OF INDEPENDENCE

When in the Course of human events, it becomes necessary for one people to dissolve the political bands which have connected them with another, and to assume among the Powers of the earth, the separate and equal station to which the Laws of Nature and of Nature's God entitle them, a decent respect to the opinions of mankind requires that they should declare the causes which impel them to the separation.

We hold these truths to be self-evident, that all men are created equal, that they are endowed by their Creator with certain unalienable Rights, that among these are Life, Liberty and the pursuit of Happiness. That to secure these rights, Governments are instituted among Men, deriving their just powers from the consent of the governed, That whenever any Form of Government becomes destructive of these ends, it is the Right of the People to alter or to abolish it, and to institute new Government, laying its foundation on such principles and organizing its powers in such form, as to them shall seem most likely to effect their Safety and Happiness. Prudence, indeed, will dictate that Governments long established should not be changed for light and transient causes; and accordingly all experience hath shown, that mankind are more disposed to suffer, while evils are sufferable, than to right themselves by abolishing the forms to which they are accustomed. But when a long train of abuses and usurpations, pursuing invariably the same Object evinces a design to reduce them under absolute Despotism, it is their right, it is their duty, to throw off such Government, and to provide new Guards for their future security.

☆ ☆ ☆

Here was buried
Thomas Jefferson
Author of the
Declaration
of American Independence
of the
Statute for Virginia
for
Religious Freedom
and Father of the
University of Virginia.
Born April 2, 1743 O.S.
Died July 4, 1826

FAMILY GRAVEYARD
MONTICELLO, VIRGINIA

☆ ☆ ☆

Since the days when Jefferson expounded his code of political philosophy, the whole world has become his pupil.

MICHAEL MAC WHITE

☆ ☆ ☆

PURPOSE

To preserve freedom and for no other purpose the people of the United States created a government under our Constitution.

They realized that no simple democracy could long survive the lure of political demagogues leading to the dictator, and they deliberately limited the power of their government and divided it into three separate parts: legislative, executive, and judicial.

This was intended to be a check on each department so that no one of them might become supreme.

The purpose of the Constitution was not to convey rights to individual citizens, but to specify the limitations imposed by free citizens on government.

LAWRENCE H. SMITH

☆ ☆ ☆

FIFTIETH ANNIVERSARY

We have now lived almost fifty years under the Constitution framed by the sages and patriots of the Revolution. The conflicts in which the nations of Europe were engaged during a great part of this period, the spirit in which they waged war against each other, and our intimate commercial connections with every part of the civilized world rendered it a time of much difficulty for the Government of the United States.

We have had our seasons of peace and of war, with all the evils which precede or follow a state of hostility with powerful nations.

We encountered these trials with our Constitution yet in its infancy, and under the disadvantages which a new and untried govern-

ment must always feel when it is called upon to put forth its whole strength without the lights of experience to guide it or the weight of precedents to justify its measures. But we have passed triumphantly through all these difficulties.

Our Constitution is no longer a doubtful experiment, and at the end of nearly half a century we find that it has preserved unimpaired the liberties of the people, secured the rights of property, and that our country has improved and is flourishing beyond any former example in the history of nations.

ANDREW JACKSON

☆ ☆ ☆

The Constitution does not provide for first and second class citizens.

WENDELL WILLKIE

☆ ☆ ☆

BATTLE FOR RIGHTS

In the cause of freedom, we have to battle for the rights of people with whom we do not agree, and whom, in many cases, we may not like. These people test the strength of the freedoms which protect all of us. If we do not defend their rights, we endanger our own.

HARRY S. TRUMAN

☆ ☆ ☆

LOVE OF LIBERTY

What constitutes the bulwark of our liberty and independence? It is not our frowning battlements, our bristling seacoast, our army and our navy. These are not our reliance against tyranny. All of those may be turned against us without making us weaker for the struggle. Our reliance is in the love of liberty which God has planted in us. Our defense is in the spirit which prizes liberty as the heritage of all men, in all lands everywhere.

ABRAHAM LINCOLN

☆ ☆ ☆

☆ ☆ ☆

KEEPING THE FAITH

We know how far from perfect realization is the ideal of our democracy. But it has never been destroyed.

Not by a civil war, four years long and slaughtering the best of our youth, a million of them.

Not by prosperity, a mighty tidal rise of it, nor by the ebb of numerous depressions.

Today we still believe in the same ideal which was declared in the first breath of life this nation drew.

"All men are created free and equal." That was so bold a thing to say that the men who signed our Declaration might have been signing their death warrant; they knew that if they failed to justify their faith in this new idea, this new country, they would be hanged as traitors.

But the army of our Revolution, that ragged, ill-trained little force of farmers, clerks, tinkers, tailors, raw lads from raw young towns, fought for that faith for seven years, against the King's drilled troops, and won.

So we grew bolder in our faith; we carried it across the land; we fought another war, to free the slaves. Fraternity has now become a habit with us.

DONALD CULROSS PEATTIE

☆ ☆ ☆

INDIVIDUAL LIBERTY

While democracy must have its organization and controls, its vital breath is individual liberty.

CHARLES EVANS HUGHES

☆ ☆ ☆

Citizenship is man's basic right, for it is nothing less than the right to have rights.

EARL WARREN

☆ ☆ ☆

MAN AND LAW

No man is above the law, and no man is below it.

THEODORE ROOSEVELT

☆ ☆ ☆

SPIRIT OF LIBERTY

The spirit of liberty is the spirit which is not too sure that it is right.

The spirit of liberty is the spirit which seeks to understand the minds of other men and women.

The spirit of liberty is the spirit which weighs their interests alongside its own without bias.

The spirit of liberty remembers that not even a sparrow falls to the earth unheeded.

The spirit of liberty is the spirit of Him who, nearly two thousand years ago, taught mankind that lesson it has never learned but has never quite forgotten—that there may be a kingdom where the least shall be heard and considered side by side with the greatest.

LEARNED HAND

☆ ☆ ☆

GOOD CITIZENSHIP

A manly assertion by each of his individual rights, and a manly concession of equal rights to every other man, is the boast and the law of good citizenship.

BENJAMIN HARRISON

☆ ☆ ☆

HAVENS OF REFUGE

Under our constitutional system, courts stand against any winds that blow as havens of refuge for those who might otherwise suffer because they are helpless, weak, outnumbered, or because they are non-conforming victims of prejudice and public excitement.

HUGO L. BLACK

☆ ☆ ☆

IN BEHALF OF JEWS IN AMERICA

We have marched forward on this road together with America as a whole.

We have marched with her bold pioneers across the continent toward her vanishing frontiers.

We have toiled and struggled and suffered together with them.

We have marched with America onward toward the expanding boundaries of her industry and commerce, her science and invention, her literature, her music, her drama, her art.

We have sat in the councils of her statesmen, we have fought and bled and died on her battlefields.

Do we owe a debt to America? Indeed we do!

It is the same debt that is owed by all others who live under her sheltering wings. It is a continuous debt that is never liquidated. We have paid it and shall continue to pay it gladly and proudly.

RUFUS LEARSI

☆　☆　☆

Government laws are needed to give us civil rights, and God is needed to make us civil.

RALPH W. SOCKMAN

☆　☆　☆

LIBERTY BELL

One of the most cherished symbols of American independence is the famous Liberty Bell, now preserved in Independence Hall, Philadelphia. It has been rung on a number of occasions, the most important of which were the following:

On July 4, 1776, the bell was rung to announce the official adoption of the Declaration of Independence. This was actually the birthday of the nation, and marks the most important single event in its history.

October 14, 1781, it was rung to celebrate the surrender of Lord Cornwallis of the En-glish forces, and the virtual close of the Revolutionary War.

April 6, 1783, it announced the proclamation of peace with Great Britain.

September 29, 1824, it was rung to welcome Lafayette, the famous French general who had assisted Washington, to Independence Hall.

July 4, 1826, it tolled to announce the death of Thomas Jefferson, principal author of the Declaration of Independence.

July 14, 1826, it ushered in "The Year of Jubilee," the fiftieth anniversary of the American Republic.

July 4, 1831, the famous bell rang for the last time on Independence Day.

February 22, 1832, the bell was rung to commemorate the birth of George Washington. Later in the same year it tolled to announce the death of the last surviving signer of the Declaration of Independence—Charles Carroll of Carrollton, Georgia.

July 21, 1834, it tolled again for the death of the Marquis de Lafayette.

July 8, 1835, while it was being tolled for the death of Chief Justice John Marshall, a crack developed in the bell. It started from the brim and inclined in a righthand direction toward the crown.

On February 22, 1843, when an attempt was being made to ring the bell on Washington's birthday, the fracture increased to such an extent that no effort has been made to ring it since that time.

RELIGIOUS TELESCOPE

☆　☆　☆

LAW AND ETHICS

We ought not to separate the science of public law from that of ethics. States or bodies politic are to be considered as moral persons having a public will capable and free to do right and wrong.

JAMES KENT

☆   ☆   ☆

If the Ten Commandments provide a standard of conduct for a virtuous individual, then the Ten Amendments which make our Bill of Rights are the ten commandments for a virtuous government.

PIERSON M. HALL

☆   ☆   ☆

THE BILL OF RIGHTS

I. Congress shall make no law respecting an establishment of religion, or prohibiting the free exercise thereof; or abridging the freedom of speech, or of the press; or the right of the people peaceably to assemble, and to petition the Government for a redress of grievances.

II. A well-regulated Militia, being necessary to the security of a free State, the right of the people to keep and bear Arms, shall not be infringed.

III. No Soldier shall, in time of peace, be quartered in any house, without the consent of the Owner, nor in time of war, but in a manner to be prescribed by law.

IV. The right of the people to be secure in their persons, houses, papers, and effects, against unreasonable searches and seizures, shall not be violated, and no Warrants shall issue, but upon probable cause, supported by Oath or affirmation, and particularly describing the place to be searched, and the persons or things to be seized.

V. No person shall be held to answer for a capital, or otherwise infamous crime, unless on a presentment or indictment of a Grand Jury, except in cases arising in the land or naval forces, or in the Militia, when in actual service in time of War or public danger; nor shall any person be subject for the same offence to be twice put in jeopardy of life or limb; nor shall be compelled in any criminal case to be a witness against himself, nor be deprived of life, liberty, or property, without due process of law; nor shall private property be taken for public use, without just compensation.

VI. In all criminal prosecutions, the accused shall enjoy the right to a speedy and public trial, by an impartial jury of the State and district wherein the crime shall have been committed, which district shall have been previously ascertained by law, and to be informed of the nature and cause of the accusation; to be confronted with the witnesses against him; to have compulsory process for obtaining witnesses in his favor, and to have the Assistance of Counsel for his defence.

VII. In Suits at common law, where the value in controversy shall exceed twenty dollars, the right of trial by jury shall be preserved, and no fact tried by a jury, shall be otherwise re-examined in any Court of the United States, than according to the rules of the common law.

VIII. Excessive bail shall not be required, nor excessive fines imposed, nor cruel and unusual punishments inflicted.

IX. The enumeration in the Constitution, of certain rights, shall not be construed to deny or disparage others retained by the people.

X. The powers not delegated to the United States by the Constitution, nor prohibited by it to the States, are reserved to the States respectively, or to the people.

☆   ☆   ☆

It does not require a lawyer to interpret the provisions of the Bill of Rights. They are as clear as the Ten Commandments.

HERBERT HOOVER

☆   ☆   ☆

Man became free when he recognized that he was subject to law.

WILL DURANT

☆   ☆   ☆

AMERICA'S BEACON

The Bill of Rights is America's beacon flaming from every hill and spire, proclaiming man's inalienable rights, declaring man's imperishable urge to exercise those rights under God and America's law with full freedom and security.

The Bill of Rights is America's pledge to peoples yet unborn both near and far to pass on God's torch of liberty, its light undimmed by the mock light of alien minds.

The Bill of Rights is America's glory, for in this land liberty was born, in this land freedom to exercise rights was won, in this land hunted minorities found haven and home, in this land enterprise and labor prosper.

The Bill of Rights is God's gift to America.

The Bill of Rights is pledge of God's hope in America.

FRANCIS JOSEPH SPELLMAN

☆　☆　☆

We want a state of things which allows every man the largest liberty compatible with the liberty of every other man.

RALPH WALDO EMERSON

☆　☆　☆

ABIDING PRINCIPLE

Every genuine American holds to the ideals of justice for all men, of independence, including free speech and free action within the limits of law, of obedience to law, of universal education, of material well-being for all the well-behaving and industrious, of peace and good-will among men.

These, however far short the nation may fail in expressing them in its actual life, are, no one will deny it, the ideals of our American democracy.

And it is because America represents these ideals that the deepest love for his country glows in the heart of the American, and in-

spires him with that patriotism which counts no cost, which esteems no sacrifice too great to maintain and to increase the influence of these principles which embody themselves in the fair shape of his native land, and have their expressive symbol in her flag.

The spirit of his patriotism is not an intermittent impulse; it is an abiding principle; it is the strongest motive of his life; it is his religion.

CHARLES ELIOT NORTON

☆　☆　☆

REVERENCE FOR LAWS

Let reverence for the laws be breathed by every American mother to the lisping babe that prattles on her lap; let it be taught in schools, in seminaries, and in colleges; let it be written in primers, spelling books, and in almanacs; let it be preached from the pulpit, proclaimed in legislative halls, and enforced in courts of justice. And, in short, let it become the political religion of the nation; and let the old and the young, the rich and the poor, the grave and the gay of all sexes and tongues and colors and conditions, sacrifice unceasingly upon its altars.

ABRAHAM LINCOLN

☆　☆　☆

PERSONAL RESPONSIBILITY

Laws have their proper place, but the responsibility of worthy citizenship is a personal one. We each have a separate and individual share in eradicating social evils and in refusing to perpetuate practices odious to a free nation.

HERBERT BROWNELL, JR.

☆　☆　☆

The immediate future of the world has been laid on the doorstep of the individual American.

WILLIAM B. HUIE

☆　☆　☆

103

STRENGTH

The ballot is stronger than the bullet.

ABRAHAM LINCOLN

☆ ☆ ☆

INDIVIDUAL IMPORTANCE

Every individual has a place to fill in the world, and is important in some respect, whether he chooses to be so or not.

NATHANIEL HAWTHORNE

☆ ☆ ☆

EPITAPH FOR HENRY DEVINE

During the protracted illness which preceded his death the deceased often expressed a wish only to live long enough to vote for Henry Clay for the Presidency. His wish was granted. The last act of his life was to vote the Whig ticket having done which he declared that he died satisfied.

WINTERGREEN CEMETERY
PORT GIBSON, MISSISSIPPI

☆ ☆ ☆

GRAVESTONE ADMONITION

Kind friends I've
    Left behind
Cast your vote for
    Jennings Bryan.

BETHEL METHODIST CEMETERY
MONTGOMERY CITY, MISSOURI

☆ ☆ ☆

MY SACRED BALLOT

The blood of free men stains my ballot sheet. Whatever others may do, I shall not carelessly make my mark. I vote not because I can, but because I must. Those who died for this, my voice in my Government, had a right to expect that I would use it wisely, honestly, and courageously. They did not die that blind partisans, or the reckless, might make a game of free elections.

Only my secret heart knows whether I justify the definition of "Voter" as they wrote it in the reddening sand. If I love my country as they did, I question my qualifications again and again.

I carefully study the issues and candidates to determine not what is best for me, but for my country.

I will not be confused or deceived by propaganda, slogans, or histrionics. I shield my eyes to the glitter of personalities, purge my mind of passion and prejudice, and search diligently for the hidden truth. I must be free of all influence save conscience and justice.

I vote as if my ballot alone decided the contest. I may lose my preference, but I will not throw away my sacred vote. For within the booth I hold in my humble hand the living proxy of all my country's honored dead.

RALPH BUSHNELL POTTS

☆ ☆ ☆

AMERICAN SPOKESMAN

William Jennings Bryan was the last great spokesman of the America of the nineteenth century—of the America of the Middle West and the South, the America of the farm and the country town, the America that read its Bible and went to Chautauqua, distrusted the big city and Wall Street, believed in God and the Declaration of Independence. He was, himself, one of these people. He thought their thoughts, and he spoke the words they were too inarticulate to speak. Above all, he fought their battles. He never failed to raise his voice against injustice; he never failed to believe that in the end justice would be done.

HENRY STEELE COMMAGER

☆ ☆ ☆

LESSON

Anglo-Saxon civilization has taught the individual to protect his own rights. American civilization will teach him to respect the rights of others.

WILLIAM JENNINGS BRYAN

104

☆ ☆ ☆

UNITED NATIONS CHARTER
PREAMBLE

We, the peoples of the United Nations, determined to save succeeding generations from the scourge of war, which twice in our lifetime has brought untold sorrow to mankind, and

To reaffirm faith in fundamental human rights, in the dignity and worth of the human person, in the equal rights of men and women and of nations large and small, and

To establish conditions under which justice and respect for the obligations arising from treaties and other sources of international law can be maintained, and

To promote social progress and better standards of life in larger freedom, and for these ends

To practice tolerance and live together in peace with one another as good neighbors, and

To unite our strength to maintain international peace and security, and

To insure, by the acceptance of principles and the institution of methods, that armed force shall not be used, save in the common interest, and

To employ international machinery for the promotion of the economic and social advancement of all peoples, have resolved to combine our efforts to accomplish these aims.

ADOPTED IN SAN FRANCISCO

JUNE 26, 1945

☆ ☆ ☆

A PRAYER FOR UNITED NATIONS

God of the free, we pledge our hearts and lives today to the cause of all free mankind.

Grant us victory over the tyrants who would enslave all free men and nations. Grant us faith and understanding to cherish all those who fight for freedom as if they were our brothers. Grant us brotherhood in hope and union, not only for the space of this bitter war, but for the days to come which shall and must unite all the children of earth.

Our earth is but a small star in the great universe. Yet of it we can make, if we choose, a planet unvexed by war, untroubled by hunger or fear, undivided by senseless distinctions of race, color or theory. Grant us the courage and foreseeing to begin this task today that our children and our children's children may be proud of the name of man.

The spirit of man has awakened and the soul of man has gone forth. Grant us the wisdom and the vision to comprehend the greatness of man's spirit, that suffers and endures so hugely for a goal beyond his own brief span. Grant us honor for our dead who died in the faith, honor for our living who work and strive for the faith, redemption and security for all captive lands and peoples. Grant us patience with the deluded and pity for the betrayed. And grant us the skill and the valor that shall cleanse the world of oppression and the old base doctrine that the strong must eat the weak because they are strong.

Yet most of all, grant us brotherhood, not only for this day but for all years—a brotherhood not of words but of acts and deeds. We are all of us children of earth—grant us that simple knowledge. If our brothers are oppressed, then we are oppressed. If they hunger, we hunger. If their freedom is taken away, our freedom is not secure. Grant us a common faith that man shall know bread and peace—that he shall know justice and righteousness, freedom and security, and equal opportunity and an equal chance to do his best, not only in our own lands, but throughout the world. And in that faith let us march toward the clean world our hands can make.

STEPHEN VINCENT BENÉT

☆ ☆ ☆

105

From AD PATRIAM

            Land of my heart,
What future is before thee? Shall it be
To lie at ease, content with thy bright
    past,
Heedless of all the world, till idleness
Relax thy limbs, and swollen with wealth
    and pride
Thou shalt abandon justice and the poor?
Or shalt thou, reawakened, scatter wide
The glorious tidings of a liberty
That lifts the latch of opportunity
First to thy children—then to all mankind?
Love of my soul—God keep thee strong and
    pure,
That thou shalt be a fitting messenger
To carry hope to all the sons of men.

WILLIAM DUDLEY FOULKE

☆   ☆   ☆

Law is the crystallization of the habit and thought of society.

WOODROW WILSON

☆   ☆   ☆

PLEDGE TO ALL MEN

We cannot solve our problems with a law or in an instant, but we can begin to weld laws and men together in an effort to provide fulfillment of the pledge America makes to all men.

ROBERT F. KENNEDY

☆   ☆   ☆

Man's capacity for justice makes democracy possible, but man's inclination to injustice makes democracy necessary.

REINHOLD NIEBUHR

☆   ☆   ☆

The acts of governments are transitory while relations between peoples are lasting.

SUMNER WELLES

☆   ☆   ☆

God grant that not only the Love of Liberty but a thorough knowledge of the rights of man may pervade all the nations of the earth, so that a philosopher may set his feet anywhere on its surface and say, "This is my country."

BENJAMIN FRANKLIN

☆   ☆   ☆

UNFINISHED TASK

What strange doubts assail this timid generation of today as it beholds the challenges to both liberty and equality. We seem beset with fear not faith, with doubt not confidence, with compromise not conviction, with dismay not dedication. We are drenched with the literature of fear and doubt. Survival has become the main theme. The fall-out shelter from which the stars of hope and courage cannot be seen has become the symbol of our fears and misgivings.

Are we to become fearful, unworthy legatees in a blessed, united land where the earth is fertile to our every need, where the skills and ingenuity of men are boundless, where the burdens are bearable, where decent living is within the reach of all, and where the genius to produce is unlimited?

Perhaps we have lost our sense of continuity? Perhaps we have forgotten that we move in that same endless stream which began with our forefathers and which will flow on and on to embrace our children and our children's children. If we have, there will have gone with it that sense of individual responsibility which is the last best hope that a nation conceived in liberty and dedicated to equality can long endure.

Comes then the reminder from the man from Illinois. Men died here and men are sleeping here who fought under a July sun that the nation might endure, united, free, tolerant, and devoted to equality. The task was unfinished. It is never quite finished.

EVERETT MC KINLEY DIRKSEN

IX

AND CROWN THY GOOD
WITH BROTHERHOOD

☆　　☆　　☆

The torch held high in the hand of liberty scatters the darkness of
natural inequality and reveals the royal kinship of all men in God.

ROBERT I. GANNON

From SPEECH TO THOSE WHO SAY COMRADE

The brotherhood is not by the blood certainly,
But neither are men brothers by speech—by saying so:
Men are brothers by life lived and are hurt for it.

Hunger and hurt are the great begetters of brotherhood:
Humiliation has gotten much love:
Danger I say is the nobler father and mother.

Those are as brothers whose bodies have shared fear
Or shared harm or shared hurt or indignity.
Why are the old soldiers brothers and nearest?

ARCHIBALD MAC LEISH

☆   ☆   ☆

BOUND TOGETHER

Ours is the only country in the world's history where men are bound together not by a common territory, not by a common racial source, or a single body of theological beliefs. We are bound together by a sense of the ultimate simple decency of human dignity. Nothing binds us together but this sense of frail, fallible, aspiring human beings.

FELIX FRANKFURTER

☆   ☆   ☆

TEST

The time to test a true gentleman is to observe him when he is in contact with individuals of a race less fortunate than his own.

BOOKER T. WASHINGTON

☆   ☆   ☆

Liberty is the one thing you cannot have unless you are willing to give it to others.

WILLIAM ALLEN WHITE

☆   ☆   ☆

NATION OF IMMIGRANTS

One trait derives more than any other from our past as a nation of immigrants. Without underrating the material motives that helped bring the Old World to the New, we can believe that idealistic impulses counted for much more.

The Puritans were a people as religiously dedicated as any in history. On their heels came colonists athirst for liberty, toleration, and social equality.

The spirit of Penn, Roger Williams, and Nathaniel Bacon went into the American soul when it was still young. Thereafter, generation by generation, countless people came because they hated oppression, injustice, and violence, and hoped to help create peace, brotherhood, and freedom.

No growing nation had such numerous and powerful contributions to its idealism. It would have been strange if, in the world's tremendous crises, the American people had not made an exhibition of idealism unprecedented in strength and scope.

ALLAN NEVINS

☆   ☆   ☆

THE NEW PATRIOT

Who is the patriot? He who lights
    The torch of war from hill to hill?
Or he who kindles on the heights
    The beacon of a world's good will?

Who is the patriot? It is he
    Who knows no boundary, race, nor creed;
Whose nation is humanity,
    His countrymen all souls that need.

Who is the patriot? Only he
    Whose business is the general good;
Whose keenest sword is sympathy,
    Whose dearest flag is brotherhood.

FREDERIC L. KNOWLES

CREATIVE MINORITY

Democracy cannot survive without the guidance of a creative minority.

HARLAN F. STONE

☆ ☆ ☆

From LET AMERICA BE AMERICA AGAIN

Let America be America again.
Let it be the dream it used to be.
Let it be the pioneer on the plain
Seeking a home where he himself is free. . . .

Let America be the dream the dreamers
    dreamed —
Let it be that great strong land of love
Where never kings connive nor tyrants
    scheme
That any man be crushed by one above. . . .

O, let my land be a land where Liberty
Is crowned with no false patriotic wreath,
But opportunity is real, and life is free,
Equality is in the air we breathe. . . .

O, let America be America again —
The land that never has been yet —
And yet must be —
The land where *every* man is free.
The land that's mine —
The poor man's, Indian's, Negro's, ME —
Who made America,
Whose sweat and blood, whose faith and
    pain,
Whose hand at the foundry, whose plow in
    the rain,
Must bring back our mighty dream again. . . .

We, the people, must redeem
Our land, the mines, the plants, the rivers,
The mountains and the endless plain —
All, all the stretch of these great green
    states —
And make America again!

LANGSTON HUGHES

☆ ☆ ☆

PRAYER

Almighty God, eternal Spirit, we for whom thou art the only hope of life acknowledge our need of thee now.

By the skill of head and hand, man has shortened the distance between the homes of his fellows, till all on our globe are now neighbors.

Help us, O God, joyful Spirit of universal love, to make this new closeness a blessing to us all. Help us to believe in our heart's core that none of us can know joy, safety, content, if others do not know hope.

By the skill of head and hand, man has brought forth such wealth of material goods as no other generation has known. Help us to know that none of us is safe in the enjoyment of our man-made wealth if all cannot have a share.

Almighty God, move us to put our whole trust in thee and thy all-powerful spirit of love. May we draw from thee that faith in the human spirit which alone gives meaning to efforts for the common good. Inspire us with that universal faith in the might of goodness, which means wholeness and life for all human souls.

DOROTHY CANFIELD FISHER

☆ ☆ ☆

EXPECTATION

This country demands that its sons and daughters whatever their race—however intense or diverse their religious connections—be merely American citizens.

LOUIS D. BRANDEIS

☆ ☆ ☆

110

THE AMERICAN WAY

To me, the American way of living means the understanding way, the cooperative way, the good-will way, the brotherly way. A colleague of mine once put it rather humorously but truly when he wrote that America must always be the land where a Christian of German origin might go with his Jewish friend into a Greek restaurant, and order Italian spaghetti, as they discuss plans together to hire a French guide for a fishing trip to Canada.

MORTON J. COHN

☆   ☆   ☆

DEMOCRATIC IDEAS

The idea that every child has a right to
    grow;
the idea that every one in the community has
    a right to be protected from violence;
the idea that all people can speak out and
    say what they think;
the idea that a man has a right to be different
    in looks, beliefs, interests, and talents
    if he does not injure others;
the idea that truth is a search that must
    never stop, that both reason and imagina-
    tion are necessary to that search, that the
    scientific method is necessary, too, and
    cannot be interfered with except when
    human life is jeopardized or profound
    human values cheapened;
the idea that the way a thing is done, the
    means used, are as important as the end
    sought;
the basic idea: that God is the ultimate con-
    cern beyond all men, that he is the supreme
    symbol, and that his laws of love and
    brotherhood and mercy and compassion
    must be obeyed.

LILLIAN SMITH

☆   ☆   ☆

America is a tune. It must be sung together.

GERALD STANLEY LEE

☆   ☆   ☆

In America there is no forgotten man, no common man, no average man. There is only our fellow man.

RICHARD M. NIXON

☆   ☆   ☆

He serves his country best
Who lives pure life, and doeth righteous
    deed,
And walks straight paths however others
    stray,
And leaves his sons as uttermost bequest
A stainless record which all men may read.
No drop but serves the slowly lifting tide,
No dew but has an errand to some flower,
No smallest star but sheds some helpful ray,
And man by man, each helping all the rest,
Make the firm bulwark of the country's
    power.

SUSAN COOLIDGE

☆   ☆   ☆

WORKABLE LIBERTY

The only kind of liberty which is workable in the real world is the liberty of the man who can follow what his heart desires without transgressing what is right.

WALTER LIPPMANN

☆   ☆   ☆

Every city is a world of some sort. San Francisco is the whole world recreated as a single work of art: a painting, a work of sculpture, a poem, a symphony, a story. It is the whole world brought together for the eye of man to behold and the heart to understand. It is all the nations of the world brought together in time and place, to test mortality. To see whether the experiment can be successful. To see if fraternity and brotherhood among the living is possible. In San Francisco there is only one race. The race of the living.

WILLIAM SAROYAN

TEN COMMANDMENTS OF GOODWILL

1. I will respect all men and women regardless of their race or religion.

2. I will protect and defend my neighbor and my neighbor's children against the ravages of racial or religious bigotry.

3. I will exemplify in my own life the spirit of goodwill and understanding.

4. I will challenge the philosophy of superiority by whomsoever it may be proclaimed whether by kings, dictators, or demagogues.

5. I will not be misled by the lying propaganda of those who seek to set race against race or nation against nation.

6. I will refuse to support any organization that has for its purpose the spreading of anti-Semitism, anti-Catholicism, or anti-Protestantism.

7. I will establish comradeship with all those who seek to exalt the spirit of love and reconciliation throughout the world.

8. I will attribute to those who differ from me the same degree of sincerity that I claim for myself.

9. I will uphold the civil rights and religious liberties of all citizens and groups whether I agree with them or not.

10. I will do more than live and let live; I will live and help live.

WALTER W. VAN KIRK

☆ ☆ ☆

Our history books tell us that the American Revolution ended in Yorktown. But the American Revolution will not be complete until the ideals of independence, equality and freedom which kept men fighting at Valley Forge are a reality not only for Americans but for peoples throughout the world.

RICHARD M. NIXON

☆ ☆ ☆

From STANZAS ON FREEDOM

Is true freedom but to break
Fetters for our own dear sake,
And with leathern hearts forget
That we owe mankind a debt?
No! true freedom is to share
All the chains our brothers wear,
    And, with heart and hand, to be
    Earnest to make others free.

They are slaves who fear to speak
For the fallen and the weak;
They are slaves who will not choose
Hatred, scoffing, and abuse,
Rather than in silence shrink
From the truth they needs must think;
    They are slaves who dare not be
    In the right with two or three.

JAMES RUSSELL LOWELL

☆ ☆ ☆

Service is both the inspiration and the accomplishment of quite everything worth while which impels us onward and upward. With service which the Nazarene would approve are associated all our ideals and our finer aspirations.

WARREN G. HARDING

☆ ☆ ☆

FRONTIERS

As man increases his knowledge of the heavens, why should he fear the unknown on earth?

As man draws nearer to the stars, why should he not also draw nearer to his neighbor?

As we push ever more deeply into the universe, probing its secrets, discovering its way, we must also constantly try to learn to cooperate across the frontiers that really divide earth's surface.

LYNDON B. JOHNSON

☆ ☆ ☆

Our skill and ingenuity may have made of the world a single neighborhood, but we have thus far singularly failed to make of it a single brotherhood.

THEODORE FRIEDMAN

☆　☆　☆

LAND WHERE HATE SHOULD DIE

This is the land where hate should die—
No feuds of faith, no spleen of race,
No darkly brooding fear should try
Beneath our flag to find a place.

Lo! every people here has sent
Its sons to answer freedom's call;
Their lifeblood is the strong cement
That builds and binds the nation's wall.

This is the land where hate should die—
Though dear to me my faith and shrine,
I serve my country well when I
Respect beliefs that are not mine.

He little loves his land who'd cast
Upon his neighbor's word a doubt,
Or cite the wrongs of ages past
From present rights to bar him out.

This is the land where hate should die—
This is the land where strife should cease,
Where foul, suspicious fear should fly
Before our flag of light and peace.

Then let us purge from poisoned thought
That service to the State we give,
And so be worthy as we ought
Of this great land in which we live!

DENIS A. MC CARTHY

☆　☆　☆

Democracy means not "I am as good as you are" but "You are as good as I am."

THEODORE PARKER

☆　☆　☆

A democracy is more than a form of government. It is primarily a mode of associated living, of conjoint communicated experience.

JOHN DEWEY

☆　☆　☆

PRAYER

We pray for America

Not alone because she is a land between two oceans, rich in soil and substance. All lands possess treasures of the earth.

Not alone because her power awes the nations, her might stretches across the seven seas, or that her word silences the sound of lesser voices. The merciful dust of the centuries has covered grandeurs once as great as hers.

Not alone because this is our fatherland to whom devotion shall be given forever. There breathes no man with soul so dead that he owns no native land.

We pray for America

Because the age-old hope of humanity for freedom was here first made manifest in men and laws dedicated to life, liberty, and the pursuit of happiness.

Because for generations she opened her arms to all who sought haven from oppression, a new chance for life, and a place on earth upon which human dignity could be proclaimed.

Because here is established that freedom, acknowledging God as its Author, which grants to each man, without distinction as to color, or class, or creed, equal justice under law, liberty of conscience, and the holy privilege of worshiping the Eternal God in spirit and in truth.

Because America, if she be willing to use the power to be the servant and not the master of mankind, may lead the nations into that world community of all humanity which has been the quest of the enlightened and the free of all ages.

RUSSELL J. CLINCHY

X

WITH PEACE
OUR BORDERS BLESS

☆   ☆   ☆

*Peace is the healing and elevating
influence of the world.*

WOODROW WILSON

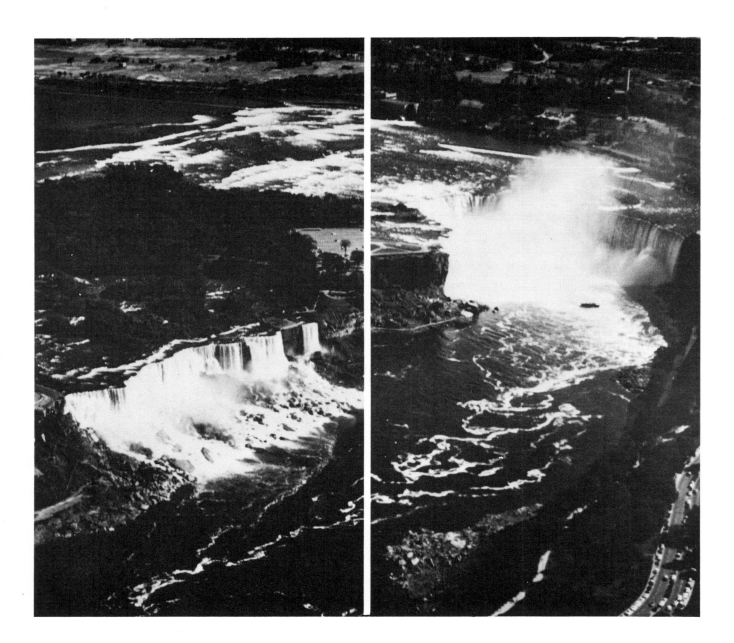

DEDICATION

It is given to us, of this generation, to achieve real peace—if not for ourselves, for our children.

It is given to us to reassert the right of a man to live as the image of God.

To those who say that these unlimited objectives are unthinkable, impossible, let us reply that it is the alternative to them which is unthinkable, impossible for Americans to contemplate.

Let us dedicate ourselves to the achievement of these unlimited objectives as boldly and as surely and as confidently as did Columbus and Washington and all the countless millions of Americans, from the Pilgrims to the pioneers, who have proved that in this unconquerably and justifiably optimistic nation nothing undertaken by free men and free women is impossible.

ROBERT E. SHERWOOD

☆　☆　☆

GARDEN OF PEACE

In almost the exact center of North America, on the border of the Province of Manitoba and the State of North Dakota, in a hilly country called the Turtle Mountains, there is an area of some 2,000 acres called the "Garden of Peace." Beneath the flags of our two nations is a stone cairn on which are the words, "To God in his glory we two nations dedicate this garden, and pledge ourselves that as long as man shall live we will not take up arms against one another."

W. J. SHERIDAN

☆　☆　☆

If civilization is to survive, we must cultivate the science of human relationships—the ability of all peoples, of all kinds, to live together in the same world at peace.

FRANKLIN D. ROOSEVELT

☆　☆　☆

From CENTENNIAL ODE

Long as thine art shall love true love,
Long as thy science truth shall know,
Long as thine eagle harms no dove,
Long as thy law by law shall grow,
Long as thy God is God above,
Thy brother every man below,
So long, dear land of all my love,
Thy name shall shine, thy fame shall glow!

SIDNEY LANIER

☆　☆　☆

PIONEER IDEALS

The paths of the pioneer have widened into broad highways. The forest clearing has expanded into affluent Commonwealths. Let us see to it that the ideals of the pioneer in his log cabin shall enlarge into the spiritual life of a democracy where civic power shall dominate and utilize individual achievement for the common good.

FREDERICK JACKSON TURNER

☆　☆　☆

HYMN

God of the strong, God of the weak,
Lord of all lands, and our own land;
Light of our souls, from thee we seek
Light from thy light, strength from thy hand.

In suffering thou hast made us one,
In mighty burdens one are we;
Teach us that lowliest duty done
Is highest service unto thee.

Teach us, great Teacher of mankind,
The sacrifice that brings thy balm;
The love, the work that bless and bind;
Teach us thy majesty, thy calm.

Teach thou, and we shall know, indeed,
The truth divine that maketh free;
And knowing, we may sow the seed
That blossoms through eternity.

RICHARD WATSON GILDER

117

☆　☆　☆

LETTER TO SIR JOSEPH BANKS

I join with you most cordially in rejoicing at the return of peace. I hope it will be lasting, and that mankind will at length, as they call themselves reasonable Creatures, have reason and sense enough to settle their differences without cutting throats; for, in my opinion, there never was a good war, or a bad peace.

What vast additions to the conveniences and comforts of living might mankind have acquired, if the money spent in wars had been employed in works of public utility!

What an extension of agriculture, even to the tops of our mountains; what rivers rendered navigable, or joined by canals; what bridges, aqueducts, new roads, and other public works, edifices, and improvements, rendering England a complete paradise, might have been obtained by spending those millions in doing good, which in the last war have been spent in doing mischief; in bringing misery into thousands of families, and destroying the lives of so many thousands of working people, who might have performed the useful labor!

BENJAMIN FRANKLIN
JULY 27, 1783

☆　☆　☆

AMERICAN DREAM

Perhaps the greatest contribution which America has made to the world is the American dream—the dream of a land where life shall be richer and fuller and better, with opportunity for every man according to his ability and achievement. That dream must be kept. It is the brightest beacon in our war-darkened world. It will be the chief light toward a just peace.

RALPH W. SOCKMAN

☆　☆　☆

I know that vast problems remain, conflicts between great powers, conflicts between small neighbors, disagreements over disarmament, persistence of ancient wrongs in the area of human rights, residual problems of colonialism, and all the rest. But men and nations, working apart, created these problems and men and nations working together must solve them.

LYNDON B. JOHNSON

☆　☆　☆

AMERICA FIRST

America first, not only in things material,
But in things of the spirit.
Not merely in science, invention, motors,
  skyscrapers,
But also in ideals, principles, character.
Not merely in the calm assertion of rights,
But in the glad assumption of duties.

Not flouting her strength as a giant,
But bending in helpfulness over a sick and
  wounded world like a Good Samaritan.
Not in splendid isolation,
But in courageous cooperation.
Not in pride, arrogance, and disdain of
  other races and peoples,
But in sympathy, love and understanding.
Not in treading again the old, worn, bloody
  pathway which ends inevitably in chaos and
  disaster,
But blazing a new trail along which, please
  God, other nations will follow into the
  new Jerusalem where wars shall be no
  more.

Some day, some nation must take that path—
  unless we are to lapse into utter barbar-
  ism—and that honor I covet for my
  beloved America.
And so in that spirit and with these hopes,
  I say with all my heart and soul, "America
  First."

G. ASHTON OLDHAM

118

☆   ☆   ☆

Could I have but a line a century hence crediting a contribution to the advance of peace, I would gladly yield every honor which has been accorded me in war.

DOUGLAS MAC ARTHUR

☆   ☆   ☆

LETTER TO HIS WIFE

What a cruel thing is war: to separate and destroy families and friends and mar the purest joys and happiness God has granted us in this world, to fill our hearts with hatred instead of love for our neighbors, and to devastate the fair face of this beautiful world.

ROBERT E. LEE

☆   ☆   ☆

THE WORLD IS ONE

The world is one; we cannot live apart,
  To earth's remotest races we are kin;
God made the generations of one blood;
  Man's separation is a sign of sin.

What though we solve the secret of the stars,
  Or from the vibrant ether pluck a song,
Can this for all man's tyranny atone
  While Mercy weeps and waits and suffers
    long?

Put up the sword, its day of anguish past;
  Disarm the forts, and then, the war-flags
    furled,
Forever keep the air without frontiers,
  The great, free, friendly highway of the
    world.

So that at last to rapture men may come,
  And hear again the music of the spheres,
And stand erect, illumined, radiant, free,
  The travail and the triumph of the years.

HINTON WHITE

☆   ☆   ☆

CRY OF THE COLONIAL
TOWN CRIER

Hear ye, hear ye all men and maids:
A light here maids, hang out your lights
And see your horns be clear and bright,
That so your candle clear may shine
Continuous from six till nine
That honest men that walk along
May see to pass safe without wrong.

☆   ☆   ☆

HOME TOWN

I have Bloomington to thank for the most important lesson I have learned: that in quiet places reason abounds, that in quiet people there is vision and purpose, that many things are revealed to the humble that are hidden from the great.

ADLAI E. STEVENSON

☆   ☆   ☆

INNER AND OUTER PEACE

The inner peace of a well-integrated life is something that must be continually achieved; the outer peace of a world in which nations live together in a spirit of brotherhood is something that must be continually earned.

DWIGHT D. EISENHOWER

☆   ☆   ☆

From UNITED NATIONS ADDRESS

On behalf of the United States I would say that we believe that international peace is an attainable goal. That is the premise that underlies all our planning. We propose never to desist, never to admit discouragement, but confidently and steadily so to act that peace becomes for us a sustaining principle of action.

JOHN FOSTER DULLES

☆   ☆   ☆

Who lives for humanity must be content to lose himself.

OCTAVIUS BROOKS FROTHINGHAM

TREATY WITH THE INDIANS

"We meet," said William Penn, "on the broad pathway of good faith and good will; no advantage shall be taken on either side, but all shall be openness and love. The friendship between you and me I will not compare to a chain; for that the rains might rust or the falling tree might break. We are the same as if one man's body were to be divided into two parts; we are all one flesh and blood."

"We will live in love with William Penn and his children," said the Indians, "as long as the sun and moon shall shine."

The simple-minded natives kept the history of this treaty by means of strings of wampum, and they would often count over the shells on a clean piece of bark and rehearse its provisions. "It was the only treaty never sworn to, and the only one never broken." On every hand the Indians waged relentless war with the colonies, but they never shed a drop of Quaker blood.

A BRIEF HISTORY OF THE UNITED STATES (1871)

☆ ☆ ☆

LOVE AND PROTECTION

James Oglethorpe, a warm-hearted English officer, settled at Savannah in 1733. He made peace with the Indians, conciliating them by presents and his kindly disposition.

One of the chiefs gave him in return a buffalo's skin with the head and feathers of an eagle painted on the inside of it.

"The eagle," said the chief, "signifies swiftness; and the buffalo, strength. The English are swift as a bird to fly over the vast areas, and as strong as a beast before their enemies. The eagle's feathers are soft and signify love; the buffalo's skin is warm and means protection; therefore love and protect our families."

A BRIEF HISTORY OF THE UNITED STATES (1871)

☆ ☆ ☆

RED MAN'S WORDS

A few more moons, a few more winters—and not one of the descendants of the mighty hosts that once moved this broad land or lived in happy homes, protected by the Great Spirit, will remain to mourn over the graves of a people once more powerful and hopeful than yours. But why should I mourn at the untimely fate of my people? Tribe follows tribe, and nation follows nation, like the waves of the sea. It is the order of nature, and regret is useless. Your time of decay may be distant, but it will surely come, for even the White Man cannot be exempt from the common destiny. We may be brothers after all. We will see.

CHIEF SEATTLE

☆ ☆ ☆

FACE OF AMERICA

Let us present once more the true face of America—warm and modest and friendly, dedicated to the welfare of all mankind, and demanding nothing except a chance for all to live and let live, to grow and govern as they wish, free from interference, free from intimidation, free from fear.

ADLAI E. STEVENSON

☆ ☆ ☆

From UNESCO CHARTER

Since wars begin in the minds of men, it is in the minds of men that the defenses of peace must be constructed.

☆ ☆ ☆

HIGH COST

No human precaution can protect a nation from the sacrifices which war levies upon future talent—the undiscovered scientists, the gifted minds, the intellectual and spiritual leaders upon whom each generation must build the hope and promise of the generation to come.

RAYMOND B. FOSDICK

From THE PEOPLE, YES

What did Hiamovi, the red man, Chief of
   the Cheyennes, have?
To a great chief at Washington and to a
   chief of peoples across the waters,
     Hiamovi spoke:
"There are birds of many colors—red, blue,
   green, yellow,
Yet it is all one bird.
There are horses of many colors—brown,
   black, yellow, white,
Yet it is all one horse.
So cattle, so all living things, animals,
   flowers, trees.

So men in this land, where once were only
   Indians, are now men of many colors—
     white, black, yellow, red.
Yet all one people.
That this should come to pass was in the
   heart of the Great Mystery.
It is right thus—and everywhere there
   shall be peace."
Thus Hiamovi, out of a tarnished and
   weatherworn heart of old gold, out of
     a living dawn gold.

                     CARL SANDBURG

☆   ☆   ☆

No true and permanent fame can be founded
except in labors which promote the happiness
of mankind.

                    CHARLES SUMNER

☆   ☆   ☆

All the languages in the world are but local
differentiations of one planetary tongue.

                    THORNTON WILDER

☆   ☆   ☆

A man's feet should be planted in his country,
but his eyes should survey the world.

                    GEORGE SANTAYANA

☆   ☆   ☆

VICTORIES OF PEACE

Let us ever remember that our interest is in
concord not in conflict, and that our real
eminence as a nation lies in the victories of
peace, not those of war.

                    WILLIAM MC KINLEY

☆   ☆   ☆

THE PEOPLE'S THANKSGIVING

Not alone for mighty empire,
   Stretching far o'er land and sea,
Not alone for bounteous harvests,
   Lift we up our hearts to thee:
Standing in the living present,
   Memory and hope between,
Lord, we would with deep thanksgiving
   Praise thee more for things unseen.

Not for battle-ship and fortress,
   Not for conquests of the sword,
But for conquests of the spirit
   Give we thanks to thee, O Lord;
For the heritage of freedom,
   For the home, the church, the school,
For the open door to manhood
   In a land the people rule.

For the armies of the faithful,
   Lives that passed and left no name;
For the glory that illumines
   Patriot souls of deathless fame;
For the people's prophet-leaders,
   Loyal to thy living word,—
For all heroes of the spirit,
   Give we thanks to thee, O Lord.

God of justice, save the people
   From the war of race and creed,
From the strife of class and faction,
   Make our nation free indeed;
Keep her faith in simple manhood
   Strong as when her life began,
Till it find its full fruition
   In the brotherhood of man!

                 WILLIAM PIERSON MERRILL

XI

FIRST IN THE HEARTS
OF HIS COUNTRYMEN

☆   ☆   ☆

*First in war, first in peace, and first in the hearts of his countrymen,
he was second to none in the humble and enduring scenes of private
life. Pious, just, humane, temperate, and sincere—uniform, dignified, and commanding—his example was as edifying to all around
him as were the effects of that example lasting.*   HENRY LEE

Washington, the brave—the wise—the good.
Washington, supreme in War, in Council,
and in Peace.
Washington, valiant without ambition—dis-
creet without fear—confident without
presumption.
Washington, in disaster calm, in success
moderate, in all, himself.
Washington, the Hero—the Patriot—the
Christian.
The Friend of Nations, the Friend of Mankind, who, when he had won all, re-
nounced all, and sought, in the bosom of
his Family and of Nature, retirement—
and in the Hope of Religion, Immortality.

ANDREW REED

☆　☆　☆

THE STAMP OF WASHINGTON
The man who had set out across the Delaware
as a Virginia farmer, as a foxhunter, became
on the other shore something else, a man of
incredible stature, a human being in some
ways more godly and more wonderful than
any other who has walked on this earth. For
he became, as with no other man in history,
the father of a nation that was to be peopled
by the wretched and the oppressed of every
land on earth. As simple, as burnished as this
sounds, it is no use to plead otherwise; the
stamp of George Washington is indelibly and
forever set upon America—and for the good.

HOWARD FAST

☆　☆　☆

LETTER TO WASHINGTON
Were an energetic and judicious system to be
proposed with your signature it would be a
circumstance highly honorable to your fame
and doubly entitle you to the glorious republican epithet, *The Father of your Country.*

HENRY KNOX

☆　☆　☆

ON WASHINGTON
His integrity was most pure, his justice the
most inflexible I have ever known, no motives
of interest or consanguinity, of friendship or
hatred, being able to bias his decision. He
was, indeed, in every sense of the words, a
wise, a good, and a great man.

His person, you know, was fine, his stature
exactly what one would wish, his deportment
easy, erect, and noble; the best horseman of
his age, and the most graceful figure that
could be seen on horseback.

On the whole, his character was, in its mass,
perfect, in nothing bad, in few points indif-
ferent; and it may truly be said, that never
did nature and fortune combine more perfectly to make a man great, and to place him
in the same constellation with whatever worthies have merited from man an everlasting
remembrance.

THOMAS JEFFERSON
LETTER TO DR. WALTER JONES
JANUARY 2, 1814

☆　☆　☆

We can't all be Washingtons, but we can all be
patriots and behave ourselves in a humane
and Christian manner.

CHARLES F. BROWNE

☆　☆　☆

From ODE TO NAPOLEON BONAPARTE
Where may the wearied eye repose
　When gazing on the great;
Where neither guilty glory glows,
　Nor despicable state?
Yes—one—the first—the last—the best—
The Cincinnatus of the West,
　Whom envy dared not hate,
Bequeathed the name of Washington,
To make man blush there was but one!

GEORGE GORDON BYRON

☆　☆　☆

History is sometimes the shadow of a great man.

PIERRE VAN PAASSEN

☆ ☆ ☆

We call him father.

He was the architect of a New Nation.

He was a builder whose hammer was a sword and whose timbers were Liberty and Justice.

He bequeathed us freedom to live and speak and grow under the Stars and Stripes.

He was 6 feet 3 1/2 inches tall and as straight as an Indian.

He walked with the majestic dignity of the English aristocrats from whom he was descended.

He had lively blue eyes.

His hair was red under his white wig.

He could ride the wildest horse and rode to hounds with the gusto of an English squire.

He had that dashing magnetic quality that marks the born leader of men.

He was a man of character "who labored to keep alive in his heart that celestial bit of fire called conscience."

He was an idealist who spoke with the eloquence of action, not words.

He raised an army of a thousand men, at his own expense, and marched to the relief of Boston.

He sacrificed the quietness and happiness of Mt. Vernon for the danger of the firing line.

His courageous spirit inspired ragged, barefoot soldiers to fight on in what seemed a hopeless cause.

In the dark days of Valley Forge his great faith alone kept the spark of freedom aglow.

He was the first signer of the Constitution of the United States of America.

He was a man so royal of character that he refused to become king.

We are the sons of this great American.

We are the divinely appointed heirs of the way of life he won for us.

We are the guardians of his ideals of liberty and justice for all.

It is our mighty task today to keep the torch of Washington aflame!

WILFERD A. PETERSON

☆ ☆ ☆

LETTER TO MARTHA

It has been determined in Congress, that the whole army raised for the defence of the American cause shall be put under my care, and that it is necessary for me to proceed immediately to Boston to take upon me the command of it.

You may believe me, my dear Patsy, when I assure you in the most solemn manner that, so far from seeking this appointment, I have used every endeavor in my power to avoid it, not only from my unwillingness to part with you and the family, but from a consciousness of its being a trust too great for my capacity, and that I should enjoy more real happiness in one month with you at home than I have the most distant prospect of finding abroad. . . .

It was utterly out of my power to refuse this appointment, without exposing my character to such censure as would have reflected dishonor upon myself, and have given pain to my friends. . . .

I shall rely, therefore, confidently on that Providence which has heretofore preserved and been bountiful to me, not doubting but that I shall return safe to you in the fall.

GEORGE WASHINGTON

☆ ☆ ☆

We must meet the hero on heroic grounds.

HENRY DAVID THOREAU

☆ ☆ ☆

126

GUIDANCE

The character, the counsels, and example of Washington will guide us through the doubts and difficulties that beset us. They will guide our children and our children's children in the paths of prosperity and peace, while America shall hold her place in the family of nations.

EDWARD EVERETT

☆　☆　☆

From WASHINGTON

Simple and brave, his faith awoke
　Ploughmen to struggle with their fate;
Armies won battles when he spoke,
　And out of CHAOS sprang the state.

ROBERT BRIDGES

☆　☆　☆

WASHINGTON AT VALLEY FORGE

O noble heart! that ne'er from duty swerved,
Nor thought of self through all the weary
　hours!
O noble life! that did for others live,
And for our nation gave its wondrous
　powers!
There were dark days, when clouds the sun-
　shine hid,
And laid upon that heart a load of care;
But yet unshaken through the storm it stood,
Nor bowed itself save for new strength—in
　prayer!

And there were days of toil—of weary march
Through winter's snow and sleet, when
　hearts, though sad,
Pressed on, cheered by the voice of him who
　led—
The noblest chief that ever soldier had!
When destitution came upon them all,
And with it murmurs of their sore distress,
Ah! then he lent his strength thereon to
　aid,
Nor failed in aught of brother's tenderness.

O days long past! that held his glorious
　life!
We hold with joy the precious legacy
Of his great name! the name of Washington!
And by each tongue that name must honored
　be;
And as through clouds of sorrow and dismay
Men looked to him as to their guiding star,
So we within our hearts his memory hold,
Nor with disloyal breath its brightness
　mar!

HARPER'S WEEKLY (1873)

☆　☆　☆

HISTORIANS' APPRAISAL

Washington was a giant in stature, a tireless and methodical worker, a firm ruler yet without the ambitions of a Caesar or a Cromwell, a soldier who faced hardships and death without flinching, a steadfast patriot, a hardheaded and practical director of affairs. Technicians have long disputed the skill of his strategy; some have ascribed the length of the war to his procrastination; others have found him wanting in energy and decision; but all have agreed that he did the one thing essential to victory—he kept some kind of army in the field in adversity as well as in prosperity and rallied about it the scattered and uncertain forces of a jealous and individualistic people.

CHARLES AND MARY BEARD

☆　☆　☆

FOREVER REMEMBERED

That name descending with all time, spreading over the whole earth, and uttered in all the languages belonging to all tribes and races of men, will forever be pronounced with affectionate gratitude by everyone in whose breast there shall arise an aspiration for human rights and liberty.

DANIEL WEBSTER

☆　☆　☆

THE NAME OF WASHINGTON

America, the land beloved,
Today reveres the name of him
Whose character was free from guile,
Whose fame the ages cannot dim.

They called him proud, but erred therein;
No lord was he, though high of birth;
Though sprung from England's lofty peers,
He served the lowliest of earth.

He turned his back on pride of name,
On motherland and luxury,
To weld a horde of quarreling men
Into a nation proudly free.

Wherever liberty is found,
Wherever shines fair freedom's sun,
Men count America a friend
And bless the name of Washington.

ARTHUR GORDON FIELD

☆   ☆   ☆

PORTRAIT

In response to a request from England for a description of Col. George Washington, his aide-de-camp, John Francis Mercer, wrote:

"He may be described as being as straight as an Indian, measuring six feet two inches in his stockings and weighing 175 pounds when he took his seat in the House of Burgesses in 1759. His frame is padded with well developed muscles, indicating great strength. His bones and joints are large, as are his feet and hands.

"He is wide shouldered, but has not a deep or round chest; is neat waisted, but is broad across the hips, and has rather long legs and arms. His head is well shaped though not large, but is gracefully poised on a superb neck. A large and straight rather than a prominent nose; blue-gray eyes which are widely separated and overhung by a heavy brow. His face is long rather than broad, with high round cheek bones, and terminates in a good firm chin. He has a clear though rather colorless pale skin, which burns with the sun. A pleasing, benevolent, though a commanding countenance, dark brown hair, which he wears in a cue.

"His mouth is large and generally firmly closed, but which from time to time discloses some defective teeth. His features are regular and placid, though flexible and expressive of deep feeling when moved by emotion."

☆   ☆   ☆

AT MOUNT VERNON

Along this path he walked, great Washington,
Who built a nation out of selfish men;
These trees he planted, here he stood and
    mused
On spring's first blossoms, or on autumn's
    gain.
By this loved river, flowing wide and free,
He sighed for rest from all the cares of
    state.
How dear his home! And yet he could not
    pause
While traitors tore his land with greed and
    hate;
He could not free himself, whose character
Was part and parcel of his country's name.
He found no lasting rest, though worn and
    spent,
Till death relieved him from the bonds of
    fame.
Through all the years, till freedom's day is
    run,
One name shall shine with splendor—
    Washington.

THOMAS CURTIS CLARK

☆   ☆   ☆

EXTRAORDINARY CHARACTERS

Had America produced nothing more than the extraordinary characters of Washington and Lincoln, her existence as a nation would be justified to the world.

JAMES E. FREEMAN

FAREWELL TO HIS ARMIES

It only remains for the Comdr in Chief to address himself once more, and that for the time, to the Armies of the U States . . . and to bid them an affectionate, a long farewell. . . .

It is universally acknowledged, that the enlarged prospects of happiness, opened by the conformation of our independence and sovereignty, almost exceeds the power of description. And shall not the brave men, who have contributed so essentially to these inestimable acquisitions, retiring victorious from the field of War to the field of agriculture, participate in all the blessings which have been obtained; in such a republic, who will exclude them from the rights of Citizens and the fruits of their labour?

To those hardy Soldiers, who are actuated by the spirit of adventure the Fisheries will afford ample and profitable employment, and the extensive and fertile regions of the West will yield a most happy asylum to those, who, fond of domestic enjoyments are seeking for personal independence. . . .

The Commander in Chief conceives little is now wanting to enable the Soldiers to change the military character into that of the Citizen, but that steady and decent tenor of behavior which has generally distinguished, not only the Army under his immediate command, but the different detachments and separate Armies through the course of the war. From their good sense and prudence he anticipates the happiest consequences; and while he congratulates them on the glorious occasion, which renders their services in the field no longer necessary, he wishes to express the strong obligations he feels himself under for the assistance he has received from every Class, and in every instance. . . .

To the various branches of the Army the General takes this last and solemn opportunity of professing his inviolable attachment and friendship. He wishes more than bare professions were in his power, that he were really able to be useful to them all in future life. . . .

And being now to conclude these his last public Orders, to take his ultimate leave in a short time of the military character, and to bid a final adieu to the Armies he has so long had the honor to Command, he can only again offer in their behalf his recommendations to their grateful country, and his prayers to the God of Armies.

May ample justice be done them here, and may the choicest of heaven's favours, both here and hereafter, attend those who, under the divine auspices, have secured innumerable blessings for others; with these wishes, and this benediction, the Commander in Chief is about to retire from Service. The curtain of separation will soon be drawn, and the military scene to him will be closed for ever.

GEORGE WASHINGTON

☆   ☆   ☆

His work well done, the leader stepped aside
Spurning a crown with more than kingly
  pride.
Content to wear the higher crown of worth,
While time endures, "First citizen of earth."

JAMES J. ROCHE

☆   ☆   ☆

From FAREWELL ADDRESS

Of all the dispositions and habits which lead to political prosperity, religion and morals are indispensable supports.

Let us with caution indulge the supposition that morality can be maintained without religion.

Whatever may be conceded to the influence of refined education on minds of peculiar stature, both reason and experience forbid us to expect that national morality can prevail in exclusion of religious principle.

GEORGE WASHINGTON

130

XII

THE GREAT EMANCIPATOR

☆   ☆   ☆

There is no name in all our country's story
So loved as his today:
No name which so unites the things of glory
With life's plain, common way.

ROBERT WHITAKER

There is no new thing to be said of Lincoln. There is no new thing to be said of the mountains, or of the sea, or of the stars. The years go their way, but the same old mountains lift their granite shoulders above the drifting clouds, and the same mysterious sea beats upon the shore, and the same silent stars keep holy vigil above a tired world. But to mountain and sea and star, men turn forever in unwearied homage.

And thus with Lincoln. For he was mountain in grandeur of spirit, he was sea in under-voice of mystic loneliness, he was star in steadfast purity of purpose and of service. And he, too, abides forever.

The years go their way, but with the name of Lincoln childhood still learns to voice a patriot's devotion, and with the name of Lincoln tears are called from old men's eyes.

HOMER HOCH

☆　☆　☆

THE HANDS OF LINCOLN

Strong as the cedar trees, grey-gnarled and
  long,
Supple at dawn, they were a woodsman's
  pride;
His title-deeds to life, his right to hearth
And home; he scarce had any help beside.

Young hands that labored in green summer
  fields,
Sun-tanned and cooled by winds, their virile
  length
Downed men like saplings; in a few years
  more
The nation feared the omen of their
  strength.

Hands of a man, they pushed the great woods
  back,
Cut friendly paths for life, sweat in the
  gloam;

His good wife knew the records of their love
And faithfulness. She watched them build
  a home.

A father's hands, they bore his children up
The dusklit stairs to bed; upon the street
They clasped his sons like massive hoops of
  steel
And sheltered them against the winter's
  sleet.

They gestured hope when war made men
  afraid
And gave, unceasing, all that love could
  give—
Life's very blood and brawn, glad that
  their strength
Should fail if these United States might
  live.

PHILIP JEROME CLEVELAND

☆　☆　☆

PARABLE

God does things in his own peculiar way.

When he wants a liberator, he goes into a desert and picks out a shepherd who stutters. When he is seeking a great artist to sing poems of faith, he picks out another shepherd, David, and makes him a king. When he is looking for the first king of Israel, he picks Saul, a farmer boy plowing between oxen.

One day God parted the clouds with his hands and looked down. He said to the angels, "Do you see what I see?" One of them said, "All I see is a little log cabin in Kentucky, and I hear the cry of a baby." Then God said, "Go down and kiss that child for he will be an emancipator and leader of men."

So the angel went down and kissed the child, and the child grew up. And one day he stood on the battlefield at Gettysburg and made a speech. He said, "The world will little note nor long remember what we say here." But the world does remember and always will. And this is the glory of America and mankind.

EDGAR F. MAGNIN

133

GOODNESS AND GREATNESS

It is the great boon of such characters as Mr. Lincoln's, that they reunite what God has joined together and man has put asunder. In him was vindicated the greatness of real goodness and the goodness of real greatness.

PHILLIPS BROOKS

☆ ☆ ☆

WHY WE LOVE LINCOLN

Let's skip all the things you've read about him, all the things you heard too often or too young.

Forget the face on the penny, the statue in Washington, the Emancipation Proclamation, the speech at Gettysburg. Forget the official things, and look at the big thing.

Why do we love this man, dead long before our time, yet dear to us as a father? What was there about Abraham Lincoln?

He came out of nowhere special—a cabin like any other out West. His folks were nobody special—pleasant, hard-working people like many others. Abe was a smart boy. He could do a good day's work on the farm. He told funny stories. He was strong and kind. He'd never try to cheat you, or fool you.

Young Abe worked at odd jobs and read law books at night. Eventually he found his way into local politics. And it was then that people, listening to his speeches, began to know there was something special about Abe Lincoln.

Abe talked about running a country as if it were something you could do. It was just a matter of people getting along.

He had nothing against anybody, rich or poor, who went his own way and let the other fellow go his. No matter how mixed up things got, Abe made you feel that the answer was somewhere among those old rules that everybody knows: no hurting, no cheating, no fooling.

Abe had a way of growing without changing. So it seemed perfectly natural to find him in the White House one day, paddling around in his slippers, putting his feet on a chair when he had a deep one to think about—the same Abe Lincoln he had always been, and yet the most dignified and the strongest and the steadiest man anybody had ever known.

And when the terrible war came that might have torn his country apart, no one doubted what Abe would do. He was a family man; he resolved to keep the American family together.

Abe Lincoln always did what most people would have done, said what most people wanted said, thought what most people thought when they stopped to think about it. He was everybody, grown a little taller—the warm and living proof of our American faith that greatness comes out of everywhere when it is free.

LOUIS REDMOND

☆ ☆ ☆

HOUSE IN SPRINGFIELD

Here in this simple house his presence clings
    To tranquil, sunlit rooms and quiet nooks,
About the silent hearth, and faded prints,
    The sturdy desk, and rocking chairs, and
        books.

He has not known the tomb upon the hill
    Where mortal dust reposes in long rest;
The formal grandeur of his distant shrine
    Could never seem so singularly blest.

For here alone we sense the man who
        crossed
    This portal and emerged into the ages:
The peer of all greathearted souls in earth's
    Most noble company of saints and sages.

GAIL BROOK BURKET

☆ ☆ ☆

134

From LINCOLN, THE MAN OF THE PEOPLE

The color of the ground was in him, the red
    earth;
The smack and tang of elemental things:
The rectitude and patience of the cliff;
The goodwill of the rain that loves all
    leaves;
The friendly welcome of the wayside well;
The courage of the bird that dares the sea;
The gladness of the wind that shakes the
    corn;
The pity of the snow that hides all scars;
The secrecy of streams that make their way
Under the mountain to the rifted rock;
The tolerance and equity of light
That gives as freely to the shrinking flower
As to the great oak flaring to the wind—
To the grave's low hill as to the Matterhorn
That shoulders out the sky. Sprung from the
    West,
He drank the valorous youth of a new world.
The strength of virgin forests braced his
    mind,
The hush of spacious prairies stilled his
    soul.
His words were oaks in acorns; and his
    thoughts
Were roots that firmly gript the granite
    truth.

                        EDWIN MARKHAM

☆   ☆   ☆

The range of the personality of Abraham
Lincoln ran far, identifying itself with the
tumults and follies of mankind, keeping
touch with multitudes and solitudes. The
free-going and friendly companion is there
and the man of the cloister, of the lonely
corner of thought, prayer, and speculation.
The man of public affairs, before a living au-
dience announcing decisions, is there, and
the solitary inquirer weaving his abstractions
related to human freedom and responsibility.

Perhaps no other American held so definitely in himself both those elements—the
genius of the Tragic, the spirit of the Comic.
The fate of man, his burdens and crosses, the
pity of circumstance, the extent of tragedy in
human life, these stood forth in word
shadows of the Lincoln utterance, as testa-
mentary as the utter melancholy of his face in
repose. And in contrast he came to be known
nevertheless as the first authentic humorist to
occupy the executive mansion in Washington,
his gift of laughter and his flair for the funny
being taken as a national belonging.

                        CARL SANDBURG

☆   ☆   ☆

WE WALK WITH LINCOLN

When we remember him, his awkward ways,
His clothing, plain and homespun, his rough
    hands,
We walk beside him through the lonely days
Then leave him, as he draws aside and stands
Alone, his dreams full-flowering before the
    fire,
Dry prairie grass and moon-wind in his hair;
The floor-strewn books are pushed aside;
    desire
Beyond his reasoning burns otherwhere.
The sparks that smouldered in his heart's
    deep wedge,
A consecrated love for righted wrong,
Inflamed him to redeem his firelight pledge
When years were filled with sorrow's tragic
    song.
A nation stands in reverence at his name
Whose prairie home nursed him with living
    flame.

                        LEILA PIER KING

☆   ☆   ☆

He leaves for America's history and biogra-
phy, so far, not only its most dramatic
reminiscence—he leaves, in my opinion, the
greatest, best, most characteristic, artistic,
moral personality.

                        WALT WHITMAN

☆ ☆ ☆

THE ROAD LINCOLN TRAVELED

Feel discouraged occasionally? The next time discouragement hits you, remember the case of a young man of limited background, possessing little more than a self-administered education. Upon completion of military service, he decided to enter politics by running for a seat in the state legislature. He was soundly defeated.

He retired from politics to try his hand at the storekeeper's trade. The store went bankrupt, and he spent the next seventeen years of his life paying off the debts.

He fell in love with a young woman . . . and suffered the heartbreaking experience of watching her die from typhoid fever.

He again entered politics, this time as a candidate for Congress. He was elected by a narrow margin, but when he ran for re-election, was defeated.

He sought a position with the United States land office. He failed to get the job.

He became a candidate for the United States Senate—and was defeated.

He was nominated for the Vice Presidency at the Presidential convention of a major political party. He lost to a political unknown on the final ballot.

Running again for the Senate, he waged a campaign which captured the attention of the nation, but which netted him only defeat.

Instead, he continued to dedicate himself to the ideals and principles in which he believed.

His eventual reward is familiar to everyone. For Abraham Lincoln, although often discouraged during his lifetime, attained undying fame.

LINCOLN SAVINGS AND LOAN ASSOCIATION
LOS ANGELES

☆ ☆ ☆

ABRAHAM LINCOLN

Remember he was poor and country-bred;
   His face was lined; he walked with awk-
      ward gait.
Smart people laughed at him sometimes and
   said,
   "How can so very plain a man be great?"
Remember he was humble, used to toil.
   Strong arms he had to build a shack, a
      fence,
Long legs to tramp the woods, to plow the
   soil,
   A head chuck full of backwoods common
      sense.
Remember all he ever had he earned.
   He walked in time through stately White
      House doors;
But all he knew of men and life he learned
   In little backwoods cabins, country stores.
Remember that his eyes could light with fun;
   That wisdom, courage, set his name apart;
But when the rest is duly said and done,
   Remember that men loved him for his
      heart.

MILDRED PLEW MEIGS

☆ ☆ ☆

From COMMEMORATION ODE

For him her Old World moulds aside she
   threw,
And, choosing sweet clay from the breast
   Of the unexhausted West,
With stuff untainted shaped a hero new,
Wise, steadfast in the strength of God,
   and true. . . .
His was no lonely mountain-peak of mind,
Thrusting to thin air o'er our cloudy bars,
A sea-mark now, now lost in vapors blind;
Broad prairie rather, genial, level-lined,
Fruitful and friendly for all human kind,
Yet also nigh to heaven and loved of lof-
   tiest stars. . . .
New birth of our new soil, the first
   American.

JAMES RUSSELL LOWELL

☆ ☆ ☆

ABRAHAM LINCOLN WALKS AT MIDNIGHT

It is portentous, and a thing of state
That here at midnight, in our little town
A mourning figure walks, and will not rest,
Near the old court-house pacing up and
    down.

Or by his homestead, or in shadowed yards
He lingers where his children used to play,
Or through the market, on the well-worn
    stones
He stalks until the dawn-stars burn away.

A bronzed, lank man! His suit of ancient
    black,
A famous high top-hat and plain worn shawl
Make him the quaint great figure that men
    love,
The prairie-lawyer, master of us all.

He cannot sleep upon his hillside now.
He is among us:—as in times before!
And we who toss and lie awake for long
Breathe deep, and start, to see him pass
    the door.

His head is bowed. He thinks on men and
    kings.
Yes, when the sick world cries, how can he
    sleep?
Too many peasants fight, they know not why,
Too many homesteads in black terror weep.

The sins of all the war-lords burn his
    heart.
He sees the dreadnaughts scouring every
    main.
He carries on his shawl-wrapped shoulders
    now
The bitterness, the folly and the pain.

He cannot rest until a spirit-dawn
Shall come;—the shining hope of Europe
    free:

The league of sober folk, the Workers'
    Earth,
Bringing long peace to Cornland, Alp and
    Sea.

It breaks his heart that kings must murder
    still,
That all his hours of travail here for men
Seem yet in vain. And who will bring white
    peace
That he may sleep upon his hill again?

VACHEL LINDSAY

☆ ☆ ☆

WHAT HE STOOD FOR

The least among us can always stand for the greatest things. It is not difficult to see the operation of this principle in those capacious personalities that have bestridden the world.

One sees it plainly, for example, in a character like Abraham Lincoln. Abstract from Lincoln the things he came to stand for and we have a queer remainder. For Lincoln, taken by himself, was unprepossessing and ungainly. He came from lowly origins and small opportunities. He had no superficial graces that cover inward lack. Rather, like a very plain wire grown incandescent, Abraham Lincoln shone with what he came to stand for. He achieved a personal suggestiveness that is one of the marvels of our history.

Think of him and see how inevitably you are reminded of magnanimity, patience, steadfastness under strain, devotion to the nation's unity, love of liberty, deepening faith, and spiritual life! He came to stand for those things which man must love or else perish.

And so, plain man though he was, he achieved an undying name.

HARRY EMERSON FOSDICK

☆ ☆ ☆

From ANOTHER WASHINGTON

Some opulent force of genius, soul, and
  race,
Some deep life-current from far centuries
Flowed to his mind and lighted his sad eyes,
And gave his name, among great names, high
  place.

JOEL BENTON

☆　☆　☆

INSCRIPTION

Out of me unworthy and unknown
The vibrations of deathless music,
"With malice toward none, with charity for
  all."
Out of me forgiveness of millions toward
  millions,
And the beneficent face of a nation
Shining with justice and truth.
I am Ann Rutledge who sleep beneath these
  weeds,
Beloved of Abraham Lincoln,
Wedded to him, not through union,
But through separation.
Bloom forever, O Republic,
From the dust of my bosom.

OAKLAND CEMETERY
PETERSBURG, ILLINOIS
(WRITTEN BY EDGAR LEE MASTERS)

☆　☆　☆

ON INAUGURATION DAY

The position of Abraham Lincoln, on the day
of his inauguration, was apparently one of
helpless debility. A bark canoe in a tempest
on mid-ocean seemed hardly less safe.

The new President himself was, according
to his own description, a man of defective
education, a lawyer by profession, knowing
nothing of administration beyond having
been master of a very small post office,
knowing nothing of war but as a captain of
volunteers in a raid against an Indian chief,
repeatedly a member of the Illinois legislature, once a member of Congress.

He spoke with ease and clearness, but not
with eloquence. He wrote concisely and to the
point, but was unskilled in the use of the pen.
He had no accurate knowledge of the public
defenses of the country, no exact conception
of its foreign relations, no comprehensive
perception of his duties.

The qualities of his nature were not suited
to hardy action. His temper was soft and
gentle and yielding, reluctant to refuse anything that presented itself to him as an act of
kindness, loving to please and willing to con-
fide, not trained to confine acts of good will
within the stern limits of duty. He was of the
temperament called melancholic, scarcely
concealed by an exterior of lightness of hu-
mor, having a deep and fixed seriousness,
jesting lips, and wanness of heart.

GEORGE BANCROFT

☆　☆　☆

THE BOOK HE READ

Lincoln's indebtedness to the Bible is obvious
and beyond dispute. He read it in his boy-
hood and its influence over him increased
with the years.

In his public addresses he quoted from the
Bible more often than from any other book,
and this was the smallest part of his debt to it.
The Bible influenced his literary style, which
indeed was modeled on the writings of the
great prophets of Israel, as is especially evi-
dent in his deeply moving Second Inaugural,
which reads like a leaf from Isaiah.

And more, the Bible gave direction to his
thought. To an extent probably unparalleled
among modern statesmen, Abraham Lincoln
thought in terms of Biblical ideas and convictions.

ERNEST FREMONT TITTLE

☆　☆　☆

To live in mankind is far more than to live in
a name.

VACHEL LINDSAY

139

☆　☆　☆

From WHEN LILACS LAST IN THE
DOORYARD BLOOM'D

Coffin that passes through lanes and streets,
Through day and night with the great cloud
　darkening the land,
With the pomp of the inloop'd flags with
　the cities draped in black,
With the show of the States themselves as
　of crape-veil'd women standing,
With processions long and winding and the
　flambeaus of the night,
With the countless torches lit, with the
　silent sea of faces and the unbared heads,
With the waiting depot, the arriving coffin,
　and the sombre faces,
With dirges through the night, with the
　thousand voices rising strong and solemn,
With all the mournful voices of the dirges
　pour'd around the coffin,
The dim-lit churches and the shuddering
　organs—where amid these you journey,
With the tolling tolling bells' perpetual
　clang,
Here, coffin that slowly passes,
I give you my sprig of lilac.

WALT WHITMAN

☆　☆　☆

AT LINCOLN'S TOMB

On the night of Good Friday, 1865, he left us
to join a blessed procession, in neither doubt
nor fear, but his soul does indeed go
marching on. For this was the Bible-reading
lad come out of wilderness, following a
prairie star, filled with wonder at the world
and its Maker, who all his life, boy and man,
not only knew the Twenty-third Psalm but,
more importantly, knew the Shepherd.

Now it seems possible that we shall never
see his like again. This is a sobering thought,
but it should be a kindling one, for upon us
now, as a people and a party, has been laid
perhaps the greatest responsibility any nation
was ever asked to shoulder, yet certainly not
greater than we can bear.

Our days are no longer than were Lincoln's, our nights are no darker, and if there
is any difference between his time and this it
lies in the tremendous advantage that is ours,
that he stood so tall before us. In such a time
and at such a moment we surely can say then,
from hopeful, brimful hearts:

We are standing, Father Abraham, devoted
millions strong, firm in the faith that was
yours and is ours, secure in the conviction
bequeathed by you to us that right does make
might and that if we but dare to do our duty
as we understand it, we shall not only
survive—we shall prevail.

EVERETT MC KINLEY DIRKSEN

☆　☆　☆

AMERICA'S MESSAGE

Our Constitution and our history speak of
liberty and of the struggles and sacrifices by
which liberty was won. To all the world they
proclaim the glory of a nation created not to
make its leaders strong but to make its people
free. And to all Americans they hold a message vital in its import, compelling in its ur-
gency.

With the privileges that liberty brings
comes the responsibility of upholding it. But,
runs a solemn assurance, in our battle to keep
men free, we do not fight alone. Behind each
of us is the past free life of America. Back of
all of us is the spirit of the Founders, which
our national shrines immortalize.

Washington is with us, and Jefferson and
Lincoln. All who fought for freedom, all who
knew the great devotion, are still our com-
rades and exemplars. With such a comradeship, we cannot hesitate. With such a leader-
ship, we cannot fail. Under such a responsibility, we dare not falter. We must hold
high the light of liberty. That is America's
message to all her citizens.

RAYMOND PITCAIRN

XIII.

THE STARS AND STRIPES FOREVER

☆　☆　☆

Our flag carries American ideas, American history, and American feelings. Beginning with the Colonies, and coming down to our time, in its sacred heraldry, in its glorious insignia, it had gathered and stored chiefly this chief idea: divine right of liberty in man. Every color means liberty; every thread means liberty; every form of star and beam or stripe of light means liberty.

HENRY WARD BEECHER

From THE AMERICAN FLAG

Flag of the free heart's hope and home!
    By angel hands to valor given;
Thy stars have lit the welkin dome,
    And all thy hues were born in heaven.
Forever float that standard sheet!
    Where breathes the foe but falls before us,
With Freedom's soil beneath our feet,
    And Freedom's banner streaming o'er us!

JOSEPH RODMAN DRAKE

☆   ☆   ☆

BY ACT OF CONGRESS

(APRIL 4, 1818)

Section 1. Be it enacted, etc., that from and after the fourth of July next, the flag of the United States be thirteen horizontal stripes, alternate red and white; that the Union have twenty stars, white in a blue field.

Section 2. And be it further enacted, that on the admission of every new state into the Union, one star be added to the union of the flag; and that such addition shall take effect on the fourth of July next succeeding such admission.

☆   ☆   ☆

A COMMITTEE OF CONGRESS VISITS BETSY ROSS

The committee asked her if she thought she could make a flag from a design, a rough drawing of which General Washington exhibited. She replied with diffidence and becoming modesty that "she did not know, but would try."

She noticed, however, that the stars, as drawn, had six points, and informed the committee that the correct star should have but five points. They answered that they understood this, but that a great number of stars would be required, and the more regular form with six points could be more easily made than one with five. She responded in a practical way, by deftly folding a scrap of paper, and then, with a single clip of her scis-

sors, she displayed a true, symmetrical, five-pointed star.

After the design was partially redrawn on the table in her little back parlor, she was left to make her sample flag according to her own ideas of the arrangement of the stars, the proportions of the stripes, and the general form of the whole.

Some time after its completion, it was presented to Congress, and the committee soon thereafter had the pleasure of reporting to her that her flag was accepted as the national standard, and she was authorized to proceed at once to the manufacture of a large number for disposal by the Continental Congress.

GEORGE CANBY

☆   ☆   ☆

The nation's strength is in the people.
The nation's prosperity is in their prosperity.
The nation's glory is in the equality of her
    justice.
The nation's perpetuity is in the patriotism of
    all her people.

GROVER CLEVELAND

☆   ☆   ☆

O Columbia! the gem of the ocean,
The home of the brave and the free,
The shrine of each patriot's devotion,
A world offers homage to thee.
Thy mandates make heroes assemble,
When liberty's form stands in view;
Thy banners make tyranny tremble,
When borne by the red, white and blue.

When war wing'd its wide desolation,
And threatened the land to deform,
The ark then of freedom's foundation,
Columbia, rode safe through the storm;
With garlands of vict'ry around her,
When so proudly she bore her brave crew;
With her flag proudly floating before her,
The boast of the red, white and blue.

TIMOTHY DWIGHT

☆ ☆ ☆

THE STAR-SPANGLED BANNER

O say, can you see, by the dawn's early
 light,
  What so proudly we hail'd at the
   twilight's last gleaming?
Whose broad stripes and bright stars,
  thro' the perilous fight,
  O'er the ramparts we watch'd, were so
   gallantly streaming?
And the rockets' red glare, the bombs
  bursting in air,
Gave proof thro' the night that our flag
  was still there.
O say, does that star-spangled banner yet
 wave
O'er the land of the free and the home of
 the brave?

On the shore dimly seen thro' the mists
  of the deep,
  Where the foe's haughty host in dread
   silence reposes,
What is that which the breeze, o'er the
  towering steep,
  As it fitfully blows, half conceals, half
   discloses?
Now it catches the gleam of the morning's
 first beam,
In full glory reflected now shines on the
 stream:
'Tis the star-spangled banner: O, long may
  it wave
O'er the land of the free and the home of
 the brave!

And where is that band who so vauntingly
  swore
  That the havoc of war and the battle's
   confusion,
A home and a country should leave us no
 more?
  Their blood has wash'd out their foul
   footsteps' pollution.
No refuge could save the hireling and slave

From the terror of flight or the gloom of
  the grave:
  And the star-spangled banner in triumph
   doth wave
O'er the land of the free and the home of
  the brave.

O thus be it ever when free-men shall
  stand
  Between their lov'd homes and the war's
   desolation;
Blest with vict'ry and peace, may the
   heav'n-rescued land
  Praise the Pow'r that hath made and
   preserv'd us a nation!
Then conquer we must, when our cause it is
  just,
And this be our motto: "In God is our trust!"
And the star-spangled banner in triumph
  shall wave
O'er the land of the free and the home of
  the brave!

FRANCIS SCOTT KEY

☆ ☆ ☆

The flag is the embodiment, not of sentiment,
but of history.

WOODROW WILSON

☆ ☆ ☆

LETTER TO HIS WIFE

The second day of July, 1776, will be the most
memorable epoch in the history of America.

I am apt to believe that it will be celebrated
by succeeding generations as the great anniversary festival. It ought to be commemo-
rated as the day of deliverance, by solemn
acts of devotion to God Almighty.

It ought to be solemnized with pomp and
parade, with shows, games, sports, guns,
bells, bonfires, and illuminations, from one
end of this continent to the other, from this
time forward forevermore.

JOHN ADAMS

144

☆ ☆ ☆

FIFTIETH ANNIVERSARY

Respected Sir: The kind invitation I received from you, on the part of the citizens of the city of Washington, to be present with them at their celebration of the Fiftieth Anniversary of American Independence, as one of the surviving signers of an instrument, pregnant with our own and the fate of the world, is most flattering to myself, and heightened by the honorable accompaniment proposed for the comfort of such a journey. It adds sensibly to the sufferings of sickness, to be deprived by it of a personal participation in the rejoicings of that day; but acquiescence is a duty under circumstances not placed among those we are permitted to control.

I should, indeed, with peculiar delight, have met and exchanged there congratulations, personally, with the small band, the remnant of that host of worthies who joined with us on that day, in the bold and doubtful election we were to make, for our country, between submission and the sword; and to have enjoyed with them the consolatory fact that our fellow citizens, after half a century of experience and prosperity, continue to approve the choice we made.

May it be to the world, what I believe it will be, (to some parts sooner, to others later, but finally to all,) the signal of arousing men to burst the chains, under which monkish ignorance and superstition had persuaded them to bind themselves, and to assume the blessings and security of self-government. The form which we have substituted restores the free right to the unbounded exercise of reason and freedom of opinion. All eyes are opened or opening to the rights of man. The general spread of the light of science has already laid open to every view the palpable truth, that the mass of mankind has not been born with saddles on their backs, nor a favored few, booted and spurred, ready to ride them legitimately, by the grace of God.

These are grounds of hope for others; for ourselves, let the annual return of this day forever refresh our recollections of these rights, and an undiminished devotion to them.

THOMAS JEFFERSON
JUNE 24, 1826

☆ ☆ ☆

THE FOURTH OF JULY

Day of glory! Welcome Day!
Freedom's banners greet thy ray;
See! how cheerfully they play
With thy morning breeze,
On the rocks where pilgrims kneeled,
On the heights where squadrons wheeled,
When a tyrant's thunder pealed
O'er the trembling seas.

God of armies! did thy stars
On their courses smite his cars;
Blast his arm, and wrest his bars
From the heaving tide?
On our standards! lo! they burn.
And, when days like this return,
Sparkle o'er the soldier's urn
Who for freedom died.

God of peace! whose spirit fills
All the echoes of our hills,
All the murmur of our rills,
Now the storm is o'er,
O let freemen be our sons,
And let future Washingtons
Rise, to lead their valiant ones
Till there's war no more!

JOHN PIERPONT

☆ ☆ ☆

The United States is the only country with a known birthday.

JAMES G. BLAINE

☆ ☆ ☆

145

FLAG DAY

What's a flag? What's the love of country for which it stands? Maybe it begins with love of the land itself. It is the fog rolling in with the tide at Eastport, or through the Golden Gate and among the towers of San Francisco. It is the sun coming up behind the White Mountains, over the Green, throwing a shining glory on Lake Champlain and above the Adirondacks. It is the storied Mississippi rolling swift and muddy past St. Louis, rolling past Cairo, pouring down past the levees of New Orleans. It is lazy noontide in the pines of Carolina, it is a sea of wheat rippling in Western Kansas, it is the San Francisco peaks far north across the glowing nakedness of Arizona, it is the Grand Canyon and a little stream coming down out of a New England ridge, in which are trout.

It is men at work. It is the storm-tossed fishermen coming into Gloucester and Provincetown and Astoria. It is the farmer riding his great machine in the dust of harvest, the dairyman going to the barn before sunrise, the lineman mending the broken wire, the miner drilling for the blast. It is the servants of fire in the murky splendor of Pittsburgh, between the Allegheny and the Monongahela, the trucks rumbling through the night, the locomotive engineer bringing the train in on time, the pilot in the clouds, the riveter running along the beam a hundred feet in the air. It is the clerk in the office, the housewife doing the dishes and sending the children off to school. It is the teacher, doctor and parson tending and helping, body and soul, for small reward.

It is small things remembered, the little corners of the land, the houses, the people that each one loves. We love our country because there was a little tree on a hill, and grass thereon, and a sweet valley below; because the hurdy-gurdy man came along on a sunny morning in a city street; because a beach or a farm or a lane or a house that might not seem much to others were once, for each of us, made magic. It is voices that are remembered only, no longer heard. It is parents, friends, the lazy chat of street and store and office, and the ease of mind that makes life tranquil. It is Summer and Winter, rain and sun and storms. These are flesh of our flesh, bone of our bone, blood of our blood, a lasting part of what we are, each of us and all of us together.

It is stories told. It is the Pilgrims dying in their first dreadful Winter. It is the minute man standing his ground at Concord Bridge, and dying there. It is the army in rags, sick, freezing, starving at Valley Forge. It is the wagons and the men on foot going westward over Cumberland Gap, floating down the great rivers, rolling over the great plains. It is the settler hacking fiercely at the primeval forest on his new, his own lands. It is Thoreau at Walden Pond, Lincoln at Cooper Union, and Lee riding home from Appomattox. It is corruption and disgrace, answered always by men who would not let the flag lie in the dust, who have stood up in every generation to fight for the old ideals and the old rights, at risk of ruin or of life itself.

It is a great multitude of people on pilgrimage, common and ordinary people, charged with the usual human failings, yet filled with such a hope as never caught the imaginations and the hearts of any nation on earth before. The hope of liberty. The hope of justice. The hope of a land in which a man can stand straight, without fear, without rancor.

The land and the people and the flag—the land a continent, the people of every race, the flag a symbol of what humanity may aspire to when the wars are over and the barriers are down: to these each generation must be dedicated and consecrated anew, to defend with life itself, if need be, but, above all, in friendliness, in hope, in courage, to live for.

EDITORIAL
THE NEW YORK TIMES

STAND BY THE FLAG

Stand by the Flag! Its stars like meteors
   gleaming,
    Have lighted Arctic icebergs, southern
      seas,
And shone responsive to the stormy beaming
    Of old Arcturus and the Pleiades.

Stand by the Flag! Its stripes have streamed
   in glory,
    To foes a fear, to friends a festal robe,
And spread in rhythmic lines the sacred story
    Of Freedom's triumphs over all the globe.

Stand by the Flag! On land and ocean billow
   By it your fathers stood unmoved and true,
Living defended; dying, from their pillow,
   With their last blessing passed it on to
    you.

Stand by the Flag! Immortal heroes bore it
   Through sulphurous smoke, deep moat
    and armed defense;
And their imperial Shades still hover o'er it.
   A guard celestial from Omnipotence.

              JOHN NICHOLS WILDER

☆ ☆ ☆

NATIONAL SYMBOL

The flag is the symbol of our national unity,
our national endeavor, our national aspiration.

   The flag tells of the struggle for independence, of union preserved, of liberty and union one and inseparable, of the sacrifices of brave men and women to whom the ideals and honor of this nation have been dearer than life.

   It means America first; it means an undivided allegiance.

   It means America united, strong and efficient, equal to her tasks.

   It means that you cannot be saved by the

valor and devotion of your ancestors, that to each generation comes its patriotic duty; and that upon your willingness to sacrifice and endure as those before you have sacrificed and endured rests the national hope.

   It speaks of equal rights, of the inspiration of free institutions exemplified and vindicated, of liberty under law intelligently conceived and impartially administered. There is not a thread in it but scorns self-indulgence, weakness, and rapacity.

   It is eloquent of our community interests, outweighing all divergencies of opinion, and of our common destiny.

              CHARLES EVANS HUGHES

☆ ☆ ☆

A GREETING TO STUDENTS IN HIS NINETIETH YEAR

On the eighth of March, 1862, sixty-nine years ago, the sloop *Cumberland* was sunk by the *Merrimac* off Newport News. The vessel went down with her flag flying, and when a little later my regiment arrived to begin the campaign on the Peninsula I saw the flag still flying above the waters beneath which the *Cumberland* lay. It was a life-long text for a young man. Fight to the end and go down with your flag at the peak. I hope I shall be able to do it . . .

            OLIVER WENDELL HOLMES, JR.

☆ ☆ ☆

From WHO FOLLOW THE FLAG

O bright flag, O brave flag, O flag to lead
   the free!
   The hand of God thy colors blent,
   And heaven to earth thy glory lent,
   To shield the weak, and guide the strong
   To make an end of human wrong,
And draw a countless human host to follow
   after thee!

             HENRY VAN DYKE

☆ ☆ ☆

Our country is rich in patriotic and national music—songs which are a very part of our history and our development as a nation, for they have been born of the great events which have shaped our destiny and have flowed spontaneously from hearts and souls inspired by the events of the moment.

New periods of national enthusiasm and fervor will come—new songs will be sung—but there will always remain a deeper reverence for the older songs, for they are the very essence of that something which we call love of country.

PATRIOTIC SONGS OF AMERICA

☆ ☆ ☆

THE MARINES' SONG

From the Halls of Montezuma
To the shores of Tripoli
We fight our country's battles
On the land as on the sea.
First to fight for right and freedom
And to keep our honor clean;
We are proud to claim the title
Of United States Marines.

Our flag's unfurled to every breeze
From dawn to setting sun;
We have fought in every clime and place
Where we could take a gun.
In the snow of far-off Northern lands
And in sunny tropic scenes;
You will find us always on the job—
The United States Marines.

Here's health to you and to our Corps
Which we are proud to serve;
In many a strife we've fought for life
And never lost our nerve.
If the Army and the Navy
Ever look on Heaven's scenes,
They will find the streets are guarded
By United States Marines.

☆ ☆ ☆

RIGHTS AND DUTIES

We do honor to the stars and stripes as the emblem of our country and the symbol of all that our patriotism means.

We identify the flag with almost everything we hold dear on earth. It represents our peace and security, our civil and political liberty, our freedom of religious worship, our family, our friends, our home. We see it in the great multitude of blessings, of rights and privileges that make up our country.

But when we look at our flag and behold it emblazoned with all our rights, we must remember that it is equally a symbol of our duties. Every glory that we associate with it is the result of duty done. A yearly contemplation of our flag strengthens and purifies the national conscience.

CALVIN COOLIDGE

☆ ☆ ☆

We take the stars from heaven, the red from our mother country, separating it by white stripes, thus showing that we have separated from her, and the white stripes shall go down to posterity representing liberty.

GEORGE WASHINGTON

☆ ☆ ☆

From YOUR FLAG AND MY FLAG

Your flag and my flag,
  And how it flies today
In your land and my land
  And half a world away!
Rose-red and blood-red
  The stripes forever gleam;
Snow-white and soul-white—
  The good forefather's dream;
Sky-blue and true-blue, with stars to gleam
    aright—
  The gloried guidon of the day, a shelter
    through the night.

WILBUR D. NESBIT

☆ ☆ ☆

149

I AM THE FLAG

I am the flag of the United States of America.

I was born on June 14, 1777, in Philadelphia.

There the Continental Congress adopted my stars and stripes as the national flag.

My thirteen stripes alternating red and white, with a union of thirteen white stars in a field of blue, represented a new constellation, a new nation dedicated to the personal and religious liberty of mankind.

Today fifty stars signal from my union, one for each of the fifty sovereign states in the greatest constitutional republic the world has ever known.

My colors symbolize the patriotic ideals and spiritual qualities of the citizens of my country.

My red stripes proclaim the fearless courage and integrity of American men and boys and the self-sacrifice and devotion of American mothers and daughters.

My white stripes stand for liberty and equality for all.

My blue is the blue of heaven, loyalty, and faith.

I represent these eternal principles: liberty, justice, and humanity.

I embody American freedom: freedom of speech, religion, assembly, the press, and the sanctity of the home.

I typify that indomitable spirit of determination brought to my land by Christopher Columbus and by all my forefathers—the Pilgrims, Puritans, settlers at Jamestown and Plymouth.

I am as old as my nation.

I am a living symbol of my nation's law: the Constitution of the United States and the Bill of Rights.

I voice Abraham Lincoln's philosophy: "A government of the people, by the people, for the people."

I stand guard over my nation's schools, the seedbed of good citizenship and true patriotism.

I am displayed in every schoolroom throughout my nation; every schoolyard has a flag pole for my display.

Daily thousands upon thousands of boys and girls pledge their allegiance to me and my country.

I have my own law—Public Law 829, "The Flag Code"—which definitely states my correct use and display for all occasions and situations.

I have my special day, Flag Day. June 14 is set aside to honor my birth.

Americans, I am the sacred emblem of your country. I symbolize your birthright, your heritage of liberty purchased with blood and sorrow.

I am your title deed of freedom, which is yours to enjoy and hold in trust for posterity.

If you fail to keep this sacred trust inviolate, if I am nullified and destroyed, you and your children will become slaves to dictators and despots.

Eternal vigilance is your price of freedom.

As you see me silhouetted against the peaceful skies of my country, remind yourself that I am the flag of your country, that I stand for what you are—no more, no less.

Guard me well, lest your freedom perish from the earth.

Dedicate your lives to those principles for which I stand: "One nation under God, indivisible, with liberty and justice for all."

I was created in freedom. I made my first appearance in a battle for human liberty.

God grant that I may spend eternity in my "land of the free and the home of the brave" and that I shall ever be known as "Old Glory," the flag of the United States of America.

RUTH APPERSON ROUS

150

☆ ☆ ☆

AS THESE BRIGHT COLORS

Set out the flag against the wind and sun;
Set out the flag and watch the ripples run
Across the stars and bars to fade in space.
There is no line of color, creed or race
To those who hold this waving emblem dear.
To them suspicion, doubt and greed and fear
Like the white ripples blown into the sky
Across the lines of red and white must fly.
Out of the blue, into the blue, this call
Destroys dividing lines and over all
The three bright colors merge at last to one—
As these united hearts—as ripples run.

RAYMOND KRESENSKY

☆ ☆ ☆

THE ART OF GOOD CITIZENSHIP

Good citizenship is a personal thing. The
good citizen reaches out to others with an
open hand, an open mind and an open heart.
He sees the potential bigness in little people.
He lifts people up instead of letting them
down.

Good citizenship calls for action. The good
citizen gets off the side lines and takes part in
the struggle. He recognizes that humanity
moves forward not only from the mighty
shoves of its great leaders but also from the
tiny pushes of the rank and file of the people.
He uses the humble ounces of his weight to
help tip the scale for what he thinks is right.

Good citizenship applies the power of the
ballot. The good citizen uses his vote as a
flaming sword to crusade for the kind of city,
state, nation and world in which he wants to
live.

Good citizenship begins at home. The good
citizen observes the law. He helps to keep his
city clean. He keeps his house painted, his
lawn trimmed and flowers growing in his
garden. He champions worthy causes and
helps the unfortunate. He strives to be a good
neighbor and to do well the thousand and

one little things that add up to the big things
we all want.

Good citizenship calls for balanced living in
the vital areas of work, play, love and worship. The good citizen strives to do his daily
work well and thus contribute to human happiness. He takes time to play and to laugh and
to look up at the stars. He makes his home
and family the center of his activities and
takes pride in being a good parent. He leaves
room for the life of the spirit.

Good citizenship is built on faith. The good
citizen has the daring of a great faith. He lifts
his sights above doubt and fear. He believes
in the possibilities of world peace and in a
growing understanding and cooperation
between men. He thinks, talks and lives in
harmony with his faith.

The good citizen clings to his great expec-
tations. Though defeat may come and dark
clouds appear, he maintains a vibrant faith in
the future of mankind.

WILFERD A. PETERSON

☆ ☆ ☆

From BARBARA FRIETCHIE

"Shoot, if you must, this old gray head,
But spare your country's flag," she said.

A shade of sadness, a blush of shame,
Over the face of the leader came;

The nobler nature within him stirred
To life at that woman's deed and word;

"Who touches a hair of yon gray head
Dies like a dog! March on!" he said.

All day long through Frederick street
Sounded the tread of marching feet:

All day long that free flag tost
Over the heads of the rebel host.

JOHN GREENLEAF WHITTIER

☆ ☆ ☆

From THE FLAG OF OUR UNION

The union of hearts, the union of hands,
And the flag of our Union forever!

GEORGE POPE MORRIS

☆ ☆ ☆

AMERICANISM

There is one quality which we must bring to the solution of every problem—that is, an intense and fervid Americanism. We shall never be successful over the dangers that confront us; we shall never achieve true greatness, nor reach the lofty ideal which the founders and preservers of our mighty Federal Republic have set before us, unless we are Americans in heart and soul, in spirit and purpose, keenly alive to the responsibility implied in the very name of American, and proud beyond measure of the glorious privilege of bearing it.

THEODORE ROOSEVELT

☆ ☆ ☆

OUR CHOICES

This flag, which we honor and under which we serve, is the emblem of our unity, our power, our thought and purpose as a nation.

It has no other character than that which we give it from generation to generation.

The choices are ours.

It floats in majestic silence above the hosts that execute those choices, whether in peace or in war.

And yet, though silent, it speaks to us—speaks to us of the past, of the men and women who went before us, and of the records they wrote upon it.

WOODROW WILSON

☆ ☆ ☆

Patriotism is the vital condition of national permanence.

GEORGE WILLIAM CURTIS

☆ ☆ ☆

MEANINGS

What does the flag mean to you? Is it simply a strip of glorified bunting, beautiful in itself, but nothing more? Each person creates his own flag, and if his nature is cheap and tawdry, his flag is the same. If his nature is exalted and reverential, he sees in the flag those qualities which make it precious to him.

To every person who loves and honors the flag of his country it has a peculiar significance which is for him alone. To one it means personal freedom from a harsh ruler, to another it means freedom of achievement, to still another it is intellectual or religious liberty.

One man sees in the flag the pageant of history, the upward struggle of the common man, the promise of the day when there shall dawn the glorious realization of equality of opportunity.

These and thousands of other concepts are woven into the flag if one cares to see them. Beyond these things is that elusive something which moves our hearts and kindles ideals of human service. That something is the incredible sacrifice which has been made that the human spirit may indeed be free.

CARRIE BONEBRAKE SIMPSON

☆ ☆ ☆

From THE FLOWER OF
LIBERTY

What flower is this that greets the morn,
Its hues from heaven so freshly born?
With burning star and flaming band
It kindles all the sunset land;
O tell us what its name may be—
Is this the flower of liberty?
    It is the banner of the free,
    The starry flower of liberty!

OLIVER WENDELL HOLMES

☆ ☆ ☆

XIV

BRING ME MEN TO MATCH MY MOUNTAINS

☆   ☆   ☆

The soil out of which such men are made is good to be born on,
good to live on, good to die for and to be buried in.

JAMES RUSSELL LOWELL

AMERICA FIFTY YEARS AFTER INDEPENDENCE

We live in an extraordinary age. It is impossible to look around us without alternate emotions of exultation and astonishment.

What shall we say of one revolution, which created a nation out of thirteen feeble colonies, and founded the empire of liberty upon the basis of the perfect equality in rights and representation of all its citizens? which commenced in a struggle by enlightened men for principles, and not for places, and in its progress and conclusion exhibited examples of heroism, patriotic sacrifices, and disinterested virtue, which have never been surpassed in the most favored regions?

What shall we say of this nation, which has in fifty years quadrupled its population, and spread itself from the Atlantic to the Rocky Mountains, not by the desolations of successful war, but by the triumphant march of industry and enterprise?

JOSEPH STORY

☆　☆　☆

FULL-FLEDGED AMERICAN

Were I to have a vision of a full-fledged American it would be something like this: A man who, with sufficient knowledge of the past, would walk fairly constantly with the thought that he was bloodbrother, if not by actual race then by the equally subtle method of mental vein transfusing into mental vein, of Washington and Lincoln, of Jefferson and Lee, and of all the men like them. Who would walk, because of this, carefully and proudly, and also humbly, lest he fail them. And, with a keen sense of the present and the future, would say to himself: "I am an American and therefore what I do, however small, is of importance."

STRUTHERS BURT

☆　☆　☆

In any region of life, produce a true frontiersman, and he will find frontiers.

W. J. CAMERON

☆　☆　☆

From THE COMING AMERICAN

Bring me men to match my mountains,
　Bring me men to match my plains—
Men with empires in their purpose
　And new eras in their brains.
Bring me men to match my prairies,
　Men to match my inland seas,
Men whose thought shall prove a highway
　Up to ampler destinies,
Pioneers to clear thought's marshlands
　And to cleanse old error's fen;
Bring me men to match my mountains—
　Bring me men!

Bring me men to match my forests,
　Strong to fight the storm and blast,
Branching toward the skyey future,
　Rooted in the fertile past.
Bring me men to match my valleys,
　Tolerant of sun and snow,
Men within whose fruitful purpose
　Time's consummate blooms shall grow,
Men to tame the tigerish instincts
　Of the lair and cave and den,
Cleanse the dragon slime of nature—
　Bring me men!

Bring me men to match my rivers,
　Continent cleavers, flowing free,
Drawn by the eternal madness
　To be mingled with the sea;
Men of oceanic impulse,
　Men whose moral currents sweep
Towards the wide-infolding ocean
　Of an undiscovered deep;
Men who feel the strong pulsation
　Of the Central Sea, and then
Time their currents to its earth throb—
　Bring me men!

SAM WALTER FOSS

155

☆ ☆ ☆

HEARTBEAT OF DEMOCRACY

"Sure, we can," said the man.
And his tone was the bone,
Was the spirit and bone,
With which freedom was sown,
The firm strength of his mood
Was as sleep and as food
To the wavering-willed;
And their spirits were thrilled
To the one effort more
That seemed hopeless before.

There is faith that is fact,
Not a wraith, but an act
That comes up from the earth
With conviction and worth.
It is big and sincere
And holds liberty dear
As its life. Said the man,
"Sure, we can. Sure, we can!"
And the air seemed to fill
With the words, "And we will!"

VIRGINIA BRASIER

☆ ☆ ☆

LABOR IN FREEDOM

Everything that is really great and inspiring is
created by individuals who labor in freedom.

ALBERT EINSTEIN

☆ ☆ ☆

From NEW ENGLAND PLANTATION
(1630)

Now I will tell you of some discommodities,
that are here to be found.

First, in the summer season, for these three
months, June, July, and August, we are troubled much with little flies called mosquitoes,
being the same they are troubled with in Lin-
colnshire and the fens; and they are nothing
but gnats, which, except they be smoked out
of their houses, are troublesome in the night
season.

Secondly, in the winter season, for two
months' space, the earth is commonly covered with snow, which is accompanied with
sharp biting frosts, something more sharp
than is in Old England, and therefore are
forced to make great fires.

Thirdly, this country being very full of
woods and wildernesses, doth also much
abound with snakes and serpents, of strange
colors and huge greatness. Yea, there are
some serpents, called rattlesnakes, that have
rattles in their tails, that will not fly from a
man as others will, but will fly upon him and
sting him so mortally that he will die within a
quarter of an hour after, except the party
stinged have about him some of the root of an
herb called snake-weed to bite on, and then
he shall receive no harm. But yet seldom falls
it out that any hurt is done by these. About
three years since an Indian was stung to
death by one of them; but we heard of none
since that time.

Fourthly and lastly, here wants as yet the
good company of honest Christians, to bring
with them horses, kine and sheep, to make
use of this fruitful land. Great pity it is to see
so much good ground for corn and for grass
as any is under the heavens, to lie altogether
unoccupied, when so many honest men and
their families in Old England, through the
populousness thereof, do make very hard
shift to live one by the other.

FRANCIS HIGGINSON

☆ ☆ ☆

CHALLENGE

My fellow Americans: ask not what your
country can do for you; ask what you can do
for your country.

My fellow citizens of the world: ask not
what America will do for you, but what together we can do for the freedom of man.

JOHN F. KENNEDY

☆ ☆ ☆

From THE DEVIL AND DANIEL WEBSTER

Every time there's a thunderstorm around Marshfield, they say you can hear his rolling voice in the hollows of the sky. And they say that if you go to his grave and speak loud and clear, "Dan'l Webster—Dan'l Webster!" the ground'll begin to shiver and the trees begin to shake. And after a while you'll hear a deep voice saying, "Neighbor, how stands the Union?" Then you better answer the Union stands as she should, rock bottomed and copper sheathed, one and indivisible, or he's liable to rear right out of the ground. At least, that's what I was told when I was a youngster.

You see, for a while, he was the biggest man in the country. He never got to be President, but he was the biggest man. There were thousands that trusted in him right next to God Almighty, and they told stories of patriarchs and such. They said, when he stood up to speak, stars and stripes came right out in the sky, and once he spoke against a river and made it sink into the ground. A man with a mouth like a mastiff, a brow like a mountain and eyes like burning anthracite—that was Dan'l Webster in his prime.

STEPHEN VINCENT BENÉT

☆ ☆ ☆

NOTHING SO PERFECT

Never, in these United States, has the brain of man conceived, or the hand of man fashioned, so perfect a thing as the clipper ship.

SAMUEL ELIOT MORISON

☆ ☆ ☆

From TWO YEARS BEFORE THE MAST

There is a witchery in the sea, its songs and stories, and in the mere sight of a ship, and the sailor's dress, especially to a young mind, which has done more to man navies, and fill merchantmen, than all the pressgangs of Europe. Many are the boys, in every seaport, who are drawn away, as by an almost irresistible attraction, from their work and schools, and hang about the decks and yards of vessels, with a fondness which, it is plain, will have its way.

RICHARD HENRY DANA

☆ ☆ ☆

CLIPPER SHIPS AND CAPTAINS

There was a time before our time,
It will not come again,
When the best ships still were wooden ships
But the men were iron men.

From Stonington to Kennebunk
The Yankee hammers plied
To build the clippers of the wave
That were New England's pride.

The "Flying Cloud," the "Northern Light,"
The "Sovereign of the Seas"—
There was salt music in the blood
That thought of names like these.

"Sea Witch," "Red Jacket," "Golden Age,"
And "Chariot of Fame,"
The whole world gaped to look at them
Before the steamship came.

Their cargoes were of tea and gold,
Their bows a cutting blade;
And, on the bridge, the skippers walked,
Lords of the China trade.

The skippers with the little beards
And the New England drawl,
Who knew Hong Kong and Marblehead
And the Pole Star over all.

Stately as churches, swift as gulls,
They trod the oceans, then —
No man had seen such ships before
And none will see again.

ROSEMARY *AND* STEPHEN VINCENT BENÉT

☆ ☆ ☆

OPPORTUNITIES

Wherever we look upon this earth, the opportunities take shape within the problems.

NELSON A. ROCKEFELLER

☆ ☆ ☆

ACQUAINTANCE

As long as I live I'll hear waterfalls and birds and winds sing. I'll interpret the rocks, learn the language of flood, storm, and the avalanche. I'll acquaint myself with the glaciers and wild gardens, and get as near the heart of the world as I can.

JOHN JAMES AUDUBON

☆ ☆ ☆

DANIEL BOONE

Daniel Boone at twenty-one
Came with his tomahawk, knife, and gun
Home from the French and Indian War
To North Carolina and the Yadkin shore.
He married his maid with a golden band,
Builded his house and cleared his land;
But the deep woods claimed their son again
And he turned his face from the homes of
    men.
Over the Blue Ridge, dark and lone,
The Mountains of Iron, the Hills of Stone,
Braving the Shawnee's jealous wrath,
He made his way on the Warrior's Path.
Alone he trod the shadowed trails;
But he was lord of a thousand vales
As he roved Kentucky, far and near,
Hunting the buffalo, elk, and deer.
What joy to see, what joy to win
So fair a land for his kith and kin,
Of streams unstained and woods unhewn!
"Elbow room!" laughed Daniel Boone.

On the Wilderness Road that his axmen
    made
The settlers flocked to the first stockade;
The deerskin shirts and the coonskin caps
Filed through the glens and the mountain
    gaps;

And hearts were high in the fateful spring
When the land said "Nay!" to the stubborn
    king.
While the men of the East of farm and town
Strove with the troops of the British Crown,
Daniel Boone from a surge of hate
Guarded a nation's westward gate.
Down in the fort in a wave of flame
The Shawnee horde and the Mingo came,
And the stout logs shook in a storm of lead;
But Boone stood firm and the savage fled.
Peace! And the settlers flocked anew,
The farm lands spread, the town lands grew;
But Daniel Boone was ill at ease
When he saw the smoke in his forest trees.
"There'll be no game in the country soon.
Elbow room!" cried Daniel Boone.

Straight as a pine at sixty-five—
Time enough for a man to thrive—
He launched his bateau on Ohio's breast
And his heart was glad as he oared it west;
There were kindly folk and his own true
    blood
Where great Missouri rolls his flood;
New woods, new streams, and room to spare,
And Daniel Boone found comfort there.
Yet far he ranged toward the sunset still,
Where the Kansas runs and the Smoky Hill,
And the prairies toss, by the south wind
    blown;
And he killed his bear on the Yellowstone.
But ever he dreamed of new domains
With vast woods and wider plains;
Ever he dreamed of a world-to-be
Where there are no bounds and the soul is
    free.
At fourscore-five, still stout and hale,
He heard a call to a farther trail;
So he turned his face where the stars are
    strewn;
"Elbow room!" sighed Daniel Boone.

ARTHUR GUITERMAN

☆ ☆ ☆

From THE FOUNDERS OF OHIO

Their fame shrinks not to names and dates
  On votive stone, the prey of time;
Behold where monumental States
  Immortalize their lives sublime.

WILLIAM H. VENABLE

☆   ☆   ☆

LETTER TO DR. BENJAMIN RUSH

I wish to mention to you in confidence that I have obtained authority from Congress to undertake the long desired object of exploring the Missouri & whatever river, heading with that, leads into the Western ocean. About 10 chosen woodsmen headed by Capt. Lewis my secretary will set out on it immediately & probably accomplish it in two seasons.

It would be very useful to state for him those objects on which it is most desirable he should bring us information.

For this purpose I ask the favor of you to prepare some notes of such particulars as may occur in his journey & which you think should draw his attention & enquiry. He will be in Philadelphia about 2 or 3 weeks hence & will wait on you.

THOMAS JEFFERSON

☆   ☆   ☆

LEWIS AND CLARK

Lewis and Clark
Said, "Come on, let's embark
For a boating trip up the Missouri!
It's the President's wish
And we might catch some fish,
Though the river is muddy as fury."

So they started away
On a breezy May day,
Full of courage and lore scientific,
And, before they came back,
They had blazed out a track
From St. Louis straight to the Pacific.

Now, if *you* want to go
From St. Louis (in Mo.)
To Portland (the Ore. not the Me. one),
You can fly there in planes
Or board limited trains
Or the family car, if there be one.

It may take you two weeks,
If your car's full of squeaks
And you stop for the sights and the
   strangers,
But it took them (don't laugh!)
Just one year and a half,
Full of buffalo, Indians and dangers.

They ate prairie-dog soup
When they suffered from croup,
For the weather was often quite drizzly.
They learned "How do you do?"
In Shoshone and Sioux,
And how to be chased by a grizzly.

They crossed mountain and river
With never a quiver,
And the Rockies themselves weren't too big
   for them,
For they scrambled across
With their teeth full of moss,
But their fiddler still playing a jig for
   them.

Missouri's Great Falls,
And the Yellowstone's walls
And the mighty Columbia's billows,
They viewed or traversed,
Of all white men the first
To make the whole Northwest their pillows.

And, when they returned,
It was glory well-earned
That they gave to the national chorus.
They were ragged and lean
But they'd seen what they'd seen,
And it spread out an Empire before us.

ROSEMARY AND STEPHEN VINCENT BENÉT

☆ ☆ ☆

TRIBUTE TO LEWIS

I had now had opportunities of knowing him intimately. Of courage undaunted; possessing a firmness and perseverance of purpose which nothing but impossibilities could divert from its direction; careful as a father of those committed to his charge, yet steady in the maintenance of order and discipline; intimate with the Indian character, customs, and principles; habituated to the hunting life; guarded, by exact observation of the vegetables and animals of his own country, against losing time in the description of objects already possessed; honest, disinterested, liberal, of sound understanding, and a fidelity to truth so scrupulous that whatever he should report would be as certain as if seen by ourselves,—with all these qualifications, as if selected and implanted by nature in one body for this express purpose, I could have no hesitation in confiding the enterprise to him.

THOMAS JEFFERSON

☆ ☆ ☆

We cross the prairie as of old
  The pilgrims crossed the sea,
To make the West, as they the East,
  The homestead of the free.

JOHN GREENLEAF WHITTIER

☆ ☆ ☆

THE MAP MAKERS

Take the surveyors out of American history and the gaps become appalling. George Washington handled the chain and compass in the rough valleys of western Pennsylvania. William Clark, discoverer of the Columbia River, ran county lines in the Blue Ridge Mountains before he was nineteen years old and was surveyor-general of Illinois twenty years later. Abraham Lincoln ran section lines over the low hills that hem the Sangamon. Even Henry David Thoreau, a transcendentalist at heart, measured the strict bounds of Concord township and located many farmers' corners. Hosts of men shared in that task that was as broad as the continent, using the light of Aldebaran and Polaris and the sun's rays to fix a net of invisible lines across America.

It must have left a mark on them as well as on their maps. They pushed ahead of settlement into new country, not roving like traders and hunters but methodically following a compass needle, taking measurements, calculating elevations, fixing exact and unalterable benchmarks.

They waded the swamps and climbed the ridges, they set up their tripods in creek beds and hacked a way through thickets to run their uncompromising lines. So they learned a way of doing. There were no detours, no evasions and circumventions in their profession.

They learned a way of thinking. Their lines ran straight over rough, confused and difficult country.

They learned a way of living. For long seasons they took the fortunes of weather and isolation. They waited, sometimes weeks on end, for an observation of the stars to clinch their meridian.

They fought wolves and camp rats and mosquitoes, they shook with ague and bled from the furious little wounds of the black fly, they counted their chain links over quaking swamps and snow-bleak prairies.

They advanced into a country that was land merely, and they left it invisibly and forever changed. Their field notes were the basis of a future civilization. With every sight and measurement they gave the land a pattern as fixed and final as the ordered stars.

No men in America did more lasting work than theirs.

WALTER HAVIGHURST

☆ ☆ ☆

161

THE COVERED WAGON

The bold, pioneering emigrants who led the way across the Great Plains would never have suspected that their symbol would be the humble and utilitarian vehicle in which they made their journey. As the long rifle and the log cabin stand for the settling of the first frontier across the Alleghenies, the sturdy covered wagon will forever call to mind the winning of the West.

Its disadvantages were obvious—it was slow, heavy, cumbersome, subject to breakage, difficult to take across rivers, ravines, and mountains or through rocky country. But it served as a moving home, involved less daily unpacking and repacking, allowed more pounds to be transported per animal, supplied an ambulance for the sick, and—when properly placed in formation—offered a fortress against attack.

GEORGE R. STEWART

☆　☆　☆

ENDEAVOR

If a man constantly aspires, is he not elevated? Did ever a man try heroism, magnanimity, truth, sincerity, and find that there was not advantage in them—that it was a vain endeavor?

HENRY DAVID THOREAU

☆　☆　☆

THE OLD COUNTRY STORE

One can imagine a country customer in the age of Jackson coming to the store from a remote corner of the township with a load of hemlock bark, exchanging jocular greetings with the relaxed gentlemen occupying the liars' bench on the store porch, before he proceeded with his business.

The dress of the rural male in pioneer times, amounting almost to a uniform, was a blue hunting shirt, vest of striped linsey, the yarn dyed at home with alum, copperas, madder, walnut, or butternut bark, and pantaloons of coarse blue cloth dyed with indigo, a country store staple for generations.

The farmer would be shod in boots or leggings and moccasins. His trading was a slow business. The dealer had to measure the bark to determine the quantity, examine it for condition.

The price discussed and agreed on was set down on the credit side of the ledger. We do not have to imagine what the purchases were, for they still may be deciphered in old account books: salt, sugar, snuff, powder and shot, molasses by the jugful, and "a looking glass to see your face."

GERALD CARSON

☆　☆　☆

THE WEST IN 1857

The hurry of life in the Western part of this country, the rapidity, energy, and enterprise with which civilization is there being carried forward, baffles all description, and, I think, can hardly be believed by those who have seen it.

Cities of magnificent streets and houses, with wharves, and quays, and warehouses, and storehouses, and shops full of Paris luxuries, and railroads from and to them in every direction, and land worth its weight in gold by the foot, and populations of fifty and hundreds of thousands, where, within the memory of men, no trace of civilization existed, but the forest grew and the savage wandered.

I was at a place called Milwaukee, on Lake Michigan, a flourishing town where they invited me to go and read Shakespeare to them, which I mention as an indication of advanced civilization, and one of the residents, a man not fifty years old, told me that he remembered the spot on which stood the hotel where I was lodging, a tangled wilderness through which ran an Indian trail. Does not all that sound wonderful?

FANNY KEMBLE

☆ ☆ ☆

WESTERN IDEALISM

Western democracy has been from the time of its birth idealistic.

The very fact of the wilderness appealed to men as a fair, blank page on which to write a new chapter in the story of man's struggle for a higher type of society.

The Western wilds, from the Alleghanies to the Pacific, constituted the richest free gift that was ever spread out before civilized man.

To the peasant and artisan of the Old World, bound by the chains of social class, as old as custom and as inevitable as fate, the West offered an exit into a free life and greater well-being among the bounties of nature, into the midst of resources that demanded manly exertion, and that gave in return the chance for indefinite ascent in the scale of social advance.

The existence of this land of opportunity has made America the goal of idealists from the days of the Pilgrim Fathers.

FREDERICK JACKSON TURNER

☆ ☆ ☆

FRONTIER PEOPLE

Much of our district was new settlements, formed and forming; hard, long rides, cabin parlors, straw beds and bedsteads, made out of barked saplings, and puncheon bedcords. But the people were kind and clever, proverbially so; showing the real pioneer or frontier hospitality. The men were a hardy, industrious, enterprising, game catching, and Indian driving set of men. The women were also hardy; they would think no hardship of turning out and helping their husbands raise their cabins, if need be; they would mount a horse and trot ten or fifteen miles to meeting, or to see the sick and minister to them, and home again the same day.

PETER CARTWRIGHT

☆ ☆ ☆

HOOVER DAM MEMORIAL

The United States of America
will continue to remember
that many who toiled here
found their final rest
while engaged in the building
of this dam.

They died to make
the desert bloom.

☆ ☆ ☆

Go West, young man, and grow up with the country.

HORACE GREELEY

☆ ☆ ☆

Be sure you are right, then go ahead.

DAVID CROCKETT

☆ ☆ ☆

WANTED

God, give us men! A time like this demands
Strong minds, great hearts, true faith, and
    ready hands;
    Men whom the lust of office does not kill;
Men whom the spoils of office cannot buy;
    Men who possess opinions and a will;
Men who have honor; men who will not lie;
Men who can stand before a demagogue
    And damn his treacherous flatteries without winking!
Tall men, sun-crowned, who live above the
    fog
    In public duty and in private thinking;
For while the rabble, with their thumb-worn
    creeds,
Their large professions and their little
    deeds,
Mingle in selfish strife, lo! Freedom weeps,
Wrong rules the land, and Justice sleeps.

JOSIAH GILBERT HOLLAND

☆ ☆ ☆

Learn to think continentally.

ALEXANDER HAMILTON

☆　☆　☆

The generation that subdued the wild land and broke up the virgin prairies inspires respect and compels admiration.

WILLA CATHER

☆　☆　☆

CHILDREN OF NATURE

Not many generations ago, where you now sit, encircled with all that exalts and embellishes civilized life, the rank thistle nodded in the wind and the wild fox dug his hole unscared.

Here lived and loved another race of beings. Beneath the same sun that rolls over your heads, the Indian hunter pursued the panting deer; gazing on the same moon that smiles for you, the Indian lover wooed his dusky mate.

Here the wigwam blaze beamed on the tender and helpless, and the council-fire glared on the wise and daring. Now they dipped their noble limbs in your sedgy lakes, and now they paddled the light canoe along your rocky shores. Here they warred; the echoing whoop, the bloody grapple, the defying death-song, all were here; and when the tiger-strife was over, here curled the smoke of peace.

Here, too, they worshiped; and from many a dark bosom went up a fervent prayer to the Great Spirit. He had not written his laws for them on tables of stone, but he had traced them on the tables of their hearts. The poor child of nature knew not the God of Revelation, but the God of the universe he acknowledged in every thing around. He beheld him in the star that sank in beauty behind his lonely dwelling; in the sacred orb that flamed on him from his midday throne; in the flower that snapped in the morning breeze; in the lofty pine that defied a thousand whirlwinds; in the timid warbler that never left its native grove; in the fearless eagle, whose untired pinion was wet in clouds; in the worm that crawled at his feet; and in his own matchless form, glowing with a spark of that light, to whose mysterious source he bent in humble though blind adoration.

As a race they have withered from the land. Their arrows are broken, their springs are dried up, their cabins are in the dust. Their council-fire has long since gone out on the shore, and their war-cry is fast fading to the untrodden west.

Slowly and sadly they climb the distant mountains and read their doom in the setting sun. They are shrinking before the mighty tide which is pressing them away; they must soon hear the roar of the last wave which will settle over them forever.

CHARLES SPRAGUE

☆　☆　☆

The frontier, for all its savage brutal habits, had created, if only now and then, characters that rose superior to destiny.

ELLEN GLASGOW

☆　☆　☆

They that can give up essential liberty to obtain a little temporary safety deserve neither liberty nor safety.

BENJAMIN FRANKLIN

☆　☆　☆

TRAIN SCHEDULE

The startings and arrivals of the cars are now the epochs of the village day. They go and come with such regularity and precision, and their whistle can be heard so far, that the farmers set their clocks by them, and thus one well-conducted institution regulates a whole country.

HENRY DAVID THOREAU

☆　☆　☆

AMERICA'S WEALTH

The wealth of a nation like ours is not stored in static reservoirs but is a fluid value created each day of our lives by the dynamic interplay of our powers as a people.

The wealth of a nation like ours is the constant flow of new ideas from the creative mind of our industrial science, the unrestrained push and probe of the men who work in laboratories, and the always ready response of industrial enterprise to today's reality and tomorrow's promise.

The wealth of a nation like ours lies in its workers and their workmanship, in their earning power, in their yearning power, and in their purchasing power.

The wealth of a nation like ours lies in the freedom of our people to want and to have, through the free exchange of their individual goods and services.

The wealth of a nation like ours lies in its partnership of people and in the harmony that exists between science and industry, worker and employer, producer and consumer, you and me.

PARTNERS

☆　☆　☆

AMERICAN SELF-RELIANCE

This country was not built by men who relied on somebody else to take care of them. It was built by men who relied on themselves, who dared to shape their own lives, who had enough courage to blaze new trails—enough confidence in themselves to take the necessary risks.

This self-reliance is our American legacy. It is the secret of that something which stamped Americans as Americans. Some call it individual initiative, others backbone. But whatever it is called, it is a precious ingredient in our national character, one which we must not lose.

The time has come for us to re-establish the rights for which we stand—to re-assert our inalienable rights to human dignity, self-respect, self-reliance—to be again the kind of people who once made America great.

Such a crusade for renewed independence will require a succession of inspired leaders—leaders in spirit and in knowledge of the problem, not just men with political power, but men who are militantly for the distinctive way of life that was America. We are likely to find such leaders only among those that promote self-reliance and who practice it with strict devotion and understanding.

J. OLLIE EDMUNDS

☆　☆　☆

The dogmas of the quiet past are inadequate to the stormy present.

ABRAHAM LINCOLN

☆　☆　☆

To be as good as our fathers we must be better.

WENDELL PHILLIPS

☆　☆　☆

PRINCIPLES OF MANHOOD

When a teacher of the future comes to point out to the youth of America how the highest rewards of intellect and devotion can be gained, he may say to them—not by subtlety and intrigue, not by wire-pulling and demagoguery, not by shiftiness in following expediency; but by being firm in devotion to the principles of manhood and the courage of righteousness in public life; by being a man without guile, without fear, without selfishness, and with devotion to duty, devotion to his country and his God.

ELIHU ROOT

☆　☆　☆

The history of every nation is eventually written in the way in which it cares for its soil.

FRANKLIN D. ROOSEVELT

☆ ☆ ☆

From AMERICA WAS PROMISES

America was promises—to whom?

Jefferson knew:
Declared it before God and before history:
Declares it still in the remembering tomb.
The promises were Man's: the land was his—
Man endowed by his Creator:
Earnest in love: perfectible by reason:
Just and perceiving justice: his natural nature
Clear and sweet at the source as springs in
    trees are.
It was Man the promise contemplated.
The times had chosen Man: no other:
Bloom on his face of every future:
Brother of stars and of all travelers:
Brother of time and of all mysteries:
Brother of grass also: of fruit trees.
It was Man who had been promised: who
    should have.
Man was to ride from the Tidewater: over the
    Gap:
West and South with the water: taking the
    book with him:
Taking the wheat seed: corn seed: pip of
    apple:
Building liberty a farmyard wide:
Breeding useful labor: for good looks:
For husbandry: humanity: for pride—
Practising self-respect and common decency.

ARCHIBALD MAC LEISH

☆ ☆ ☆

Americans are always moving on.

STEPHEN VINCENT BENÉT

☆ ☆ ☆

REQUIREMENT

That nation is proudest and noblest and most
exalted which has the greatest number of
truly great men.

SINCLAIR LEWIS

☆ ☆ ☆

GOETHALS, THE PROPHET ENGINEER

A man went down to Panama,
Where many a man had died,
To slit the sliding mountains
And lift the eternal tide;
A man stood up in Panama,
And the mountains stood aside.

For a poet wrought in Panama
With a continent for his theme,
And he wrote with flood and fire
To forge a planet's dream,
And the derricks rang his dithyrambs
And his stanzas roared in steam.

Where old Balboa bent his gaze
He leads the liners through,
And the Horn that tossed Magellan
Bellows a far halloo,
For where the navies never sailed
Steamed Goethals and his crew.

So nevermore the tropic routes
Need poleward warp and veer,
But on through the Gates of Goethals
The steady keels shall steer,
Where the tribes of man are led toward
    peace
By the prophet engineer.

PERCY MAC KAYE

☆ ☆ ☆

WORTHY PURSUITS

To direct the genius and resources of our
country to useful improvements, to the sciences, the arts, education, the amendment of
the public mind and morals, in such pursuits
lie real honor and the nation's glory.

ROBERT FULTON
HALL OF FAME INSCRIPTION

☆ ☆ ☆

167

Never in history have a nation and people had the opportunity that we now have to display greatness.

RALPH J. BUNCHE

☆　☆　☆

HISTORICAL FOOTNOTE

The occasion had not been arranged and rehearsed as I suspect the sending of the first message over the Morse telegraph had been years before, for instead of that noble first telegraphic message—"What hath God wrought?"—the first message of the telephone was: "Mr. Watson, come here, I want you." Perhaps if Mr. Bell had realized that he was about to make a bit of history, he would have been prepared with a more sounding and interesting sentence.

THOMAS A. WATSON

☆　☆　☆

CHARLES A. LINDBERGH

Alone?

Is he alone at whose right side rides Courage, with Skill within the cockpit and Faith upon the left? Does solitude surround the brave when Adventure leads the way and Ambition reads the dials? Is there no company with him, for whom the air is cleft by Daring and the darkness made light by Emprise?

True, the fragile bodies of his fellows do not weigh down his plane; true, the fretful minds of weaker men are lacking from his crowded cabin; but as his airship keeps her course he holds communion with those rare spirits that inspire to intrepidity and by their sustaining potency give strength to arm, resource to mind, content to soul.

Alone? With what other companions would man fly to whom the choice were given?

HAROLD MAC DONALD ANDERSON

☆　☆　☆

AMERICA'S STRENGTH

America is a nation of strengths. Its industrial might gives its people the highest living standard in the world. Its powerful defenses safeguard its heritage of independence and freedom.

America is a nation of strong people. They have courageously resisted the cold war tactics of an alien doctrine, and bravely stemmed the advances of aggressors.

America is a nation of shining ideals. It has held proudly in trust "the preservation of the sacred fire of liberty," as George Washington said. It has always been a nation "under God," as the pledge of allegiance states.

America is a nation of growing spiritual strength. In its early years, scarcely more than a tenth of its citizens were connected with religious groups. Since then we have put on much spiritual armor. Today a majority of the population are church and synagogue members. More than half attend worship services regularly.

We are on the high road to deeper spiritual power and material progress.

AMERICAN LIFE PROGRAM

☆　☆　☆

PROMISED LAND

Idealism must always prevail on the frontier, for the frontier, whether geographical or intellectual, offers little hope to those who see things as they are. To venture into the wilderness, one must see it, not as it is, but as it will be. The frontier, being the possession of those only who see its future, is the promised land which cannot be entered save by those who have faith. America, having been such a Promised Land, is therefore inhabited by men of faith: idealism is ingrained in the character of the people.

CARL BECKER

☆　☆　☆

168

XV

AMERICAN SCHOOLS
AND SCHOLARS

☆　☆　☆

If, almost on the day of their landings, our ancestors founded schools and endowed colleges, what obligations do not rest upon us, living under circumstances so much more favorable, both for providing and for using the means of education?　DANIEL WEBSTER

NEW ENGLAND BUILDS A COLLEGE

After God had carried us safe to New England, and we had builded our houses, provided necessaries for our livelihood, reared convenient places for God's worship, and settled the civil government, one of the next things we longed for and looked after was to advance learning and perpetuate it to posterity, dreading to leave an illiterate ministry to the churches when our present ministers shall lie in the dust. And as we were thinking and consulting how to effect this great work, it pleased God to stir up the heart of one Mr. Harvard (a godly gentleman and lover of learning, there living amongst us) to give the one half of his estate (it being in all about £1700) towards the erecting of a college, and all his library. After him, another gave £300, others after them cast in more, and the public hand of the state added the rest. The college was, by common consent, appointed to be at Cambridge (a place very pleasant and accommodate) and is called (according to the name of the first founder) Harvard College.

From NEW ENGLAND'S FIRST FRUITS (1643)

☆　☆　☆

The schools of democracy should be concerned to give each child an opportunity to express himself in that kind of purposeful functioning which is mind.

JOHN L. CHILDS

☆　☆　☆

WORTHY WORK

If we work upon marble, it will perish. If we build temples, they will crumble into dust. But if we work on immortal souls, if we imbue them with just principles of action—the fear of wrong, the love of right—we engrave upon those tablets something which no time can obliterate and which will brighten and heighten through all eternity.

DANIEL WEBSTER

☆　☆　☆

In a nation which holds sacred the dignity and worth of the individual, education is first and foremost an instrument for serving the aspirations of each person. It is not only the means for earning a living, but for enlarging life—for maintaining and improving liberty of the mind, for exercising both the rights and obligations of freedom, for understanding the world in which we live.

DWIGHT D. EISENHOWER

☆　☆　☆

SCHOOLS IN LINCOLN COUNTRY

I know the kind of schools Lincoln attended, and in spite of their grave limitations I have a high sense of their value.

Even the discipline of those schools, severe as it was, and combining "lickin' and l'arnin' " with a liberal allowance for the licking, was not without its worth.

If the teachers were ignorant, so were the pupils and their parents; if the teacher could cipher to the rule of three, that was quite as far as most of the pupils had any occasion to go.

The schoolhouses were bare, log buildings, with the cracks unchinked. They were built upon slopes high enough at one end for hogs to rest under the floor and fill the place with fleas—a situation only partly remedied by the penny-royal which the pupils brought in by the armful and tramped upon in the aisle.

The benches were of puncheon and had no backs, and it was thought a needless concession to love of luxury to saw off the legs where they projected upward through the surface of the seat.

But the children departed from those schools a little less ignorant than they were when they entered.

WILLIAM E. BARTON

☆　☆　☆

171

A system of general instruction which shall reach every description of our citizens from the richest to the poorest, as it was the earliest, so will it be the latest of all the public concerns in which I shall permit myself to take an interest.

THOMAS JEFFERSON

☆　☆　☆

JEFFERSON'S HOPE FOR THE UNIVERSITY OF VIRGINIA

We fondly hope that the instruction which may flow from this institution, kindly cherished, by advancing the minds of our youth with the growing science of the time, and elevating the views of our citizens generally to the practice of the social duties and the functions of self-government, may ensure to our country the reputation, the safety, the prosperity, and all the other blessings which experience proves to result from the cultivation and improvement of the general mind.

THOMAS JEFFERSON

☆　☆　☆

IN BEHALF OF DARTMOUTH COLLEGE

It is, Sir, as I have said, a small college. And yet there are those who love it.

DANIEL WEBSTER

☆　☆　☆

A well-instructed people alone can be permanently a free people.

JAMES MADISON

☆　☆　☆

America's future will be determined by the home and the school. The child becomes largely what it is taught. Hence we must watch what we teach it, and how we live before it.

JANE ADDAMS

☆　☆　☆

I want to see education as common as grass and as free for all as sunshine and rain.

BOOKER T. WASHINGTON

☆　☆　☆

AMERICA WAS SCHOOLMASTERS

America was forests,
America was grain,
Wheat from dawn to sunset,
And rainbows trailing rain.

America was beavers,
Buffalo in seas,
Cornsilk and the johnnycake,
Songs of scythes and bees.

America was brown men
With eyes full of the sun,
But America was schoolmasters,
Tall one by lonely one.

They hewed oak, carried water,
Their hands were knuckleboned,
They piled on loads of syntax
Till the small boys groaned.

They taught girls such manners
As stiffened them for life,
But made many a fine speller,
Good mother and good wife.

They took small wiry children,
Wild as panther-cats,
And turned them into reasoning,
Sunny democrats.

They caught a nation eager,
They caught a nation young,
They taught the nation fairness,
Thrift, and the golden tongue.

They started at the bottom
And built up strong and sweet,
They shaped our minds and morals
With switches on the seat!

ROBERT P. TRISTRAM COFFIN

172

The truest glory of our forefathers is in that system of public instruction, which they instituted by law, and to which New England owes more of its character, its distinction, and its prosperity, than to all other causes.

JOSEPH STORY

☆   ☆   ☆

AMERICA'S SCHOOLMASTER

A woman's prayers, overheard in a lonely forest, launched the career of one of America's foremost educators, William Holmes McGuffey. While riding along a trail in 1818, the Reverend Thomas Hughes, a prominent pioneer, heard a woman praying that her children might receive an education. As a result of his investigation he arranged to have her stepson, William McGuffey, attend the Old Stone Academy in Darlington, Pa. Though the family considered this episode a miracle, in later years McGuffey himself used to remark that his practical stepmother probably timed her prayer to be heard both by the Almighty and his earthly representative.

Born on the Pennsylvania frontier in 1800, McGuffey as a boy received only rudimentary education. Even at the academy his home duties prevented full-time attendance but he memorized his lessons and recited them aloud while at his chores.

After working his way through Washington College and teaching summers, McGuffey became a professor at Miami University in Oxford, Ohio. Here in 1833 he and his wife moved into their new home (now owned by Miami University) where the idea was born for the readers which made his name a household word. Here, with his own and neighbors' children, he tested his theories of education, often holding classes outdoors with pupils seated on logs. His highly successful series of readers incorporating his teaching methods proved far superior to ear-

lier textbooks not only in their carefully graded material but in the use of numerous illustrations which appeared in later editions.

A striking figure in his black bombazine suit and stovepipe hat, McGuffey was an unforgettable teacher and his readers had untold influence on the mental and moral development of generations of schoolchildren.

RICHARD L. DOYLE

☆   ☆   ☆

THE MC GUFFEY READERS

The Readers went west in freight wagons and with emigrant caravans; traders packed them into Indian reservations; they turned up in sod schoolhouses on the prairie, in cow towns on the plains, and mining camps in the Rockies and the Sierras. Between 1870 and 1890 the series sold sixty million copies. They were the basic schoolbooks in 37 states. Except for New England, where they never got started, the McGuffey Readers blanketed the nation.

Fifteen sets of school readers were published in America between 1820 and 1841, but for some reason the McGuffey series ran away with the race.

Perhaps the clue is in the first lesson—A is for Ax. While children learned those letters the ax was ringing in every clearing, it was hewing logs for cabins and schoolhouses, it was changing the mid-continent. Thud, thud, thud—in the sound of the ax the future of America was beating like a pulse. The picture showed a boy not as tall as the ax helve leaning against a stump. It was a real ax, from the child's real world, the roughhewn, hopeful, equalitarian world of the Jacksonian West. After ax came box, cat, and dog; nut, ox, and pig; vine, wren, and yoke—all homely, familiar things. The lessons were alive with children at work, at play, at school: boys with hoops, kites, skates; girls with dolls, sleds, and jumping ropes. Reading could be fun.

WALTER HAVIGHURST

☆ ☆ ☆

Education's real challenge is to produce men and women who know how to think; and knowing how, do it; and having done it, voice their opinions.

HENRY T. HEALD

☆ ☆ ☆

EDUCATION FOR ALL AMERICAN YOUTH

1. Equip every youth educationally to enter an occupation suited to his abilities and offering reasonable opportunity for personal growth and social usefulness.

2. Prepare him to assume the full responsibilities of American citizenship.

3. Give him a fair chance to exercise his right to the pursuit of happiness.

4. Stimulate intellectual curiosity, engender satisfaction in intellectual achievement, and cultivate the ability to think rationally.

5. Help him to develop an appreciation of the ethical values which underlie life in a democratic society.

HARRY JAMES CARMAN

☆ ☆ ☆

Education is the result of contact. A great people is produced by contact with great minds.

CALVIN COOLIDGE

☆ ☆ ☆

SAFEGUARD OF LIBERTY

Education is a better safeguard of liberty than a standing army.

EDWARD EVERETT

☆ ☆ ☆

The public school is at once the symbol of our democracy and the most pervasive means for promoting our common destiny.

FELIX FRANKFURTER

☆ ☆ ☆

FREEDOM'S FRONTIER

The classroom—not the trench—is the frontier of freedom now and forevermore.

LYNDON B. JOHNSON

☆ ☆ ☆

EDUCATION FOR SURVIVAL

Fortunately or otherwise, we live at a time when the average individual has to know several times as much in order to keep informed as he did only thirty or forty years ago. Being "educated" today requires not only more than a superficial knowledge of the arts and sciences, but a sense of interrelationship such as is taught in few schools. Finally, being "educated" today, in terms of the larger needs, means preparation for world citizenship; in short, education for survival.

NORMAN COUSINS

☆ ☆ ☆

WHAT VITAL EDUCATION MEANS

Let us be honest with youth and tell them there is no magic formula of education for war or peace, no fruit of the tree of knowledge which, swiftly eaten, can make us wise as gods, knowing good and evil.

Even in these critical days, when educated persons are so desperately needed, the process of education requires time and work and striving.

The ability to think straight, some knowledge of the past, some vision of the future, some skill in useful service, some urge to fit that service into the wellbeing of the community—these are the most vital things education must try to produce.

If we can achieve them in the citizens of our land, then, given the right to knowledge and the free use thereof, we shall have brought to America the wisdom and the courage to match her destiny.

VIRGINIA C. GILDERSLEEVE

☆ ☆ ☆

COLLEGE MOTTOES

Veritas (Truth).

HARVARD UNIVERSITY (1636)

Lux et veritas (Light and truth).

YALE UNIVERSITY (1701)

Veritas et utilitas (Truth and usefulness).

HOWARD UNIVERSITY (1867)

Lux sit (Let there be light).

UNIVERSITY OF WASHINGTON (1861)

Gratia et veritas (Thankfulness and truth).

GOUCHER COLLEGE (1885)

Hope.

UNIVERSITY OF RHODE ISLAND (1892)

Quaecumque sunt vera (In any circumstances they are true).

NORTHWESTERN UNIVERSITY (1851)

Spiritus est qui vivificat (It is the Spirit that gives life).

DUQUESNE UNIVERSITY (1878)

In Deo speramus (In God we trust).

BROWN UNIVERSITY (1764)

Leges sine moribus vanae (Law without character is useless).

UNIVERSITY OF PENNSYLVANIA (1740)

Terras irradient (They illuminate the lands).

AMHERST COLLEGE (1821)

Dei sub numine viget (Under God's power she flourishes).

PRINCETON UNIVERSITY (1746)

☆ ☆ ☆

UNDERGIRDING

I have tried to suggest that freedom is the real goal of education, but that it will not be won without an undergirding of religious experience.

NATHAN M. PUSEY

☆ ☆ ☆

REFLECTION

In a democracy, the state and its schools can never do much more than reflect the spiritual climate of the community at large.

WINTHROP S. HUDSON

☆ ☆ ☆

GOAL

The goal of education is not the pursuit of knowledge for the glorification of the mind, but for the purification of the heart.

BERNARD MANDELBAUM

☆ ☆ ☆

CITIZEN'S OPPORTUNITY

The traditional American faith in the necessity of mass education, without regard to inherited privilege or opportunity, is the point of origin of the land-grant institutions. The founders of the Republic were convinced from the beginning that education should be broadened to reach all the people. Only by doing this could every citizen be provided with the opportunity to make the most of his natural talents. Education restricted to a privileged few meant perpetuating a permanent restriction upon the freedom of the individual to seek that equality which a democratic society had promised him.

MILTON S. EISENHOWER

☆ ☆ ☆

Schoolhouses are the republican line of fortifications.

HORACE MANN

☆ ☆ ☆

CHANGE AND VISION

A democracy cannot stay alive if the people in it do not urge change when change is necessary; it cannot grow unless the people have vision. Therefore, reformers, prophets, poets, and protest groups belong to the democratic way of life.

LILLIAN SMITH

☆　☆　☆

TEST OF TRUTH

When men have realized that time has upset many fighting beliefs, they may come to believe, even more than they believe the very foundations of their own conduct, that the ultimate good desired is better reached by free trade in ideas—that the best test of truth is the power of truth to get itself accepted in the market, and that truth is the only ground upon which their wishes can be carried out. That, at any rate, is the theory of our Constitution. It is an experiment, as all life is an experiment.

OLIVER WENDELL HOLMES, JR.

☆　☆　☆

PRINCIPLE

The only safe principle upon which a free America can keep its freedom is that of the free and open market in ideas.

MORRIS ERNST

☆　☆　☆

TIRELESS CRITIC

Education is society's servant but also her tireless critic, for no civilization is ever worthy of worship.

Values of crucial importance for human beings are always getting lost, or getting obscured and undervalued, in the workaday world.

A complete education has a responsibility to do more than "serve society." It has to save us from ourselves.

NATHAN M. PUSEY

☆　☆　☆

We need an America with the wisdom of experience. But we must not let America grow old in spirit.

HUBERT H. HUMPHREY

☆　☆　☆

TRIBUTE TO A TEACHER

A pine bench, with Mark Hopkins at one end of it and me at the other, is a good enough college for me.

JAMES A. GARFIELD

☆　☆　☆

AMERICA'S TEACHERS

No assembly of people, whether scientists, spacemen, or statesmen could be more impressive or important than the members of America's teaching profession, for no group wields greater power and influence over the future than you. Every pupil you have carries in his mind or heart or conscience a bit of you. Your influence, your example, your ideas and values keep marching on—how far into the future and into what realms of our spacious universe you will never know.

MARGARET E. JENKINS

☆　☆　☆

What is the business of education, but to fit men to accomplish their duties and their destiny?

JOSEPH STORY

☆　☆　☆

Education is a kind of continuing dialogue, and a dialogue assumes, in the nature of the case, different points of view.

ROBERT M. HUTCHINS

☆　☆　☆

To be an American is of itself almost a moral condition, an education, and a career.

GEORGE SANTAYANA

☆ ☆ ☆

A child's education should begin at least one hundred years before he is born.

OLIVER WENDELL HOLMES

☆ ☆ ☆

ENTRANCE
The classroom should be an entrance to the world, not an escape from it.

JOHN CIARDI

☆ ☆ ☆

PRAYER OF A BEGINNING TEACHER
Dear God, I humbly pray
  That thou, with each passing day
  Wilt give me courage, wisdom true,
To meet each problem, see it through—
  With wisdom and justice to teach each child
  To recognize the things worthwhile.
Help me to start them on the way
  To clean, brave living—day by day,
  So that tomorrow for each one
  Will be met squarely—and be won—
And as I help each little child
  To learn to love the things worthwhile,
  Lord, help me to be true;
  For I am just beginning, too.

OUIDA SMITH DUNNAM

☆ ☆ ☆

Education is both a personal interest and a national asset. For education enlarges life, not only for each of us as a person, but also for all of us as a nation.

MARION B. FOLSOM

☆ ☆ ☆

The great end of education is to discipline rather than to furnish the mind; to train it to the use of its own powers rather than fill it with the accumulations of others.

JONATHAN EDWARDS

☆ ☆ ☆

WORK OF THE UNIVERSITY
A great university has two special functions. The first is to produce a small number of scholars of the highest rank, a small number of men who, in science and literature, or in art, will do productive work of the first class. The second is to send out into the world a very large number of men who could never achieve and who ought not to try to achieve such a position in the field of scholarship, but whose energies are to be felt in every other form of activity; and who should go out from our doors with the balanced development of body, of mind, and above all, of character, which shall fit them to do work both honorable and efficient.

THEODORE ROOSEVELT

☆ ☆ ☆

FORTRESSES
Glory we owe in no small part to the all-embracing influence of our colleges and universities. They have wrought mightily in the making of America. They stand like mighty fortresses within whose protection the truth is secure.

CALVIN COOLIDGE

☆ ☆ ☆

ALMA MATER
What a man ought never to forget with regard to a college is that it is a nursery of principle and of honor.

WOODROW WILSON

☆ ☆ ☆

GREATEST DISCOVERY
The Common School is the greatest discovery ever made by man.

It is supereminent in its universality and in the timeliness of the aid it offers.

The Common School can train up children in the elements of all good knowledge and of virtue.

HORACE MANN

XVI

THERE WAS A CHILD
WENT FORTH

☆ ☆ ☆

My story is only a story of the chance in life which
America brings to all boys and girls.

HERBERT HOOVER

AMERICA'S RESOURCE

Our most important resource for the future is today's youth. I am filled with admiration for many of our young people, but I believe earnestly that we all need to do careful thinking about the kind of training our boys and girls are getting in such things as patriotism, morals, ideals, personal health, the value of hard work, pride in a job well done. Is our generation doing the things that alone can give our children and grandchildren a deep appreciation of these special values?

DWIGHT D. EISENHOWER

☆ ☆ ☆

THE AMERICAN BOY

What we have a right to expect of the American boy is that he shall turn out to be a good American man.

The boy can best become a good man by being a good boy—not a goody-goody boy, but just a plain good boy.

I do not mean that he must love only the negative virtues; I mean that he must love the positive virtues also. "Good," in the largest sense, should include whatever is fine, straightforward, clean, brave and manly.

The best boys I know—the best men I know—are good at their studies or their business, fearless and stalwart, hated and feared by all that is wicked and depraved, incapable of submitting to wrongdoing, and equally incapable of being aught but tender to the weak and helpless.

Of course the effect that a thoroughly manly, thoroughly straight and upright boy can have upon the companions of his own age, and upon those who are younger, is incalculable.

If he is not thoroughly manly, then they will not respect him, and his good qualities will count for but little; while, of course, if he is mean, cruel, or wicked, then his physical strength and force of mind merely make him so much the more objectionable a member of society.

He can not do good work if he is not strong and does not try with his whole heart and soul to count in any contest; and his strength will be a curse to himself and to every one else if he does not have a thorough command over himself and over his own evil passions, and if he does not use his strength on the side of decency, justice and fair dealing.

In short, in life, as in a football game, the principle to follow is: Hit the line hard: don't foul and don't shirk, but hit the line hard.

THEODORE ROOSEVELT

☆ ☆ ☆

POSSIBILITIES

Democracy is based upon the conviction that there are extraordinary possibilities in ordinary people.

HARRY EMERSON FOSDICK

☆ ☆ ☆

LETTER TO THOMAS JEFFERSON SMITH

Your affectionate and excellent father has requested that I would address to you something which might possibly have a favourable influence on the course of life you have to run, and I, too, as a namesake, feel an interest in that course.

Few words will be necessary, with good dispositions on your part.

Adore God. Reverence and cherish your parents. Love your neighbour as yourself, and your country more than yourself. Be just. Be true. Murmur not at the ways of Providence. So shall the life into which you have entered be the portal to one of eternal and ineffable bliss. And if to the dead it is permitted to care for the things of this world, every action of your life will be under my regard. Farewell.

THOMAS JEFFERSON

☆ ☆ ☆

From THERE WAS A CHILD WENT FORTH

There was a child went forth every day,
And the first object he look'd upon, that
   object he became,
And that object became part of him for the
   day or a certain part of the day,
Or for many years or stretching cycles of
   years.

The early lilacs became part of this child,
And grass and white and red morning-
   glories, and white and red clover, and the
   song of the phoebe-bird,
And the Third-month lambs and the sow's
   pink-faint litter, and the mare's foal and
   the cow's calf,
And the noisy brood of the barnyard or by
   the mire of the pond-side,
And the fish suspending themselves so
   curiously below there, and the beautiful
   curious liquid,
And the water-plants with their graceful flat
   heads, all became part of him.

The field-sprouts of Fourth-month and Fifth-
   month became part of him,
Winter-grain sprouts and those of the light-
   yellow corn, and the esculent roots of the
   garden,
And the apple-trees cover'd with blossoms
   and the fruit afterward, and wood-berries,
   and the commonest weeds by the road . . . .
And the schoolmistress that pass'd on her
   way to the school,
And the friendly boys that pass'd, and the
   quarrelsome boys,
And the tidy and fresh-cheek'd girls, and the
   barefoot Negro boy and girl,
And all the changes of city and country wherever he went.

WALT WHITMAN

☆ ☆ ☆

YOUNG GEORGE WASHINGTON WOULD NOT TELL A LIE

"George," said his father, "do you know who killed that beautiful little cherry tree yonder in the garden?"

This was a tough question; and George staggered under it for a moment: but quickly recovered himself: and looking at his father, with the sweet face of youth brightened with the inexpressible charm of all-conquering truth, he bravely cried out, "I can't tell a lie, Pa; you know I can't tell a lie. I did cut it with my hatchet."

"Run to my arms, you dearest boy," cried his father in transports, "run to my arms; glad am I, George, that you killed my tree; for you have paid me for it a thousand fold."

PARSON WEEMS

☆ ☆ ☆

BORN IN AMERICA

The beauty of democracy is that you never can tell when a youngster is born what he is going to do with you, and that, no matter how humbly he is born, he has got a chance to master the minds and lead the imaginations of the whole country.

WOODROW WILSON

☆ ☆ ☆

APPRAISAL AT TWENTY-THREE

If John Kennedy is characteristic of the younger generation—and I believe he is—many of us would be happy to have the destinies of this Republic handed over to his generation at once.

HENRY R. LUCE

☆ ☆ ☆

TWO JOBS

A boy has two jobs. One is just being a boy. The other is growing up to be a man.

HERBERT HOOVER

☆ ☆ ☆

182

PLEDGE OF THE 4-H CLUBS

I pledge:

My Head to clear thinking.

My Heart to great loyalty.

My Hands to larger service.

My Health to better living.

For my club, my community, and my country.

☆　☆　☆

THE BOYS' CLUB CODE

I believe in God and the right to worship according to my own faith and religion.

I believe in America and the American way of life . . . in the Constitution and the Bill of Rights.

I believe in fair play, honesty, and sportsmanship.

I believe in my Boys' Club which stands for these things.

☆　☆　☆

THE CUB SCOUT PROMISE

I promise to do my best

to do my duty to God

and my country,

to be square

and obey the Law of the Pack.

☆　☆　☆

THE BOY SCOUT OATH

On my honor, I will do my best:

To do my duty to God and my country, and to obey the Scout Law.

To help other people at all times.

To keep myself physically strong, mentally awake, and morally straight.

☆　☆　☆

THE GIRL SCOUT PROMISE

On my honor, I will try:

To do my duty to God and my country.

To help other people at all times.

To obey the Girl Scout Laws.

☆　☆　☆

FIFTH OF JULY PARADE

She hears drums marching down the street
With Sousa music in their beat;
The slender trombones stepping high,
Are sliding notes into the sky.

She cannot watch parades dry-eyed,
As this one struts in conscious pride
With pie tin drums that come from home,
And tissue paper on a comb!

RALPH W. SEAGER

☆　☆　☆

There is nothing so fine as to be twenty-one and an American. One is for a fleeting instant—and the other is forever. So live—decently, fearlessly, joyously—and don't forget that in the long run it is not the years in your life but the life in your years that counts!

ADLAI E. STEVENSON

☆　☆　☆

PRICELESS GIFT

You who have the priceless gift of youth must and can revivify the spirit of our country. Never has the earnest young man or woman lived in a time richer in possibilities, in invitations to high emprise. If you will take it so, the twilight of our time is the morning and not the evening twilight. It is the lark and not the nightingale that you are hearing.

CHRISTIAN GAUSS

☆　☆　☆

The lives of our great men belong to the country. If facts are told showing that they had weaknesses which they overcame, the force of their successful example is greater to lift the youth of the country up to emulate them than if they are painted as perfect without temptation and without weakness.

WILLIAM HOWARD TAFT

☆ ☆ ☆

MESSAGE TO YOUNG AMERICA

Girls and boys of America, you are the hope of the world!

Not men and women of America, not even young men and young women of America, but girls and boys! You who carry the un-blunted swords of ten-to-seventeen, you are the ones who are the hope of the world. Not to die for the world, but to live for it, to think for it, to work for it; to keep sharp and un-stained by rust the splendid sword of the spirit!

It is not only because you are yourselves fine and true and upright and daring and free, Young America, that the world finds its hope in you. The world knows the men, the great deeds, and the principles greater than men or deeds, that have made this America of yours and mine. The world knows that in you, whether your ancestors came over in the *Mayflower* three hundred years ago, or in the steerage of a liner twenty years ago, lives the spirit of a great tradition. The world puts its hope in you, but not only in you. It puts its hope in the great ghosts that stand behind you, upholding your arms, whispering wisdom to you, patience, perseverance, cour-age, crying, "Go on, Young America! We back you up!" Washington, first of all! And around him, Putnam, Warren, Hancock, Samuel Adams, John Adams, Hamilton, Jef-ferson, Marshall, Greene, Stark! You re-member Stark? Stark held the rail fence at Bunker Hill. Morris going from house to house, collecting dollars for the starved Con-tinentals; Ben Franklin, in France, fighting to win friends for the new nation! They are be-hind you! And there is Marion with his men living in the wilderness like Robin Hood in Sherwood.

Look behind you, Young America!

Bainbridge, Preble, Decatur!

Hull of the *Constitution* which whipped the *Guerrière*; Perry of Lake Erie; McDonough of Lake Champlain, gallant men all, stand be-hind you. Jackson is there; Jackson who whipped the troops that whipped Napoleon; that sturdy fighter for free speech, who died with his boots on in the halls of Congress —John Quincy Adams—is behind you!

Union, one and indissoluble!

You remember? Webster said that. Web-ster is behind you. Clay is behind you! Rogers and Clark are behind you, Fremont, Daniel Boone, Kit Carson, Sam Houston, Davy Crockett. You remember? The frontiersmen, the Indian fighters, the pioneers are behind you, dauntless of spirit; the colonists of Vir-ginia, Massachusetts, Connecticut, the new Netherlands, the Carolinas; the settlers in wild lands, pressing westward to Ohio, to Illi-nois, to Kansas, to California, men and women, unafraid, clear-eyed; the brave builders of the West are behind you, Young America, upholding your hands! It is a great army of ghosts, Young America, that stands back of you! And there, Sherman, Sheridan, Meade, Thomas, Farragut, Grant, silent, te-nacious, magnanimous! Stonewall Jackson, Stuart, Lee! And in the midst of them, the greatest of all, Lincoln, with his hand on your shoulder, Young America, saying, "Sonny, I'm with you. Go on!"

There's Patrick Henry! Can't you hear his words echoing down the dark places? "Is life so dear, or peace so sweet as to be purchased at the price of slavery?" Glorious ghost! Thank God, we have proved at last that we have not forgotten him!

Heroes all, Young America, as far as the eye can reach! And beyond them, into the gray distance, the heroes without name—in war, the soldiers, the sailors, the nurses, the women who waited at home; in peace, the school-teachers, the scientists, the parsons, the physicians, the workers in slums; the fighters everywhere for justice, for truth, for light; for clean cities, clean business, clean government!

HERMANN HAGEDORN

184

☆ ☆ ☆

Children are our most valuable natural resource.

HERBERT HOOVER

☆ ☆ ☆

From MY LOST YOUTH

Often I think of the beautiful town
That is seated by the sea;
Often in thoughts go up and down
The pleasant streets of that dear old town,
And my youth comes back to me.
And a verse of Lapland song
Is haunting my memory still:
"A boy's will is the wind's will,
And the thoughts of youth are long, long
  thoughts."

HENRY WADSWORTH LONGFELLOW

☆ ☆ ☆

CHALLENGE TO BOSTON YOUTH

As the boy goes on his errand he shall say, "To such duty I, too, am born. I am God's messenger."

As the young man tells the story to his sweetheart, he shall say, "We are God's children also, you and I, and we have our duties."

They look backward, only to look forward.

"God needs me, that this city may still stand in the forefront of his people's land. Here am I. God may draft me for some special duty, as he drafted Warren and Franklin. Present! Ready for service! Thank God I come from men who are not afraid in battle. Thank God, I am born from women whose walk was close to him. Thank God, I am his son."

And she shall say, "I am his daughter."

He has nations to call to his service. "Here am I."

He has causeways to build, for the march forward of his people. "Here am I."

There are torrents to bridge, highways in deserts. "Here am I."

He has oceans to cross. He has the hungry world to feed. He has the wilderness to clothe in beauty. "Here am I."

God of heaven, be with us as thou wert with the fathers.

God of heaven, we will be with thee, as the fathers were.

Boys and girls, young men and maidens, listen to the voices which speak here.

EDWARD EVERETT HALE (1897)

☆ ☆ ☆

One laugh of a child will make the holiest day more sacred still.

ROBERT G. INGERSOLL

☆ ☆ ☆

FIRST THANKSGIVING OF ALL

Peace and Mercy and Jonathan,
And Patience (very small),
Stood by the table giving thanks
The first Thanksgiving of all.
There was very little for them to eat,
Nothing special and nothing sweet;
Only bread and a little broth,
And a bit of fruit (and no tablecloth);
But Peace and Mercy and Jonathan
And Patience, in a row,
Stood up and asked a blessing on
Thanksgiving, long ago.
Thankful they were their ship had come
Safely across the sea;
Thankful they were for hearth and home,
And kin and company;
They were glad of broth to go with their
  bread,
Glad their apples were round and red,
Glad of mayflowers they would bring
Out of the woods again next spring.
So Peace and Mercy and Jonathan,
And Patience (very small),
Stood up gratefully giving thanks
The first Thanksgiving of all.

NANCY BYRD TURNER

☆ ☆ ☆

186

CIRCUS PARADE

At the turn of the century, America was witness to the full flowering of a unique art form, the art of the American circus.

Created by artisans trained in the European craft traditions, the carvings, banners, and posters of the American circus once constituted an exciting and homogeneous whole. The carvings in particular represented a level of creativity easily equal to the cigar store Indians and ships' figureheads.

From the very beginning, canny entrepreneurs realized that the necessity of taking their circus wagons through a town on the way to the fairgrounds could be turned into a virtue. Out of this necessity came the parade, small at first, but gradually growing in magnitude, until at the turn of the century one advertisement was able to boast:

"A million dollar free street parade, numbering four hundred horses, military bands, chimes of the cathedral organ, uncaged wild beasts, children's fairyland parade, happy childhood's sweetest dreams represented on beautiful floats driven by fifty Shetland ponies, moving under the iridescent sheen of a thousand shimmering banners, comprising a vision of beauty as varied as the stars and more gorgeous than the spectacle of the Caesars."

AMERICAN HERITAGE

☆　　☆　　☆

Sports constantly make demands on the participant for top performance, and they develop integrity, self-reliance, and initiative. They teach you a lot about working in groups, without being unduly submerged in the group.

BYRON R. WHITE

☆　　☆　　☆

If youth be a defect, it is one that we outgrow only too soon.

JAMES RUSSELL LOWELL

☆　　☆　　☆

P. T. BARNUM, AMERICA'S SHOWMAN, ADVERTISES HIS AMERICAN MUSEUM

After months of unwearied labor and spending

NEARLY TEN THOUSAND DOLLARS

NEARLY TEN THOUSAND DOLLARS

NEARLY TEN THOUSAND DOLLARS

in capturing and transporting them from that part of the Gulf of St. Lawrence nearest Labrador, the manager is entitled to offer his visitors

TWO LIVING WHALES

TWO LIVING WHALES

TWO LIVING WHALES

TWO LIVING WHALES

a male and a female. Everybody has read of whales

IN NURSERY TALES AND SAILOR'S YARNS

IN NURSERY TALES AND SAILOR'S YARNS

everybody has read of whales in story, song and history, and everybody

WANTS TO SEE A WHALE

WANTS TO SEE A WHALE

WANTS TO SEE A WHALE

and now they have the opportunity. Barnum has

CAPTURED TWO OF THE LEVIATHANS

CAPTURED TWO OF THE LEVIATHANS

CAPTURED TWO OF THE LEVIATHANS

has built a small ocean in his museum, filled it from the briny deep, and there

THE TWO LIVING WHALES

THE TWO LIVING WHALES

THE TWO LIVING WHALES

THE TWO LIVING WHALES

measuring respectively fifteen and twenty feet in length, may be seen at all hours sporting in their native element. Who will miss the opportunity of seeing them? Another may not offer in a lifetime. Embrace this ere it is too late.

☆　☆　☆

Whoever wants to know the heart and mind of America had better learn baseball, the rules and realities of the game, and do it by watching first some high school or small-town teams.

JACQUES BARZUN

☆　☆　☆

LAST WORDS TO HER FOURTEEN-YEAR-OLD SON

Andrew, if I should not see you again, I wish you to remember and treasure up some things I have already said to you.

In this world you will have to make your own way.

To do that you must have friends.

You can make friends by being honest and you can keep them by being steadfast.

You must keep in mind that friends worth having will in the long run expect as much from you as they give to you.

To forget an obligation or be ungrateful for a kindness is a base crime, not merely a fault or a sin, but an actual crime. Men guilty of it sooner or later must suffer the penalty.

In personal conduct be always polite but never obsequious.

None will respect you more than you respect yourself.

Avoid quarrels as long as you can without yielding to imposition. But sustain your manhood always.

Never bring a suit in law for assault and battery or for defamation. The law affords no remedy for such outrages that can satisfy the feelings of a true man.

Never wound the feelings of others. Never brook wanton outrage upon your own feelings.

If you ever have to vindicate your feelings or defend your honor, do it calmly. If angry at first, wait till your wrath cools before you proceed.

ELIZABETH HUTCHINSON JACKSON
MOTHER OF ANDREW JACKSON

☆　☆　☆

WHAT I WANT MY CHILDREN TO REMEMBER ABOUT HOME

That their father and mother loved each other.

That our home was a happy one because we all worked to keep it so.

That each child was given every possible opportunity to develop his own personality.

That each child's personal possessions were inviolable if kept in the place allotted to them.

That the books in the house were to be read if handled rightly, and there were no shelves under lock and key because of questionable contents.

That absolute truth abided there; no earnest questioner, however young, was put off with subterfuge or evasion.

That we believed in hospitality, in spite of any extra labor involved, and that our friends loved to come to us.

That Sunday was the happiest day of the week, and that we all looked forward to its coming because it was the day when we went to church together, then came home for an afternoon with father in the midst.

That though father and mother worked hard and long at their respective jobs, they found time every day to keep informed on current events, to read good books, to think through to logical conclusions, and to pray.

OPEN-CHURCH FOUNDATION

XVII

SO LONG AS THERE
ARE HOMES

☆　☆　☆

As much as I converse with sages and heroes, they have very little of my love and admiration. I long for rural and domestic scenes, for the warbling of birds and the prattling of my children.

JOHN ADAMS

From LAND HO!

Round the hearth-stone of home, in the land
   of our birth,
The holiest spot on the face of the earth.

GEORGE POPE MORRIS

☆   ☆   ☆

PIONEER HOMES

Our pioneer homes made our nation great.
They were places of industry, piety, and
democracy. The barn or wagonshed, for the
men and boys, and the kitchen for women
and girls, provided centers of industry. The
home was a sanctuary in which the family
became a congregation regularly honoring
the word of God and worshiping the eternal
Lord of Life. The dining-table and the fireside assembly were arenas of political
discussion—the prep schools of democracy.
The father was prophet, priest and
king—prophet in teaching the word of truth,
priest in leading his family in many a religious exercise, and king because he enforced
the moral law. And the home was linked to
the Church by the institution of the family
pew.

EDWARD L. R. ELSON

☆   ☆   ☆

LOG CABIN PRESIDENTS

Seven presidents were born in log cabins:

Andrew Jackson in the Waxhaw Settlement, New Lancaster County, South Carolina, on March 15, 1767.

Martin Van Buren at Kinderhook, Columbia County, New York, on December 5,
1782.

Abraham Lincoln near Hodgenville,
Hardin (Larue) County, Kentucky, on February 12, 1809.

Andrew Johnson at Raleigh, North Carolina, on December 29, 1808.

Ulysses S. Grant at Point Pleasant, Cler-
mont County, Ohio, on April 27, 1822.

James A. Garfield at Orange, Cuyahoga

County, Ohio, on November 19, 1831.

Benjamin Harrison at North Bend, Hamilton County, Ohio, on August 20, 1833.

☆   ☆   ☆

THE PIONEER MOTHER

Upon the jolting wagonseat she rode
Across the trackless prairie to the west,
Or trudged beside the oxen with a goad,
A sleeping child clasped tightly to her breast.
Frail flesh rebelling, but spirit never—
What tales the dark could tell of women's
   tears!—
Her bravery incentive to endeavor;
Her laughter spurring strong men past their
   fears.
O to her valor and comeliness
A commonwealth today owes its white domes
Of state, its fields, its highways, and its
   homes;
Its cities wrested from the wilderness,
And bends in memory above the hand
That gentled, woman-wise, a savage land.

ETHEL ROMIG FULLER

·   ☆   ☆   ☆

By profession I am a soldier and take pride in
that fact. But I am prouder, infinitely
prouder, to be a father.

DOUGLAS MAC ARTHUR

☆   ☆   ☆

We want an America of homes, illumined
with hope and happiness, where mothers,
freed from the necessity for long hours of toil
beyond their own doors, may preside as befits
the hearthstone of American citizenship. We
want the cradle of American childhood
rocked under conditions so wholesome and
so hopeful that no blight may touch it in its
development, and we want to provide that no
selfish interest, no material necessity, no lack
of opportunity shall prevent the gaining of
that education so essential to best citizenship.

WARREN G. HARDING

☆ ☆ ☆

INSCRIPTION

On the banks of the James River, a husband erected a tombstone in memory of his wife, one of those one hundred maidens who had come to Virginia in 1619 to marry the lonely settlers. The stone bore this legend:

SHE TOUCHED THE SOIL OF VIRGINIA

WITH HER LITTLE FOOT

AND THE WILDERNESS BECAME A HOME

EUDORA RAMSAY RICHARDSON

☆ ☆ ☆

HARTFORD IN 1868

Of all the beautiful towns it has been my fortune to see this is the chief. It is a city of 40,000 inhabitants, and seems to be composed almost entirely of dwelling houses—not shingle-shaped affairs, stood on end and packed together like a "deck" of cards, but massive private hotels, scattered along the broad, straight streets, from fifty all the way up to two hundred yards apart.

Each house sits in the midst of about an acre of green grass, or flower beds or ornamental shrubbery, guarded on all sides by the trimmed hedges of arborvitae, and by files of huge forest trees that cast a shadow like a thunder-cloud. Some of these stately dwellings are almost buried from sight in parks and forests of these noble trees.

Everywhere the eye turns it is blessed with a vision of refreshing green. You do not know what beauty is if you have not been here.

MARK TWAIN

☆ ☆ ☆

LETTER TO HIS WIFE

I am blessed above my kind, with another self—a life companion who is part of me—part of my heart and flesh and spirit—and not a fellow pilgrim who lags far behind, or flies ahead, or soars above me.

Side by side, my darling, we walk the ways of life; and the ray of light that falls upon the one illumines the face of the other; the cloud that darkens the hope of one casts its sable shadow upon the other; and the storms that come will beat upon no single head but both will feel their might and brave their desolation.

MARK TWAIN

☆ ☆ ☆

No nation can be destroyed while it possesses a good home life.

JOSIAH GILBERT HOLLAND

☆ ☆ ☆

The home is the most vital social unit in any democracy. It influences the actions of all society. But goodness must not only be cultivated in the home, it must be carried forth beyond its doors.

JAMES KELLER

☆ ☆ ☆

GOOD OLD DAYS

Things have changed greatly and still are changing, can they change much more? Can you think of any more improvements? My father liked his fireplace the same as I like my old iron stove, and now they have the gas and electric ranges, but I would not be surprised, when the younger generation gets old, when people of coming generations, a hundred years from now, will look back upon us as primitives.

And yet I wonder sometimes whether we are progressing. In my childhood days life was different, in many ways, we were slower, still we had a good and happy life, I think, people enjoyed more in their way, at least they seemed to be happier, they don't take time to be happy nowadays.

GRANDMA MOSES

☆ ☆ ☆

MAIN STREET

As the Nineteenth Century turned slowly into its final quarter, the life most New Englanders knew was that of the small town or the farm. In their land of long winters, the most precious time was summer when the smells, the sounds, and silences of nature were all the more acute for being crowded into so brief a span. All the world had an early-morning freshness, school was out, and ahead of every child there stretched the limitless vista of summer.

Beneath the shading elms and maples of Main Street were white houses in perverse alignment and behind them big, comfortable yards sprinkled with apple trees and honeysuckle, weathered sheds, and squeaky rope swings that lifted a child high above the vegetable patch to command, for an instant, the hills and woods beyond. Out in the meadows, insects droned their course from daisy to black-eyed Susan and boys tramped through tall grass toward still, secret pools where the big trout lay. Here and on the hilltops, where little ginghamed girls swung through forgotten clearings, looking for blueberries, only the far-off note of the dinner horn was a link with reality.

This was a world of wagons and green apples, of lemonade in tall, cool, earthenware crocks, of chicken sounds and cowbells, and dogs who wandered into church to scratch and be snickered at. There was time to laze on the warm earth, smelling the grass smell, wondering if a real agate marble was worth the trade of a jackknife with a broken blade or if the blackberry pie was for supper.

RICHARD M. KETCHUM

☆　☆　☆

DOMESTIC HEROISM

More heroism has been displayed in the household and the closet than in the most memorable battlefields of history.

HENRY WARD BEECHER

☆　☆　☆

EPITAPH FOR REBECCA JONES

Devoted Christian mother who whipped Sherman's bummers with scalding water while trying to take her dinner pot which contained a ham bone being cooked for her soldier boys.

PLEASANT GROVE CEMETERY
RALEIGH, NORTH CAROLINA

☆　☆　☆

SOUL OF A NATION

Territory is but the body of a nation. The people who inhabit its hills and valleys are its soul, its spirit, its life.

JAMES A. GARFIELD

☆　☆　☆

TOWN BELLS

Town-hall steeple bells did not customarily strike the hours in the eighteenth century, but they did strike three daytime signals: six in the morning (when most people got up), noon, and nine in the evening for curfew.

Often curfew was followed by a "count-strike" so that people could properly date their diaries before retiring.

Calls to court, town meetings, church services, and even (in small villages) announcements of births and deaths were all part of a kind of Morse code that everybody understood.

Deaths were rung only by church bell, usually after the rising peal at six; the age of the deceased was sometimes rung too. Executions were rung from the instant the gallows did its work: the toll for a man was "three times three," and for a woman, "three times two."

Town bells also rang for emergencies like fires, and to call the people to get important news in the town square as soon as a bulletin arrived by horse and rider.

ERIC SLOANE

☆　☆　☆

AMERICAN INNS

The old saying about many an American inn, that "George Washington slept here," is not necessarily so apocryphal as we sometimes assume. His campaigns kept him constantly on the move, and wherever he found himself, there was likely to be an inn nearby. On foot, on horseback, or even in a coach, a day's journey was very short by our modern standards, and accommodations had to be available nearly everywhere. New Jersey alone, just after the Revolution, had 443 inns.

In earlier days all diversions centered there. The furnishing of food and shelter to travelers and to horses, and of liquid comfort to neighbors, was not the establishment's only function. Whatever there was of novelty in entertainment or instruction went on at the inn, and it served as the gathering place for folk on scores of duties or pleasures bent. Legal notices and governmental proclamations were posted there, newspapers were on file, mail was distributed, and the taproom was a clearing house for news. A constant panorama passed within the walls and before the doors.

The inn also served the townspeople. Indeed, its importance to its local neighbors was far greater, day in and day out, than to the occasional traveler. Inns and taverns played an important part in the political and military affairs of the colonies. Law courts sat in their public rooms, not only in small towns but in the cities. A center of events, a center of alarms, the inn in many a city and town saw some of the most dramatic acts in the colonists' struggle for independence.

RUDOLF A. CLEMEN

☆ ☆ ☆

Look well to the hearthstone; therein all hope for America lies.

CALVIN COOLIDGE

☆ ☆ ☆

PARLOR PIANO

In many an humble home throughout our land the piano has gathered about it the most sacred and tender association. . .with its music each daughter. . .touched. . .the heart of her future husband.

GROVER CLEVELAND

☆ ☆ ☆

REFASHIONING

The world is constantly being fashioned and refashioned in our homes.

LELAND FOSTER WOOD

☆ ☆ ☆

THE AUTOMOBILE QUESTION

The automobile question is becoming more and more interesting daily, and signs are not wanting that our warning of some months ago to the automobilists to be careful lest they arouse the animosity of the public by a careless attitude toward the rights of the latter was not without justification.

We had hoped that the devotees of this sport would of their own initiative impose such restrictions upon the pursuit thereof as would conduce to the public safety and their own popularity.

This they do not seem to have done, and with the multiplication of accidents in the public highways much indignation against them is accreting which before long may burst forth in an overwhelming torrent of wrath.

One correspondent offers a thousand dollars to be used in the organization of a troop of minute-men armed with rifles, who shall stand on street corners and pick off automobilists as they pass, much as the minute-men of '76 picked off the offensive redcoats of the British army.

HARPER'S WEEKLY
MAY 17, 1902

☆ ☆ ☆

Every antique farmhouse and moss-grown cottage is a picture.

WASHINGTON IRVING

✩ ✩ ✩

AMERICAN FARMERS

We are American farmers. We are Americans. We are farmers.

Our grandsires freed this virgin continent, plowed it from East to West, and gave it to us. This land is for us and for our children to make richer and more fruitful.

We grow foods, fibers—fifteen times as much as we use.

We grow men and women—farmers, Presidents, and Senators, generals of industry, captains of commerce, missionaries, builders.

Communists would call us capitalists, because we own land and we own tools.

Capitalists might choose to call us laborers, because we work with our hands.

Others may call us managers, because we direct men and manage materials.

Our children call us "Dad."

We are also deacons, stockholders, mechanics, veterinarians, electricians, school board members, Rotarians, voters, scientists, neighbors, men of good will.

Our rules are Nature's rules, the laws of God.

We command the magic of the seasons and the miracles of science, because we obey Nature's rules.

Our raw materials are soil and seed, animals, the atmosphere and the rain, and the mighty sun.

We work with brains. We toil with muscles of steel, fed by the fires of lightning and by oils from the inner earth.

We are partners with the laboratory, with the factory, and with all the people.

We provide industry with ever-renewable raw materials from the inexhaustible world of plants. We buy products from the labor of every fellow-citizen.

Our efficiencies have raised great cities and happy towns, and have given all the people meat and bread.

We believe in work and in honor
We believe in freedom.

We are grateful for the American freedom that has let us earn so many blessings.

We know that liberty is our most precious possession. At the ballot-boxes and on the battlefield we shall defend it.

We have proven a new pattern of abundance. We pray that we may also help to make a pattern for peace.

WHEELER MC MILLEN

From FARM JOURNAL

✩ ✩ ✩

HOME ON THE FARM

Life on the old farm developed qualities of frugality, industry, and fortitude. Without these qualities our family would all have starved to death. I didn't die. None of our family died under eighty. The tough ones lived to 105. We raised just about everything we consumed, and manufactured nearly everything we used. It was not, perhaps, the ideal way to live, or to bring up a family—but we made out, and I suppose in our own terms we were happy. We saw little money, and it was not for frivolous use. The marketing was done as much as possible by barter, and it was a sort of Yankee bartering that undoubtedly had a huge influence on many a trade I executed later in life.

RALPH GOULD

✩ ✩ ✩

LETTER TO HER HUSBAND JOHN REGARDING WOMEN'S RIGHTS

In the new code of laws which I suppose it will be necessary for you to make I desire you would remember the ladies and be more generous and favorable to them than your ancestors.

ABIGAIL ADAMS

★ ★ ★

EVERYBODY'S HOME TOWN

The people who reside in Washington have been sent here by their fellow countrymen: farmers, scholars, merchants, professional folk, men and women from the vast expanse that is America. Others have been drawn here by the requirements of an age of big and powerful government.

This capital is a projection of all the cities, towns, hamlets, and countryside which combine to make the United States of America.

Every citizen shares in its virtues and vices, in its successes and failures, in its triumphs and trials, its honor and dishonor, its prestige and its responsibilities.

America's ideals, standards, spiritual power and character combine to form a cultural mosaic known as Washington. In its complex character, the city is a microcosm of the United States.

EDWARD L. R. ELSON

★ ★ ★

UPON ENTERING THE WHITE HOUSE

I stood for a moment over the great brass seal, bearing the national coat of arms, which is sunk in the floor in the middle of the entrance hall. "The Seal of the President of the United States," I read around the border, and now—that meant my husband!

HELEN HERRON TAFT

★ ★ ★

LETTER TO HIS WIFE

Your sentiments of the duties we owe to our country are such as become the best of women and the best of men.

Among all the disappointments and the perplexities which have fallen to my share in life, nothing has contributed so much to support my mind as the choice blessings of a wife, whose capacity enabled her to compre-

hend, and whose pure virtue obliged her to approve, the views of her husband.

In this remote situation I am deprived in a great measure of this comfort. Yet I read and read again your charming letters, and they serve me, in some faint degree, as a substitute for the company and conversation of the writer.

I want to take a walk with you in the garden, to go over to the common, the plain, the meadow. I want to take Charles in one hand and Tom in the other, and walk with you, Abby on your right hand and John upon my left, to view the cornfields, the orchards, etc.

JOHN ADAMS

★ ★ ★

Inscribed on the mantelpiece of the fireplace in the White House state dining room:

I pray heaven to bestow
the best of blessings
on this house
and on all that shall
hereafter inhabit it.
May none but honest and wise men
ever rule under this roof.

JOHN ADAMS

★ ★ ★

ABIGAIL ADAMS

My mother was an angel upon earth. She was a minister of blessing to all human beings within her sphere of action. Her heart was the abode of heavenly purity. She had no feelings but of kindness and beneficence, yet her mind was as firm as her temper was mild and gentle. She had known sorrow, but her sorrow was silent. Had she lived to the age of the patriarchs, every day of her life would have been filled with clouds of goodness and of love.

JOHN QUINCY ADAMS

★ ★ ★

197

On September 20, 1824, John Quincy Adams wandered among the tombstones of the family burial plot at Quincy musing on the past and future of his line. "Four generations, of whom very little more is known," he wrote in his *Diary*, "than is recorded upon these stones. There are three succeeding generations of us now living. Pass another century, and we shall all be mouldering in the same dust, or resolved into the same elements. Who then of our posterity shall visit this yard? And what shall he read engraved upon the stones? This is known only to the Creator of all. The record may be longer. May it be of blameless lives!"

JAMES TRUSLOW ADAMS

☆　☆　☆

WASHINGTON'S MOTHER

The mother of Washington, in forming him for those distinguished parts he was destined to perform, first taught him the duties of obedience, the better to prepare him for those of command. In the well-ordered domicile where his early years were passed, the levity and indulgence common to youth were tempered by a deference and well-regulated restraint which, while it curtailed no rational enjoyment usual in the springtime of life, prescribed those enjoyments within the bounds of moderation and propriety.

The matron held in reserve an authority which never departed from her, not even when her son had become the most illustrious of men. It seemed to say, "I am your mother, the being who gave you life, the guide who directed your steps when they needed the guidance of age and wisdom, the parental affection which claimed your love, the parental authority which commanded your obedience; whatever may be your success, whatever your renown, next to your God you owe most to me." Nor did the chief dissent from these truths, but to the last moment of the life of his venerable parent, he yielded to

her will the most dutiful, implicit obedience, and felt for her person and character the most holy reverence and attachment.

GEORGE WASHINGTON PARKE CUSTIS

☆　☆　☆

TRIBUTE TO GRACE

From our being together we seemed naturally to come to care for each other. We became engaged in the early summer of 1905 and were married at her home in Burlington, Vermont, on October fourth of that year. I have seen so much fiction written on this subject that I may be pardoned for relating the plain facts. We thought we were made for each other. For almost a quarter of a century she has borne with my infirmities, and I have rejoiced in her graces.

CALVIN COOLIDGE

☆　☆　☆

During her twelve years as First Lady, Mrs. Franklin Delano Roosevelt became unquestionably the best-known woman in the world. She travelled hundreds of thousands of miles, talked to people at every level of society, wrote articles, spoke over the radio, held press conferences, and began a newspaper column that ran for twenty-five years. No other President's wife has played a like role in government and political affairs. Eleanor Roosevelt was the President's eyes, ears, and (some said) conscience; the greatest champion of his New Deal measures to end the Depression; his representative in a thousand places he could not reach. During World War II she went as his emissary to both European and Pacific war areas. While her critics accused her of selfish motives, her admirers thought she possessed unequalled moral courage and compassion. Her life both during and after the White House years became a great protest against poverty and injustice.

AMERICAN HERITAGE

HAWTHORNE VISITS THE WHITE HOUSE

Unquestionably, Western man though he be, and Kentuckian by birth, President Lincoln is the essential representative of all Yankees, and the veritable specimen, physically, of what the world seems determined to regard as our characteristic qualities.

It is the strangest and yet the fittest thing in the jumble of human vicissitudes, that he, out of so many millions, unlooked for, unselected by any intelligible process that could be based upon his genuine qualities, unknown to those who chose him, and unsuspected of what endowments may adapt him for his tremendous responsibility, should have found the way open for him to fling his lank personality into the chair of state, where, I presume, it was his first impulse to throw his legs on the council-table, and tell the Cabinet Ministers a story.

There is no describing his lengthy awkwardness, nor the uncouthness of his movement; and yet it seemed as if I had been in the habit of seeing him daily, and had shaken hands with him a thousand times in some village street; so true was he to the aspect of the pattern American, though with a certain extravagance which, possibly, I exaggerated still further by the delighted eagerness with which I took it in.

If put to guess his calling and livelihood, I should have taken him for a country schoolmaster as soon as anything else. He was dressed in a rusty black frock-coat and pantaloons, unbrushed, and worn so faithfully that the suit had adapted itself to the curves and angularities of his figure, and had grown to be an outer skin of the man. He had shabby slippers on his feet.

His hair was black, still unmixed with gray, stiff, somewhat bushy, and had apparently been acquainted with neither brush nor comb that morning, after the disarrangement of the pillow; and as to a night-cap, Uncle Abe probably knows nothing of such effeminacies.

His complexion is dark and sallow, betokening, I fear, an insalubrious atmosphere around the White House; he has thick black eyebrows and an impending brow; his nose is large, and the lines about his mouth are very strongly defined.

The whole physiognomy is as coarse a one as you would meet anywhere in the length and breadth of the States; but, withal, it is redeemed, illuminated, softened, and brightened by a kindly though serious look out of his eyes, and an expression of homely sagacity, that seems weighted with rich results of village experience.

A great deal of native sense; no bookish cultivation, no refinement; honest at heart, and thoroughly so, and yet, in some sort, sly—at least, endowed with a sort of tact and wisdom that are akin to craft, and would impel him, I think, to take an antagonist in flank, rather than to make a bull-run at him right in front. But, on the whole, I like this sallow, queer, sagacious visage, with the homely human sympathies that warmed it; and, for my small share in the matter, would as lief have Uncle Abe for a ruler as any man whom it would have been practicable to put in his place.

NATHANIEL HAWTHORNE

☆ ☆ ☆

HOME AND COUNTRY

The man who loves home best, and loves it most unselfishly, loves his country best.

JOSIAH GILBERT HOLLAND

☆ ☆ ☆

The history of every country begins in the heart of a man or a woman.

WILLA CATHER

☆ ☆ ☆

From THE HUSKING BEE

For now, the corn house filled, the harvest
  home,
  Th' invited neighbors to the husking come;
A frolic scene, where work and mirth and
  play
  Unite their charms to cheer the hours
  away.

JOEL BARLOW

☆　☆　☆

FIRST THANKSGIVING

Our harvest being gotten in, our governor sent four men on fowling that so we might after a special manner rejoice together after we had gathered the fruits of our labors. They four killed as much fowl as with a little help beside served the company about a week. At which times among other recreations we exercised our arms, many of the Indians coming amongst us, and among the rest their greatest king Massasoyt with some ninety men, whom for three days we entertained and feasted, and they went out and killed five deer which they brought and bestow'd on our governor, and upon the captains and others.

EDWARD WINSLOW

☆　☆　☆

THANKSGIVING PROCLAMATION

Inasmuch as the Great Father has given us this year an abundant harvest of Indian corn, wheat, peas, beans, squashes, and garden vegetables, and has made the forests to abound with game and the sea with fish and clams, and inasmuch as He has protected us from the ravage of the savages, has spared us from pestilence and has granted us freedom to worship God according to the dictates of our own conscience; now, I, your magistrate, do proclaim that all ye Pilgrims, with your wives and ye little ones, do gather at ye meet-house, on ye hill, between the hours of 9 and 12 in the day time, on Thursday, November

ye 29th, of the year of our Lord one thousand six hundred and twenty-three, and the third year since ye Pilgrims landed on ye Plymouth Rock, there to listen to ye pastor and render thanksgiving to ye Almighty God for all His blessings.

WILLIAM BRADFORD

☆　☆　☆

I should like to feel that, in every American family, some place is made for an expression of our gratitude to Almighty God, and for a frank acknowledgment of our faith that he can supply that additional strength which, for these trying times, is so sorely needed.

DWIGHT D. EISENHOWER

☆　☆　☆

From AN IOWA CHRISTMAS

The tree came from down in the grove, and on it were many paper ornaments made by my cousins, as well as beautiful ones brought from the Black Forest, where the family had originally lived.

There were popcorn balls, from corn planted on the sunny slope by the watermelons, paper horns with homemade candy, and apples from the orchard.

The gifts tended to be hand-knit socks, or wool ties, or fancy crocheted "yokes" for nightgowns, tatted collars for blouses, doilies with fancy flower patterns for tables, tidies for chairs, and once I received a brilliantly polished cow horn with a cavalryman crudely but bravely carved on it.

And there would usually be a cornhusk doll, perhaps with a prune or walnut for a face, and a gay dress of an old corset-cover scrap with its ribbons still bright.

And there were real candles burning with real flames, every guest sniffing the air for the smell of scorching pine needles.

PAUL ENGLE

☆　☆　☆

The family is one of nature's masterpieces.

GEORGE SANTAYANA

☆ ☆ ☆

GENERATION TO GENERATION

I have an abiding confidence that the God of our fathers will be the God of their children—that he will be our God; that he will graciously enable us to preserve that glorious fabric, which his mercy and his goodness, not the might and strength of our ancestors, enable them to construct; and that countless generations, enjoying the rich heritage which they have transmitted to us, and which, by his blessing, we will transmit to them, will in distant ages unite in the tribute of gratitude to their memories, which, in this our day, it is our privilege to offer.

JOHN M. BERRIEN
UNITED STATES SENATE (1850)

☆ ☆ ☆

.HALL OF FAME INSCRIPTION

The day will come when man will recognize woman as his peer, not only at the fireside but in the councils of the nation. Then will there be the perfect comradeship between the sexes that shall result in the highest development of the race.

SUSAN B. ANTHONY

☆ ☆ ☆

FAMILY OF MAN

I am persuaded that whatever facilitates intercourse between the different portions of the human family will have the effect under the guidance of sound moral principles to promote the best interests of man.

SAMUEL F. B. MORSE

☆ ☆ ☆

Going to the mountains is going home.

JOHN MUIR

☆ ☆ ☆

WORTHY TEST

The highest test of the civilization of a race is its willingness to extend a helping hand to the less fortunate.

BOOKER T. WASHINGTON

☆ ☆ ☆

RULE OF THUMB

New England says, "Make do, or go without,"
So they make do.
A garment's better for a patch or two;
What's brash, new, raw, is not for them,
What's worn, indigenous, has their esteem.
By the being turned, let out and dyed
The hand-me-down is glorified,
And fifty years are not too much
To wear an ax helve smooth to touch.

Then take their weather—they
Make do with what their betters throw away;
Heat waves, cold fronts, glacial
Hurricanes or any special
Cast-off storms that no one else will take.

The Old World sent its odds and ends to make
New England—then it taught them: "Wear it out,
Eat it up, make do." One simple rule
Turns out the Yankee article
Genuine and Simon-pure,
Something which will last, which will endure.

BIANCA BRADBURY

☆ ☆ ☆

The makers of the Constitution sought to protect Americans in their beliefs, their thoughts, their emotions, and their sensations.

They conferred, as against the Government, the right to be let alone—the most comprehensive of rights and the right most valued by civilized men.

LOUIS D. BRANDEIS

✩ ✩ ✩

DUTCH CUISINE

The Pennsylvania Dutch are predominantly German in origin—with a strong admixture of Swiss, Moravians, and some Hollanders among them—and many of their favorite dishes, like sauerkraut and pickled pig's feet, are available anywhere that Germans have foregathered.

Others which the Pennsylvania Dutch can take credit for introducing, like scrapple, waffles, apple butter, and Philadelphia pepper pot, have long since joined the nationwide menu.

Still others, of course, like chicken corn soup or schnitz-un-gnepp (made with slices of dried apple soaked back to original size, dumplings, and ham or pork), are available only here.

No one else seems to know how to make a shoo-fly pie from molasses, brown sugar, flour, and spices. (The name may have come from the fact that a cook working with these ingredients on a hot summer day would have winged visitors.)

But the genius of this cuisine lies not so much in its unique dishes as in the fresh touch which these people give to the conventional American food obtainable anywhere. They have quite a way with common things.

ARCHIBALD THOMAS ROBERTSON

✩ ✩ ✩

SCHNITZ-UN-GNEPP

2 1/2 to 3 pounds smoked ham with bone
2 cups dried apples
2 tablespoons brown sugar
Dumplings

Cover ham almost completely with cold water. Bring to a boil, reduce heat, cover and simmer gently for about two hours. While the ham is simmering, put the dried apples (Schnitz) in a bowl, cover with cold water, and soak. When the ham has cooked, add drained apples and brown sugar. Simmer for another hour. Serve with dumplings, made as follows:

1 1/2 cups all-purpose flour
3 teaspoons baking powder
1/2 teaspoon salt
1 tablespoon butter
1/4 cup milk, approximately
1 egg, well beaten

Sift flour, baking powder, and salt together into a bowl. Pinch in the butter until well distributed, then stir in enough milk to make a soft dough, and add egg. Lift the cooked ham onto a hot platter and spoon apples around it. Drop dumplings (Gnepp) from a spoon into the boiling ham liquid, cover tightly, and simmer 10 to 12 minutes. Arrange the dumplings on the platter around the meat, and spoon a little of the liquid over them. Some Pennsylvania Dutch cooks thicken the liquid by stirring in a little flour mixed to a smooth paste with water; others like it unthickened. Serves 6 to 8.

THE AMERICAN HERITAGE COOKBOOK

✩ ✩ ✩

So long as there are homes to which men turn
At close of day,
So long as there are homes where children
 are—
Where women stay,
If love and loyalty and faith be found
Across these sills,
A stricken nation can recover from
Its gravest ills.

So long as there are homes where fires burn
And there is bread,
So long as there are homes where lamps are
 lit
And prayers are said;
Although a people falters through the dark
And nations grope,
With God himself back of these little homes
We still can hope.

GRACE NOLL CROWELL

XVIII

THE MAYFLOWER
IS SAILING ON

☆　☆　☆

We are in a new era. The old methods and solutions no longer suffice. We must have new thoughts, new ideas, new concepts, just as did our venerated forefathers when they faced a new world.

DOUGLAS MACARTHUR

LIVING HOPE

I think the true fulfillment of our spirit, of our people, of our mighty and immortal land, is yet to come.

I think the true discovery of our own democracy is still before us.

And I think that all these things are certain as the morning, as inevitable as noon.

I think I speak for most men living when I say that our America is Here, is Now, and beckons on before us, and that this glorious assurance is not only our living hope, but our dream to be accomplished.

THOMAS WOLFE

☆   ☆   ☆

REAFFIRMATION

Many generations ago, Benjamin Franklin pointed across the hall of the Constitutional Convention at Philadelphia to the golden half-sun engraved on the back of Washington's chair, and he remarked: "Now, at length, I have the happiness to know that it is a rising, not a setting, sun." And so today, when a single fireball can light the fires of ten thousand suns, we need to reaffirm our faith in America.

NELSON A. ROCKEFELLER

☆   ☆   ☆

I've been to the mountaintop. And I've looked over, and I've seen the Promised Land. I may not get there with you, but I want you to know that we as a people will get to the Promised Land. So I'm happy. Mine eyes have seen the glory of the coming of the Lord.

MARTIN LUTHER KING, JR.

☆   ☆   ☆

This generation of Americans has a rendezvous with destiny.

FRANKLIN D. ROOSEVELT

☆   ☆   ☆

HYMN

More light shall break from out thy word
　For pilgrim followers of the gleam,
Till, led by thy free spirit, Lord,
　We see and share the pilgrim dream!

What mighty hopes are in our care,
　What holy dreams of brotherhood;
God of our fathers, help us dare
　Their passion for the common good!

Wild roars the blast, the storm is high!
　Above the storm are shining still
The lights by which we live and die;
　Our peace is ever in thy will!

The ancient stars, the ancient faith,
　Defend us till our voyage is done—
Across the floods of fear and death
　The Mayflower still is sailing on!

ALLEN EASTMAN CROSS

☆   ☆   ☆

HOPE FOR ALL TIME

The Declaration of Independence gave liberty not alone to the people of this country, but hope to all the world, for all future time. It was that which gave promise that in due time the weights would be lifted from the shoulders of all men, and that all should have an equal chance. This is the sentiment embodied in the Declaration of Independence.

ABRAHAM LINCOLN

☆   ☆   ☆

PRAYER FROM APOLLO 8

Give us, O God, the vision which can see thy love in the world in spite of human failure. Give us the faith to trust thy goodness in spite of our ignorance and weakness. Give us the knowledge that we may continue to pray with understanding hearts, and show us what each one of us can do to set forward the coming of the day of universal peace.

FRANK BORMAN

☆ ☆ ☆

MORAL GRANDEUR
There can be no security for America unless we can establish and keep vital connections with the world's peoples, unless there is some moral grandeur to our purposes, unless what we do is directed to the cause of human life and the free man.

NORMAN COUSINS

☆ ☆ ☆

VISION
We do not honor the fathers by going back to the place where they stopped but by going on toward the things their vision foresaw.

JUSTIN WROE NIXON

☆ ☆ ☆

From THE BUILDING OF THE SHIP
Thou, too, sail on, O Ship of State!
Sail on, O Union, strong and great!
Humanity with all its fears,
With all the hopes of future years,
Is hanging breathless on thy fate!
We know what Master laid thy keel,
What Workmen wrought thy ribs of steel,
Who made each mast, and sail, and rope,
What anvils rang, what hammers beat,
In what a forge and what a heat
Were shaped the anchors of thy hope!
Fear not each sudden sound and shock,
'Tis of the wave and not the rock;
'Tis but the flapping of the sail,
And not a rent made by the gale!
In spite of rock and tempest's roar,
In spite of false lights on the shore,
Sail on, nor fear to breast the sea!
Our hearts, our hopes, are all with thee,
Our hearts, our hopes, our prayers, our tears,
Our faith triumphant o'er our fears,
Are all with thee, are all with thee!

HENRY WADSWORTH LONGFELLOW

☆ ☆ ☆

ONLY THE BEGINNING
Democracy is a way of life that looks easy and is difficult. In these confused times, when we all feel tempted to go around looking for someone upon whom to place responsibility for the world's ills, I have to keep myself reminded of the fact that no one, living or dead, can do for me my job of being free.

I like to remind myself, also, that those forefathers of ours knew what they were about: they knew that fighting for liberty was not the end, but only the beginning. Whatever illusions I may have had to the contrary must not be charged up to those fine old realists.

Washington himself handed down the challenge to his own and successive generations: "We stand now, an Independent People, and have yet to learn political tactics. We are placed among the nations of the earth, and have a character to establish; but how we shall acquit ourselves, time must discover."

We despair of democracy. But I look around the world and see no other system that is working—working in the sense that under it humans are developing a long-range capacity to behave, with cooperative intelligence, as free individuals.

BONARO W. OVERSTREET

☆ ☆ ☆

The smallest village, the plainest home, give ample space for the resources of the college-trained woman.

ALICE FREEMAN PALMER

☆ ☆ ☆

PATH OF DESTINY
Always the path of American destiny has been into the unknown. Always there arose enough of reserves of strength, balances of sanity, portions of wisdom to carry the nation through to a fresh start with ever-renewing vitality.

CARL SANDBURG

206

☆ ☆ ☆

OLD VIRTUES

The principal thing we can do, if we really want to make the world over again, is to try the use of the word "old" again. It was the "old" things that made this country the great nation it is.

There is the Old Virtue of religious faith.

There are the Old Virtues of integrity and truth.

There is the Old Virtue of incorruptible service and honor in public office.

There are the Old Virtues of economy in government, of self-reliance, thrift, and individual responsibility, and liberty.

There are the Old Virtues of patriotism, real love of country, and willingness to sacrifice for it.

These "old" ideas are very inexpensive. And they would help win hot and cold wars. I realize such suggestions will raise that odious word, "reactionary," but some of these "old" values are slipping away rapidly from American life. And if they slip too far, the lights will go out in America, even if we win the hot and cold wars.

HERBERT HOOVER

☆ ☆ ☆

I like the dreams of the future better than the history of the past.

THOMAS JEFFERSON

☆ ☆ ☆

LESSON LEARNED

The most important thing I have learned as a judge is that the heart and soul of America are sound and true and that the intuitive judgment of the ordinary man in the street is in the aggregate something infinitely penetrating and reliable.

HAROLD R. MEDINA

☆ ☆ ☆

PARTNERSHIP

Every American is a free member of a mighty partnership that has at its command all the pooled strength of Western Civilization— spiritual ideals, political experience, social purpose, scientific wealth, industrial prowess.

There is no limit, other than our own resolve, to the temporal goals we set before ourselves—as free individuals joined in a team with our fellows, as a free nation in the community of nations.

DWIGHT D. EISENHOWER

☆ ☆ ☆

LOOKING FORWARD
TO AMERICA'S FUTURE

I look forward to a great future for America—a future in which our country will match its military strength with our moral strength, its wealth with our wisdom, its power with our purpose.

I look forward to an America which will not be afraid of grace and beauty, which will protect the beauty of our natural environment, which will preserve the great old American houses and squares and parks of our national past, and which will build handsome and balanced cities for our future.

I look forward to an America which will reward achievement in the arts as we reward achievement in business or statecraft.

I look forward to an America which will steadily raise the standards of artistic accomplishment and which will steadily enlarge cultural opportunities for all of our citizens.

I look forward to an America which commands respect throughout the world not only for its strength but for its civilization as well. And I look forward to a world which will be safe for democracy and diversity but also for personal distinction.

JOHN F. KENNEDY

☆ ☆ ☆

PRAYER

Help us, our Father, to show other nations an America to imitate—not an America of loud jazz music, self-seeking indulgence, and love of money, but the America that loves fair play, honest dealing, straight talk, real freedom, and faith in God.

Make us to see that it cannot be done as long as we are content to be coupon clippers on the original investment made by our forefathers.

Give us faith in God and love for our fellow men, that we may have something to deposit, on which the young people of today can draw interest tomorrow.

By thy grace, let us this day increase the moral capital of this country.

PETER MARSHALL

☆ ☆ ☆

Now truly, as these regions have been more widely explored, it is clear that a new part of the world has been discovered by Americus Vespucius. This may be learned from his letters which are herewith printed. I see no reason why this new part of the world should not be called after Americus. That is, it should be called the land of Americus, or America, from its discoverer, a man of much wisdom.

MARTIN WALDSEEMÜLLER (1507)

☆ ☆ ☆

From HISTORIA DEL MONDO NUOVO (1565)

Columbus being at a party with many noble Spaniards, where the subject of the conversation was the Indies, one of them undertook to say, "Señor Cristóbel, even if you had not undertaken this great enterprise, we should not have lacked a man who would have made this same discovery."

Columbus made no reply but took an egg, saying, "Gentlemen, make it stand here, not with crumbs, salt, etc., but naked and without anything at all, as I will, who was the first to discover the Indies."

They all tried, and no one succeeded in making it stand up.

When the egg came round to Columbus, he fixed it by beating it down on the table, having thus crushed a little of one end.

Wherefore all remained confused, understanding what he meant: that after the deed is done, everybody knows how to do it.

GIROLAMO BENZONI

☆ ☆ ☆

From COLUMBUS

Then pale and worn, he paced his deck,
  And peered through darkness.
      Ah, that night
Of all dark nights! And then a speck—
  A light! A light! At last a light!
It grew, a starlit flag unfurled!
  It grew to be Time's burst of dawn.
He gained a world; he gave that world
  Its grandest lesson: "On! sail on!"

JOAQUIN MILLER

☆ ☆ ☆

The stile of this confederacy shall be "The United States of America."

ARTICLES OF CONFEDERATION

☆ ☆ ☆

LETTER TO WASHINGTON

I must soon quit the scene, but you may live to see our country flourish; as it will amazingly and rapidly after the War is over; like a field of young Indian corn, which long fair weather and sunshine had enfeebled and discolored, and which in that weak state, by a thunder gust of violent wind, hail, and rain, seemed to be threatened with absolute destruction; yet the storm being once past, it recovers fresh verdure, shoots up with double vigor, and delights the eye not of its owner only, but of every observing traveler.

BENJAMIN FRANKLIN

A NEW WIND A-BLOWIN'

There's a brand new wind a-blowin' down
    that Lincoln road.
There's a brand new hope a-growin' down
    where freedom's seeds are sowed.
There's a new truth we'll be knowin' that
    will lift our heavy load,
When we find out what free men can really
    do.

There's a brand new day a–comin' for the
    land called U.S.A.
New tunes we'll be a–strummin' in our
    hearts by night and day.
As we march on we'll be hummin', how our
    troubles' gone away,
'Cause we've found out what free men can
    really do.

And if you feel like dancin' then, why
    come on folks, and dance!
And if you feel like prancin' then, why
    come on folks, and prance!
'Cause I really ain't romancin' when I say
    we've got our chance
To show 'em what free men can really do.

There's a brand new wind a-blowin' thru
    a land that's proud and free.
Ev'rywhere there's folks a-wakin' to a
    truth that's bound to be.
So let's all pull together for that day
    of victory,
And we'll show 'em what free men can
    really do!

              LANGSTON HUGHES

☆ ☆ ☆

The future is no more uncertain than the
present.

              WALT WHITMAN

☆ ☆ ☆

INTERDEPENDENCE

The days of the rugged individualist are over
and the days of the cooperative individual are
here. The pioneer on his homestead was independent and could go it alone. His descendants, whether at the plow, or loom, or
desk, whether in village or city, are interde-
pendent. The pioneer forged a free world on
his own. His children's children must find
their way with all other peoples to a free
world.

              PAUL G. HOFFMAN

☆ ☆ ☆

CAUTION

The Ship of Democracy, which has weathered all storms, may sink through the mutiny
of those on board.

              GROVER CLEVELAND

☆ ☆ ☆

SECOND THOUGHT

The second, sober thought of the people is
seldom wrong, and always efficient.

              MARTIN VAN BUREN

☆ ☆ ☆

AMERICA'S SONS

We are the sons of our father, whose face
    we have never seen,
we are the sons of our father, whose voice
    we have never heard,
we are the sons of our father, to whom we
    have cried for strength in our agony,
we are the sons of our father, whose life
    like ours was lived in solitude and in
    the wilderness,
we are the sons of our father, to whom only
    can we speak out the strange, dark burden
    of our heart and spirit,
we are the sons of our father, and we shall
    follow the print of his foot forever.

              THOMAS WOLFE

☆ ☆ ☆

From I HEAR AMERICA SINGING

I hear America singing, the varied carols I
   hear,
Those of the mechanics, each singing his as
   it should be blithe and strong,
The carpenter singing his as he measures his
   plank or beam,
The mason singing his as he makes ready for
   work, or leaves off work,
The boatman singing what belongs to him in
   his boat, the deck–hand singing on the
   steamboat deck,
The shoemaker singing as he sits on his
   bench,
   the hatter singing as he stands,
The wood-cutter's song, the ploughboy's on
   his way in the morning, or at noon inter-
   mission or at sundown,
The delicious singing of the mother, or of
   the young wife at work, or the girl sewing
   or washing,
Each singing what belongs to him or her and
   to none else.

WALT WHITMAN

☆   ☆   ☆

POINT OF VIEW

There are many ways of looking at this nation
of ours. It may be seen through documents
and papers preserved in the major archives
of the land. It may be viewed from the classroom, where a skilled teacher sets forth its
saga. The economist can speak of the economic forces that brought it into being. The
sociologist can expound on the evolvement of
a new culture from the bringing together of
many ethnic groups. The psychologist can
attempt to interpret the drives that motivate
man to adventure into the wilderness and to
dare the unknown. The man of religion can
point to the hunger for new forms and patterns of religious expression. The historian
can try to bring these and other strands of
truth together into a reasonable pattern.

Having said all of this, it seems to me that
the best way to see America clearly and to
understand its greatness is to cover its countryside, cross its deserts, climb its mountains,
walk its streets in villages and metropolises,
go from the Atlantic to the Pacific and from
Canada to Mexico. And, above all else, visit
with people.

CHARLES L. COPENHAVER

☆   ☆   ☆

The American Dream is a lovely thing, but to
keep it alive, to keep it from turning into a
nightmare, every once in a while we've got to
wake up.

LOUIS ADAMIC

☆   ☆   ☆

CHALLENGE TO LEAD

America is not just rich in material things, an
industrial giant, a mighty military power.
America is the country schoolhouse, the village church, the town meeting, the humble
farmhouse, the rhythmic poetry of peaceful
countryside.

America is the mirth and laughter of its
children, the charity, the generosity, the
compassion of its people. America is the
triumph of merit and diligence over family
and caste. America is the freedom of choice
which God intended all men to have—the
right to do, to speak, to worship, to dissent, to
dream, to build, to fail, and to succeed.

America is the marriage of liberty with
authority, of individual freedom with social
organization. America is the best discovery
yet of a full and honorable way of life.

We are rich in all the things that decent
people yearn for. It is our task to live up to
these values and to make them known to
every nation, friend or foe. For on us has
fallen the challenge to lead the free. And the
truth about ourselves is more powerful than
any man-made missile.

DEAN ALFANGE

KNOWING OUR HISTORY

There is little that is more important for an American citizen to know than the history and traditions of his country. Without such knowledge, he stands uncertain and defenseless before the world, knowing neither where he has come from nor where he is going. With such knowledge, he is no longer alone but draws a strength far greater than his own from the cumulative experience of the past and a cumulative vision of the future.

Knowledge of our history is, first of all, a pleasure for its own sake. The American past is a record of stirring achievement in the face of stubborn difficulty. It is a record filled with figures larger than life, with high drama and hard decision, with valor and with tragedy, with incidents both poignant and picturesque, and with the excitement and hope involved in the conquest of a wilderness and the settlement of a continent. For the true historian—and for the true student of history—history is an end in itself. It fulfills a deep human need for understanding, and the satisfaction it provides requires no further justification.

Yet, though no further justification is required for the study of history, it would not be correct to say that history serves no further use than the satisfaction of the individual to learn, to choose goals and stick to them, to avoid making the same mistake twice—in short, to grow—so history is the means by which a nation establishes its sense of identity and purpose. The future arises out of the past, and a country's history is a statement of the values and hopes which, having forged what has gone before, will now forecast what is to come.

JOHN F. KENNEDY

MOSAIC

History is never made in the abstract. Always it is something that someone or some group has done. Moreover, history is never some solid mass achievement; on the contrary, it is a mosaic composed of countless parts, each perfected by the sacrificial devotion of undying zeal of some particular person or some specific group. As we reflect upon America, we discover that it is a living and growing thing: here a person who has caught the vision of a new day, and there a consecrated group which has launched boldly out upon a new venture in obedience to a far-laid plan.

Thus, the forces that have made history, and will continue to make it, are the uncrushable ideals men cherish, the definite plans they discipline themselves to work out, and the daring hopes by which they dynamize their souls.

Though it may not be our lot to stand as a lone individual at the crossroads of history to control and direct the onrushing stream of destiny, still we can choose to become a component part of a determined group that has espoused some high cause to which it has dedicated its all.

Therefore as weavers, all of us, of the great fabric of history, we are so close to our work, so held by the wide tangle of loose ends, that we do not see the whole pattern, much less the dim Great Hand on the other side tracing the design. There is only one wise thing for us to do today, and that is to seek the place of vision. Thither we need to go betimes, in humility and awe, to renew our sense of a destiny moving in the sources of human history, and give new vows of loyalty to those eternal things that make us grandly human and nobly divine.

W. WALDEMAR W. ARGOW

☆ ☆ ☆   ☆ ☆ ☆

America lives in her simple homes:
The weathered door, the old wisteria vine,
The dusty barnyard where the rooster roams,
The common trees like elm and oak and
  pine:
In furniture for comfort, not for looks,
In names like Jack and Pete and Caroline,
In neighbors you can trust, and honest books,
And peace, and hope, and opportunity.
She lives like destiny in Mom, who cooks
On gleaming stoves her special fricassee,
And jams and cakes and endless apple pies.
She lives in Pop, the family referee,
Absorbing Sunday news with heavy eyes;
And in the dog, and in the shouting kids
Returning home from school, to memorize
The history of the ancient pyramids.

RUSSELL W. DAVENPORT

☆　☆　☆

I LOVE AMERICA

I love America, where truth can be shouted from the housetops, instead of whispered in dismal cellars hidden from the spies and dictators.

I love America, where families can sleep peacefully without fear of secret seizure and torture in some foul prison, or purged in blood for political reasons.

I love America, where men are truly free men; not living in fear of slavery, exile, or involuntary servitude, while their homes are confiscated and loved ones are turned weeping and sorrowing from their doors.

I love America, where there are equal rights for all, and where people are not forced to hate, persecute, or kill because of religion, race, or creed.

I love America, where little children are not forced to suffer for want of bread withheld at the whim of some despot carrying out a plan for greater glory.

I love America, where men can think as they please, and where thought is not regulated by decrees, enforced with bullets and bayonets.

I love America, where there is love, laughter, hope, and opportunity, and not hate, sorrow, dejection, and futility.

I love America despite her present troubles because free men can cure them.

I love America, and I will gladly give my life to preserve the freedom our forefathers created, so that our children and their descendants can forever enjoy blessings we have inherited.

FRANKLIN E. JORDAN

☆　☆　☆

ALTAR OF LIBERTY

In America a glorious fire has been lighted upon the altar of liberty. Keep it burning, and let the sparks that continually go up from it fall on other altars, and light up in distant lands the fire of freedom.

WILLIAM HENRY HARRISON

☆　☆　☆

FOR JOHN F. KENNEDY

Out of the days of sorrowing and grief,
Let us hold fast the vision you saw best,
In spite of spirits numbed in disbelief,
We will not sleep though you are safe at
  rest.

Let peace be made. Let nations live in trust.
Let people act within the name of neighbor.
Let hyacinths bring up from hatred's dust
A fragrance that will come to bless your
  labor.

Now, let us see all citizens converge
Equal in opportunity for all,
And out of civil war at last emerge
The civil rights for which you stood so tall.
Where people care, the truth will carry on,
And this we pledge for all to witness, John.

RALPH W. SEAGER

☆　☆　☆

PRAYER

We thank thee, our Father, for life and love, for the mystery and majesty of existence, for the world of beauty which surrounds us, and for the miracle of our conscious life by which we behold the wonders of the universe.

We are grateful for the ties which bind us to our fellowmen; for our common toil in industry and marts of trade; for our joint inheritance as citizens of this nation; for traditions and customs hallowed by age through which our passions are ordered and channelled.

We thank thee for the faith of our fathers by which we claim kinship with the past and gain strength for the present; for the love of dear ones in our homes and for the enlarging responsibilities and sobering duties of our family life; for the serenity of old people who redeem us of fretfulness; and for the courage of youth through which we are saved from sloth.

We are not worthy of the rich inheritances of our common life. We confess that we have profaned the temple of this life by our selfishness and heedlessness.

Have mercy upon us that we may express our gratitude for thy many mercies by contrition for our sins, and that we may prove our repentance by lives dedicated fully to thee and to the common good.

REINHOLD NIEBUHR

☆　☆　☆

The only lasting security for any of us lies in moving constantly forward.

HENRY A. WALLACE

☆　☆　☆

I am certain that, however great the hardships and the trials which loom ahead, our America will endure and the cause of human freedom will triumph.

CORDELL HULL

☆　☆　☆

We, here in America, hold in our hands the hope of the world, the fate of the coming years; and shame and disgrace will be ours if, in our eyes, the light of high resolve is dimmed, if we trail in the dust the golden hopes of men.

THEODORE ROOSEVELT

☆　☆　☆

THE CALL

In days long gone God spake unto our sires:
"Courage! Launch out! A new world build
　for me!"
Then to the deep they set their ships, and
　sailed,
And came to land, and prayed that here
　might be
A realm from pride and despotism free,
A place of peace, the home of liberty.
Lo, in these days, to all good men and true
God speaks again: "Launch out upon the
　deep
And win for me a world of righteousness!"
Can we, free men, at such an hour still
　sleep?
O God of freedom, stir us in our night
That we set forth, for justice, truth, and
　right!

THOMAS CURTIS CLARK

☆　☆　☆

Neither race, nor tradition, nor the actual past binds the American to his countryman, but rather the future which together they are building.

HUGO MÜNSTERBERG

☆　☆　☆

All the past we leave behind,
We debouch upon a newer mightier world,
　varied world,
Fresh and strong the world we seize, world
　of labor and the march,
Pioneers! O pioneers!

WALT WHITMAN

214

ACKNOWLEDGMENTS

Acknowledgment is made to the following for permission to reprint materials as indicated:

AMERICAN HERITAGE PUBLISHING CO., INC., for extract from *The American Heritage Cookbook*, copyright © 1964 by American Heritage Publishing Co., Inc.; extract from Foreword by John F. Kennedy in *The American Heritage New Illustrated History of the United States*, copyright © 1963 by American Heritage Publishing Co., Inc.; extract from "What They Did There" by Bruce Catton in *American Heritage*, December 1954; extract from "New England Summer" by Richard M. Ketchum in *American Heritage*, August 1957; extract from "Where Gallant Spirits Still Tell Their Story" by Bruce Catton in *American Heritage*, December 1957; extract from "The Farm Boy and the Angel" in *American Heritage*, October 1962; extract from "Melting Pot in the Bayous" in *American Heritage*, December 1963; extract from "The Thundering Water" by Bruce Catton in *American Heritage*, June 1964; extract from "The President's Lady" in *American Heritage*, August 1964; extract from "Fill Yourself Up, Clean Your Plate" by Archie Robertson in *American Heritage*, April 1964; extract from "Gaudery on Wheels" in *American Heritage*, December 1964.

THE ATLANTIC MONTHLY for extract by Carl Sandburg, copyright 1947 by The Atlantic Monthly Company, Boston, Massachusetts, reprinted by permission of Harcourt, Brace & World, Inc.

CHILD LIFE for "Abraham Lincoln" by Mildred Plew Meigs, copyright 1936 by *Child Life*, reprinted by permission of *Child Life* and Marion P. Ruckel.

THE CHRISTIAN CENTURY FOUNDATION for "As These Bright Colors" by Raymond Kresensky, copyright 1943 by The Christian Century Foundation; "Shadows" by John H. Staries, copyright 1942 by The Christian Century Foundation.

THE COURIER-JOURNAL, Louisville, Kentucky, for editorial by Hazel Parker Haynes. Reprinted by permission of *The Courier-Journal* and Hazel Parker Haynes.

FARM JOURNAL for "We Are American Farmers" by Wheeler McMillen.

JOHN HANCOCK MUTUAL LIFE INSURANCE COMPANY for articles on Robert E. Lee and Abraham Lincoln by Lou Redmond; extract from *Patriotic Songs*.

HOME INSURANCE COMPANY OF NEW YORK for article by Richard L. Doyle.

LINCOLN SAVINGS AND LOAN ASSOCIATION, Los Angeles, for article on Abraham Lincoln.

NATIONAL ASSOCIATION OF MANUFACTURERS for "Beyond the Horizon."

THE NEW YORK TIMES COMPANY for Flag Day editorial; extract from "New Frontiers" by Allan Nevins in *The New York Times Magazine* (October 1958), copyright © 1958 by The New York Times Company.

NEWSWEEK for "The Message of the Bells," copyright © 1965 by Newsweek, Inc.

THE OPEN-DOOR FOUNDATION for "What I Want My Children to Remember about Home."

THE P.E.O. RECORD for "Heritage" by Irene Bennett; "And So—America" by Grace Elizabeth Bush; "Meanings" by Carrie Bonebrake Simpson.

READER'S DIGEST for "Letter from a Navy Pilot," published as "Testament of Youth" in the February 1943 issue of *Reader's Digest*. Reprinted by permission of *Reader's Digest* and *Toronto National News-Letter*.

SATURDAY REVIEW for extract from "Is America Living Half a Life?" by Norman Cousins, copyright © 1957 by Saturday Review, Inc.; extract from "Education against Helplessness" by Norman Cousins, copyright © 1960 by Saturday Review, Inc.; extract from "Setting Our Sights for Tomorrow" by Harry James Carman, copyright 1945 by Saturday Review, Inc.

SUNSHINE MAGAZINE quotation by Franklin E. Jordan; quotations titled "Fifty-Six Signers" and "Ten Tests of an American."

THIS WEEK MAGAZINE for quotation by Dean Alfange, copyright © 1959 by the United Newspapers Magazine Corporation.

Acknowledgment is made to the estates of the following persons for permission to reprint material from their writings:

Eric W. Barnes; Leslie Savage Clark for "New England Spires" from "With All Thy Heart"; Thomas Curtis Clark for "At Mount Vernon" and "The Call"; Rudolf A. Clemen; Everett McKinley Dirksen; Simon Edelstein; Frances Frost for extract from "Johnny Appleseed's Song" from *Mid-Century*, copyright 1946 by Frances Frost; Arthur Guiterman for "Daniel Boone"; Hermann Hagedorn for extract from *You Are the Hope of the World*, copyright 1917, 1945 by Hermann Hagedorn; John Haynes Holmes for "America Triumphant"; Robert F. Kennedy; Martin Luther King, Jr.; Alfred Kreymborg for "Ballad of the Common Man"; Elias Lieberman for "I Am an American" from *Paved Streets*, copyright 1918, 1946 by Elias Lieberman; Percy MacKaye for "Goethals, the Prophet Engineer" from *The Present Hour*; Edwin Markham for extract from "Lincoln, the Man of the People" from *Poems of Edwin Markham*; Raymond Pitcairn; Abba Hillel Silver for "America"; Robert Whitaker for extract from "Washington"; Allen E. Woodall for "Map of My Country."

Acknowledgment is made to the following persons for permission to reprint material from their writings:

Herbert Agar; Richard Sanders Allen; W. Waldemar W. Argow; Jacques Barzun; George S. Benson; Hugo L. Black; Harold A. Bosley; Bianca Bradbury for "Rule of Thumb"; Virginia Brasier for "Heartbeat of Democracy"; Carl Bridenbaugh; Herbert Brownell, Jr.; Ralph J. Bunche; Gail Brook Burket for "House in Springfield" and "I Love America"; Mary Ellen Chase; John Ciardi; John L. Childs; Philip Jerome Cleveland for "The Hands of Lincoln"; Russell J. Clinchy; Henry Steele Commager for extract from *There Were Giants in the Land*; Charles L. Copenhaver; Marshall B. Davidson; John Dos Passos for extract from *The Ground We Stand On*, copyright © 1941, 1969 by John Dos Passos; Ouida Smith Dunnam for "Prayer of a Beginning Teacher"; Will Durant; J. Ollie Edmunds; Deane Edwards; Milton S. Eisenhower; Edward L. R. Elson; Paul Engle; Morris L. Ernst; Marion B. Folsom; Raymond B. Fosdick; Theodore Friedman; Robert I. Gannon; Billy Graham; Pierson M. Hall; Floyd Arthur Harper; Walter Havighurst for "The McGuffey Readers" and extract from *Land of Promise*; Henry T. Heald; Paul G. Hoffman; Winthrop S. Hudson; William B. Huie; Hubert H. Humphrey; Robert M. Hutchins; Margaret E. Jenkins; Lyndon B. Johnson; James Keller for extract from *You Can Change the World*; Leila Pier King for "Tomb of the Unknown Soldier" and "We Walk with Lincoln" from *At the Hunter's Horn*; David Lawrence; Henry Cabot Lodge, Jr.; David McCord; Robert J. McCracken; Edgar F. Magnin; Bernard Mandelbaum; Harold R. Medina; Samuel Eliot Morison for extract from *The Oxford History of the American People*; Allan Nevins; Reinhold Niebuhr; Richard M. Nixon; Bonaro W. Overstreet; Ralph Bushnell Potts; Nathan M. Pusey; I. James Quillen; Eudora Ramsay Richardson; John D. Rockefeller 3rd; Nelson A. Rockefeller; Carlos P. Romulo; Ruth Apperson Rous for "I Am the Flag"; Francis Russell; Max Savelle; Ralph W. Seager for "Fifth of July Parade" from *Beyond the Green Gate*, copyright © 1958 by Ralph W. Seager, and "Eyes of Granite" and "For John F. Kennedy" from *Cup, Flagon & Fountain*, copyright © 1965 by Ralph W. Seager; W. J. Sheridan; Eric Sloane; Ralph W. Sockman; George R. Stewart; Robert Trout; Nancy Byrd Turner for "First Thanksgiving of All"; Earl Warren; Byron R. White; Theodore H. White.

INDEX OF PHOTOGRAPHS

INDEX OF FAMILIAR QUOTATIONS

BIOGRAPHICAL INDEX OF AUTHORS

(Book titles and other sources are also included)

INDEX OF POETRY

*(This index includes first lines and titles;
poets are listed in Biographical Index of Authors)*

221

INDEX OF TOPICS